LITERATURE AND LAW
IN THE MIDDLE AGES

GARLAND REFERENCE LIBRARY
OF THE HUMANITIES
(VOL. 378)

LITERATURE AND LAW
IN THE MIDDLE AGES
A *Bibliography of Scholarship*

John A. Alford
Dennis P. Seniff

GARLAND PUBLISHING, INC. • NEW YORK & LONDON
1984

Library of Congress Cataloging in Publication Data

Alford, John A., 1938-
Literature and law in the Middle Ages.

(Garland reference library of the humanities ;
v. 378)
Includes indexes.
1. Law and literature—Bibliography. 2. Middle
Ages—Bibliography. I. Seniff, Dennis P. (Dennis Paul)
II. Title. III. Series.
LAW   809'.93355   82–49117
ISBN 0–8240–9211–2

Printed on acid-free, 250-year-life paper
Manufactured in the United States of America

CONTENTS

ACKNOWLEDGMENTS

Numerous individuals have contributed to the making of this bibliography.

We would like to thank the following for calling our attention to studies that otherwise we might have overlooked: Judson B. Allen, S. G. Armistead, Cesáreo Bandera, W. F. Bolton, Dwayne E. Carpenter, Henry Ansgar Kelly, Victoria Kirkham, Giuseppe Mazzotta, Craig McDonald, Noël M. Valis, and Richard Weisberg.

We are grateful to the Michigan State University Foundation for its generous support of the project; and to our research assistants Stephen Guice, Philip McKinney, and Brigitte Merz. Kathleen Blumreich was especially helpful during the preparation and editing of the indexes.

To our friends in Madison, Wisconsin, we owe a special debt of gratitude: to Connie Seniff for her hospitality; to Lloyd Kasten of the Hispanic Seminary of Medieval Studies for wise counsel; and above all to John Nitti and Ruth Richards, also of the Hispanic Seminary, for supervising the computer typesetting of the book.

Finally we would like to thank our wives Linda and Celia who have borne the demands of the project with unfailing good cheer.

INTRODUCTION

Why literature and law? What have these two things to do with each other? And how can we justify a bibliography of studies on their connection in the Middle Ages?

In his epoch-making "Von der Poesie im Recht" (1816)—the earliest item in the bibliography [9] and the true fount of most subsequent scholarship on the topic—Jacob Grimm argues that the unity of early poetry and law inheres not in the observer's methodology but in the very nature of the two enterprises. Primitive society regarded literature, law, and religion from a single, coherent point of view [20]. Gradually these things diverged and took on separate identities. But in the period covered by this bibliography the process was not yet complete. Many medieval poets still felt that their art existed primarily to enforce obedience to God and king. The population as a whole still regarded law as the chief instrument of the divine will in human affairs; indeed, the thirteenth-century legal treatise known as *Sachsenspiegel* emphasizes that "God is Himself Law" [478]. And it was still the case that literary production was mostly in the hands of men trained for careers in law or in the Church—often both [e.g., 146, 147, 158, 224, 253, 655, 660, 661, 710, 711, 716, 795, 839, 874, 913]. In light of these facts, it is hardly surprising that the writings of the period, both secular and religious, should be pervaded by legal influence in one form or another.

As the bibliography makes clear, the study of this influence has passed through several stages, each corresponding to the scholarly preoccupations of the time. Grimm, of course, was one of the founders of historical linguistics. Both in his seminal essay of 1816 and in the introduction to his monumental *Deutsche Rechtsaltertümer* [348], he starts with language as the basic evidence for a close connection between early Germanic law and literature; and this approach is followed by numerous other scholars who stress either the "poetic" features of early legal codes, such as alliteration, rhyme, and figurative language [142, 330, 364, 366, 382], or the value of literature to the study of early legal terminology [331, 343, 365, 372, 373, 380, 551, 553]. Perhaps the clearest evidence of Grimm's influence in recent years is the work of Stephen Schwartz, who proposes comparative linguistics as the means for reconstructing Germanic law [383] and bases his own *Poetry and Law in Germanic Myth* on Grimm's "Von der Poesie im Recht."

Another approach influenced by Grimm and especially popular in the nineteenth century is the use of literature as document—a guide to the social and political life of a culture, a storehouse of *Rechtsaltertümer*. Why this approach was so popular is not hard to understand. Literary works often provided the main or only evidence historians had in certain areas. Moreover, many of the works in question were discovered only in the last century. These new finds had to be cleaned off, dated, and put in categories before they could be analyzed as "art." During the late nineteenth and early twentieth centuries, therefore, important articles on certain medieval poems appeared in legal journals [342, 352, 370, 380, 439, 793]; and often their authors were legal scholars, such as Fehr [340, 342, 402], Künssberg [364-366], or Zallinger [388, 460, 461], who saw literary texts as a means of filling the gaps in our knowledge of medieval law and custom. The assumption that contemporary legal practice is reflected in the literature has become a powerful motive even in the work of scholars with no interest in law as such [viz. 49, 72, 86, 108, 110, 126, 133 (Latin); 138, 152, 154, 171, 196, 238, 244, 247, 274, 291, 306, 313, 315, 317 (English); 400, 424, 425, 430, 433, 454, 456, 493, 494, 500 (German); 575, 581, 590, 598, 702, 703, 636, 698, 646, 657, 658, 689, 688 (French); 804, 813, 829, 856, 859, 874, 881, 897 (Spanish)]. But nowhere has the question of how far literature may be trusted as a record of legal practice been more fully or frequently debated than in the case of the Icelandic sagas [e.g., 509, 528, 534, 535, 537, 539, 544, 566], for no literature is more saturated with legal themes. As Theodore Andersson observes, "The theme of a saga is conflict" [507, p. 6], to which we may add Alan Berger's suggestion that the saga writers found in law "a catalogue of conflicts useful to a conflict-hungry literature"[512].

The preoccupation with linguistic and historical matters gave way in the early twentieth century to more purely "artistic" concerns. The focus shifted from "literature in the service of law"—the motto of Fehr's great work [340, vol. 2]—to "law in the service of literature." Increasingly, legal scholarship was being turned toward explications of the text itself. This pattern generally holds in every section of the bibliography. The entries under *Chanson de Roland* may be used to illustrate the trend. In 1871 Bresslau examined the legal antiquities preserved in the poem and judged them to be accurate [613]. In 1890 Baist attempted to trace certain aspects of the poet's handling of the judicial combat to Germanic law [611]. In 1921 Jenkins cited contemporary law as an explanation for Ganelon's rage at the first council [623]. And then in 1936 Ruggieri proposed that the trial of

Ganelon is actually the nucleus around which the poem was constructed [632]. In short, law has moved from the periphery of critical concern to center stage. The pattern is typical. Of course, the older interest in linguistic and historical elements continues to express itself, but during the past several decades legal approaches to literature have been concerned mainly with illuminating the text itself. How does legal usage contribute to the ambiguity or richness of the poet's language [280, 415, 594, 676, 680, 687, 829, 901]? What is the role of judicial rhetoric in literary debates [350, 603]? How crucial is law to certain traditional metaphors [137, 242, 399]? To what extent do legal structures (e.g., wills, contracts, trial procedures) underlie literary structures [427, 447, 575, 601, 602, 619, 632, 656, 706]?

Most recently—again corresponding to a general trend in literary studies (semiology, hermeneutic theory, etc.)—the connection between law and literature has been treated from a highly abstract, theoretical point of view. For example, what are the basic similarities between arguing a case and writing a poem [38]? How is the interpretation of a law like the interpretation of a literary text [1, 12, 13, 19]? In what sense can the text itself be considered an "inquest" [668]?

Of the four general approaches just described, this bibliography is concerned primarily with the third one, that is, with approaches that use law as a vehicle for illuminating some aspect of the literary text—language, style, imagery, structure, and theme. In this category we have included almost every relevant study known to us. But we have been selective in the case of linguistic, historical, and theoretical approaches—a course dictated by necessity. The number of individual word-studies that draw upon both legal and literary works is enormous. So is the number of social and legal histories based in part on literary evidence. The vast majority of these, however, contribute little to one's understanding of medieval literature; and to include them would inflate the book to no purpose. As for the more theoretical inquiries into law and literary interpretation, these rarely offer any medieval examples.

The scope of the bibliography is indicated by the title, *Literature and Law in the Middle Ages*. We mean "literature" in the usual sense of the word (poetry, drama, fiction, and so forth), but we have not hesitated to include studies of law in medieval sermons, chronicles, saints' lives, and other forms of writing. In any event the number is small. The literatures treated are Latin, Old and Middle English, German (with several additional entries on the Flemish *Van den Vos Reinaerde*), Icelandic, French and Provençal, Italian (dominated by the figure of Dante), and Hispanic (primarily Spanish). These form a coherent whole: they draw upon the same literary traditions, often upon the same bodies of law (Roman and canon), and show much reciprocal influence. Of course the literature of other languages (such as Celtic) might have been included as well, but we have had to draw the line at some point because of time, space, and our own linguistic backgrounds.

For the present purpose "literature" has been easier to define than "law." The medieval concept of law was extremely broad. It included not only positive law (custom, royal and papal decrees, legislative acts, etc.) but also natural law and even divine law. These various kinds of law were seen not as merely analogous to one another but rather as manifestations of a single law in different spheres [137]. In short, all law was one law. To include here only those studies of law in the modern, more restricted sense of the word would be to misrepresent the medieval reality and to separate positive law from the philosophical context that gave it meaning and authority. An appreciation of such basic ideas as *ratio* [116], *ordo* [386], and *lex aeterna* [81] is essential to the proper understanding of the place of law in medieval thought. Therefore, we have included the major studies of these ideas in both literary and theological works (e.g., *The City of God* and the *Summa theologica*), and we have done so with the confidence that most of our readers would want them included.

Finally, like "literature" and "law," the definition of "Middle Ages" is also subject to wide interpretation. In general we accept the more or less conventional dates of 800 to 1400, while making allowance for the fact that some literary historians (notably of German and English literature) would extend the *terminus ad quem* by another century. The Latin entries represent a special problem. Although the year 800 is a convenient date from which to trace the rise of vernacular literature, it is a totally arbitrary marker in the history of medieval Latin. The standard survey, Max Manitius's *Geschichte der lateinischen Literatur des Mittelalters* [57], begins with Boethius (sixth century). The Modern Language Association's bibliography of medieval Latin goes all the way back to Tertullian and Clement of Alexandria (second century A. D.). Even without these bibliographical precedents, however, we would have included such early Christian writers as Tertullian, Lactantius, and above all Augustine, for their influence had more to do with medieval literature's receptivity to legal terms and ideas than any other single cause.

Briefly put, our guiding principle throughout has been the question, "What value does this item have for the reader interested in the relationship between medieval literature and law?"

The annotations have been written with this question in mind. They are intended not as summaries of the works listed but as guides to the legal content thereof. The order of entries in each section conforms to that found in the annual bibliography of the Modern Language Association of America—that is, general and miscellaneous items first, then primary works listed in alphabetical order by author (if known, by title if not). The entire Icelandic section is treated as general and miscellaneous, since most of the items therein deal with thematic questions or several works at once. Readers who wish to identify quickly those entries that concern particular sagas should consult the index. Because the index is unusually full—citing every author or work and almost every legal term and concept in the book—cross-references have been held to a minimum.

In compiling the bibliography we have relied mainly on the following sources: *Arkiv för Nordisk Filologi, Bibliographie der deutschen Literaturwissenschaft, Cambridge Bibliography of English Literature*, Alan Deyermond, *A Literary History of Spain: The Middle Ages* (1971), *La Corónica* annual bibliography, *Dissertation Abstracts, Dissertation Abstracts International*, Stanley B. Greenfield and Fred C. Robinson, *A Bibliography of Publications on Old English Literature to the End of 1972, International Guide to Medieval Studies, International Medieval Bibliography, Modern Humanities Research Association Annual Bibliography, Modern Language Association of America International Bibliography, Old English Newsletter, Quarterly Check-List of Medievalia, Rassegna della Letteratura Italiana, Revue d'Histoire Ecclésiastique, Scandinavian Studies, The Year's Work in English Studies*, and *The Year's Work in Modern Language Studies*. In many cases, however, titles alone were no guide to legal content. We could hardly have guessed, for example, that Peter Wapnewski's "Rüdigers Schild. Zur 37. Aventiure des *Nibelungenliedes*" [458] would be of major importance to the study of law in that poem. The footnotes of other scholars, therefore, have been an indispensable help.

A number of relevant studies came to our attention too late for inclusion in the bibliography itself: Leonard Forster, "Gotelint and the Constables," *MLR*, 43 (1948), 410-411; George Nordmeyer, "The Judge in the *Meier Helmbrecht*," *MLN*, 63 (1948), 95-104 (both articles on *Helmbrecht*); David Hook, "On Certain Correspondences between the *Poema de mio Cid* and Contemporary Legal Instruments," *Iberoromania*, 11 (1980), 31-53, and "The Legal Basis of the Cid's Agreement with Abbot Sancho," *Romania*, 101 (1980), 517-526; C. Colin Smith, *The Making of the Poema de mio Cid* (Cambridge: Cambridge University Press, 1983); and Richard Weisberg, "Literature and Law," in *Interrelations of Literature*, ed. Jean-Pierre Barricelli and Joseph Gibaldi (New York: Modern Language Association of America, 1982).

The division of editorial responsibilities was as follows: General, Latin, Old and Middle English, German, Icelandic, and French sections (Alford); Italian and Hispanic (Seniff).

ABBREVIATIONS

AEM	*Anuario de estudios medievales*
AHDE	*Anuario de la historia del derecho español*
AnM	*Annuale Mediaevale*
Archiv	*Archiv für das Studium der Neueren Sprachen und Literaturen*
ASI	*Archivio Storico Italiano*
BBSIA	*Bulletin Bibliographique de la Société Internationale Arthurienne*
BGDSL	*Beiträge zur Geschichte der Deutschen Sprache und Literatur* (Tübingen)
BHS	*Bulletin of Hispanic Studies*
BSDI	*Bollettino della Società Dantesca Italiana*
CCM	*Cahiers de Civilisation Médiévale*
CeS	*Cultura e Scuola*
ChauR	*Chaucer Review*
CL	*Comparative Literature*
DDJ	*Deutsches Dante Jahrbuch*
DSARDS	*Dante Studies, with the Annual Report of the Dante Society*
DVLG	*Deutsche Vierteljahrsschrift für Literaturwissenschaft und Geistesgeschichte*
EHR	*English Historical Review*
ELH	*Journal of English Literary History*
ELN	*English Language Notes*
ES	*English Studies*
FR	*French Review*
GD	*Giornale Dantesco*
GQ	*German Quarterly*
GR	*Germanic Review*
GSLI	*Giornale Storico della Letteratura Italiana*
HR	*Hispanic Review*
IL	*L'Information Littéraire*
JEGP	*Journal of English and Germanic Philology*
KRQ	*Kentucky Romance Quarterly*
MA	*Le Moyen Âge: Revue d'Histoire et de Philologie*
M&H	*Medievalia et Humanistica*
MLN	*Modern Language Notes*
MLQ	*Modern Language Quarterly*
MLR	*Modern Language Review*
MP	*Modern Philology*
MRom	*Marche Romane*

MScan	*Mediaeval Scandinavia*
N&Q	*Notes and Queries*
NM	*Neuphilologische Mitteilungen*
NMS	*Nottingham Medieval Studies*
PLL	*Papers on Language and Literature*
PMLA	*Publications of the Modern Language Association of America*
PQ	*Philological Quarterly*
RABM	*Revista de Archivos, Bibliotecas y Museos*
RASLA	*Rivista abruzzese di scienze, lettere ed arti*
REH	*Revista de Estudios Hispánicos*
RES	*Review of English Studies*
RF	*Romanische Forschungen*
RFE	*Revista de Filología Española*
RHM	*Revista Hispánica Moderna*
RLR	*Revue des Langues Romanes*
RomN	*Romance Notes*
RPh	*Romance Philology*
RR	*Romanic Review*
RSI	*Rivista Storica Italiana*
RUGD	*Rivista Universale di Giurisprudenza e Dottrina*
SBAW	*Sitzungsberichte, Bayerische Akademie der Wissenschaften. Philosophisch-Historische Klasse*
SBoc	*Studi sul Boccaccio*
SP	*Studies in Philology*
SS	*Scandinavian Studies*
SzEP	*Studien zur Englischen Philologie*
ZDA	*Zeitschrift für Deutsches Altertum und Deutsche Literatur*
ZDP	*Zeitschrift für Deutsche Philologie*
ZRG	*Zeitschrift der Savigny-Stiftung für Rechtsgeschichte*
ZRP	*Zeitschrift für Romanische Philologie*

LITERATURE AND LAW
IN THE MIDDLE AGES

GENERAL

1   Abraham, Kenneth. "Statutory Interpretation and Literary Theory: Some Common Concerns of an Unlikely Pair." *Rutgers Law Review*, 32 (1979), 676-694.

       Focuses on the defining issue in both legal and literary interpretation: "to what extent does the text have a determinate meaning, and to what extent is the reader free to interpret it as he chooses?" Abraham shows how this distinction between objective and subjective interpretation has affected thinking about a classic case (*Riggs v. Palmer*); and he ends by suggesting that critics on opposing sides of the issue actually share a great deal of common ground. [Cf. 12, 19.]

2   Balducci, Umberto. "Literature and Law." *Interdisciplinary Essays*, 2.1. Ed. Stephen H. Good and Olaf P. Tollefsen. Emmitsburg, Md.: St. Mary's College, 1971 [1973], 15-24.

3   Barfield, Owen. "Poetic Diction and Legal Fiction." *Essays Presented to Charles Williams*. Ed. C. S. Lewis. London: Oxford University Press, 1947, pp. 106-127.

       A leisurely excursion into the question of metaphorical meaning. Barfield suggests that the history of legal fictions may serve as a "slow-motion picture" of the way in which metaphorical meaning develops in the language. His principal example is the device of "trusteeship," which grew out of the fact that a suit brought by an ousted freeholder was much more drawn-out than one brought by an ousted leaseholder: the first was a matter of *real* property, the second of *personal* property. The freeholder eventually discovered (fifteenth century) that it was to his advantage to pursue the case as the agent of a fictitious John Doe, to whom he had "leased" the land. "Has new law been made?" Barfield asks. "It is much the same as asking whether new language has been made when a metaphor disappears into a 'meaning.'" The analogy is expressed briefly in the formula "metaphor:language:meaning::legal fiction:law:social life."

4   Clanchy, M. T. *From Memory to Written Record*. Cambridge,
         Mass.: Harvard University Press, 1979.

         Although this book has little to say about literature as such, it
         makes an important argument for the connection between the growth
         of literacy in England (1066-1307) and the phenomenal increase in
         the production and retention of records (particularly of legal
         documents).

5   Derrett, John Duncan M. *Law in the New Testament*. London:
         Darton, Longman and Todd, 1970.

         A fascinating (and controversial) attempt to reconstruct the legal
         background, mainly Jewish, of the parables and sayings of Jesus.
         Derrett shows that without a knowledge of contemporary law, one is
         likely to distort the meaning of particular passages or to miss the
         point altogether. Although legal approaches to the Bible are
         relatively new, there is already an extensive literature on the subject.
         Derrett's copious notes provide a good indication of the scholarship
         thus far. (His references to medieval exegetes serve mainly to
         underscore their misunderstanding of the parables.)

6   _____. *Studies in the New Testament, I: Glimpses
         of the Legal and Social Presuppositions of the Authors*. Leiden:
         Brill, 1977.

         A continuation of the method and subject of Derrett's earlier
         book, *Law in the New Testament*.

7   Eden, Kathy Hannah. "The Influence of Legal Procedure on the
         Development of Tragic Structure." Diss. Stanford University 1980.

         An inquiry into both the theoretical and practical associations
         between law and tragic drama. The author begins with the
         Aristotelian analogy between equity and poetic fiction: both are
         instruments of knowledge "designed, by negotiating between
         universal propositions and particular instances, to discover the truth
         (cause, intention) in the context of ethical action." Chapter 2 shows
         how subsequent apologists for poetry depend on Aristotle's concept
         of fiction and "on his fundamentally legal formulation of
         intention." The final three chapters discuss the influence of legal
         procedure on tragic structure in Greek, Roman, and Elizabethan
         drama. The structure of Greek and Elizabethan tragedy is said to

reflect the accusatorial system (the visual spectacle of a contest between adversaries, conducted before a jury) in contrast to Senecan tragedy, which is said to reflect the inquisitorial system (the less visual, un-adversarial hearing before a single judge).

8   Fisher, John. "Tristan and Courtly Adultery." *CL*, 9 (1957), 150-164.

    Believes that the ambivalence toward adultery in the Tristan legend had its origin in Pictish law and tradition, specifically in the practice of matriliny (well-attested) and polyandry (or at least what appeared to be, among Roman observers, "the absence of regular marriage and the practice of promiscuous cohabitation").

9   Grimm, Jacob. "Von der Poesie im Recht." *Zeitschrift für geschichtliche Rechtswissenschaft*, 2 (1816), 25-99; rpt. *Kleinere Schriften*. Hildesheim: Olms, 1965, 6:152-191.

    This is the seminal study of the relationship between literature and law. Grimm stresses the idea that both go back to a common origin and thus share certain characteristics. The main proof is linguistic. Dozens of examples are cited (e.g., judges are called "finders," as are poets [trobadores, trouveurs]; both create, hence "schaffer, schöffen, scof"; "runes" go back etymologically to the scepters of kings; and so forth). Moreover the literary character of early law is apparent in its rhyme, alliteration, and expressiveness (e.g., distance is defined not as so many feet, but as how far the cock flies or the cat springs). Such poetic elements suffered a decline, however, with the revival of Roman law. Still under the influence of Romanticism, Grimm treats his subject somewhat wistfully, admiring the former unity of law, literature, and religion; contrasting the *Strenge* of the old law and the *Gleichgültigkeit* of the new; and stressing the earlier value attached to honesty or *Ehrlichkeit*.

10   Harnack, Adolph. *History of Dogma*. 7 vols. Trans. Neil Buchanan et al. New York: Russell and Russell, 1958.

    An encyclopedic survey of Christian dogma from its beginnings to the Reformation. The legal content of early Christian writings (above all in Tertullian) is stressed repeatedly (e.g., 3:267 ff., 5:15 ff., 6:21 ff., et passim).

11   Hexter, Ralph J. "Equivocal Oaths and Ordeals in Medieval
      Literature." (The LeBaron Russell Briggs Prize Honors Essays in
      English, 1974, Harvard University.) Cambridge, Mass.: Harvard
      University Press, 1975.

      This study traces the changing literary fortunes of the ordeal as a
      means of determining truth. In pre-thirteenth-century treatments of
      the theme, writers were generally willing to accept the equivocal oath
      as a legitimate way of saving one's skin, especially in cases where the
      accuser was even more morally corrupt. However, the banning of
      ordeals by the Fourth Lateran Council (1215) signaled a change in
      attitude. This change is first seen in the *Tristan* of Gottfried von
      Strassburg, who alters his sources in order to bring them into line
      with the new thinking. "Specifically he elevated the treatment of the
      episode of the equivocal oath as he found it in his source, intending
      to raise the question of absolute justice." The author of *Amis and
      Amiloun* (ca. 1330) actually sees in the "tricked ordeal" a sin
      demanding punishment. And Malory, writing 150 years later, "has
      completely secularized the ordeal and squared it with the beliefs of
      his age." In fact, "he treats and structures the older materials of the
      motif of the equivocal oath and ordeal and the other judicial
      combats in an original way to represent the decline of Arthur's
      society." From his own tragic experience as a political prisoner, "he
      learned only too well the slow process by which might overcomes
      right, at first by equivocation, and then by brute force."

12   Hirsch, E. D. Jr. *Validity in Interpretation*. New Haven: Yale
      University Press, 1967.

      In this important book, described by its author as "a
      contribution to general hermeneutic theory with special emphasis on
      the problem of validity," Hirsch stresses repeatedly the analogies
      involved in the interpretation of legal, biblical, and literary texts.
      Thus he suggests (pp. 124-125) that the "willed meaning" in both
      legal and literary texts is theoretically capable of embracing
      "analogous and unforeseeable implications" (e.g., there is no
      difference *in principle* between extending an old law to cover new
      technological achievements and reading a play like *Hamlet* to
      accommodate Freudian psychology). Among his several
      conclusions, based in part on a consideration of the canons of
      interpretation used in law, the following is one of the most
      important: "It may be set down as a general rule of interpretation

that there are no interpretive rules which are at once general and practical....The notion that a reliable methodology of interpretation can be built upon a set of canons is thus a mirage" (pp. 202-203).

13 Jacobson, Richard. "Law, Ritual, Absence: Towards a Semiology of Law." *University of Hartford Studies in Literature*, 9 (1977), 164-174.

In calling for a study of the semiology of law, the author makes several suggestive comparisons between the language of law and that of Jewish religious literature. Like the *Kol Nidrei* (a portion of the Jewish liturgy which begins the Day of Atonement), the ritualistic language of the law invokes "a moment beyond the word," a sanction that is "magical, mystical, and most important, *present*." At the same time, a legal code represents an *absence*—the absence of society, the king, the father. Law is "an *expropriation* of the social presence." As an example of the semiology of absence, Jacobson notes the rise of an elaborate Old Testament hermeneutics, coinciding with the end of Israelite prophecy (400 B. C.). "It is in this sense that when God ceases to speak, a text emerges to speak for him."

14 Kaminska, Alexandra Barbara. "Literary Confessions from 1215 through 1550: Development in Theme and Form of French, German, and English Confessions from the Fourth Lateran Council through the Reformation." Diss. University of Maryland 1972.

Sees the flourishing of literary confessions such as the *Roman de la Rose,* the Archpoet's *Confessio*, the German song beginning "Das pulschafft nit sünd sey," and other works as a consequence of the social reaction against Canon 21 of the Fourth Lateran Council (requiring annual auricular confession).

15 Kantorowicz, Ernst H. *The King's Two Bodies: A Study in Medieval Political Theology.* Princeton: Princeton University Press, 1957; rpt. 1981.

A monumental study of the concept of "the king's two bodies" (natural and corporate) from the eleventh to the sixteenth century. The work begins and ends with chapters on two literary figures, Shakespeare and Dante, and in-between provides illustrations from numerous other writers, e.g., Geoffrey of Monmouth, John of Salisbury, Petrarch, Fortescue, et al. Especially noteworthy are

Kantorowicz's blending of legal and literary sources, and his many references to the same practice among medieval jurists; for example, in the case of certain ideas ("Fictio imitatur naturam"), "the jurists not only fell in with the literary and artistic theories, but may have had even the function of pathfinders..." (p. 307n), and "Albericus de Rosate (d. 1354) repeatedly referred...to Dante (especially to *Monarchia*, III) as a juristic authority..." (p. 457n). In addition to Kantorowicz's very full exposition of the subject, his copious footnotes serve as an invaluable source of information on texts, legal commentaries, and modern scholarship. [Cf. 710.]

16   Liermann, Hans. "Die Gottheit im Recht. Ein historisch-dogmatischer Versuch." *SBAW*, 1968 (Heft 6).

Describes several aspects of the historical relation between the concepts of law and divinity. The primitive concept of *mana* is eventually personified; "God" becomes a legal person, capable of making law (viz. *Sachsenspiegel*), owning property (everything on earth is held of God, a "loan"), entering into contracts (e.g., the agreement between Thor and Freyja in *Edda*, and medieval literary treatments of the rainbow—a sign of God's covenant with mankind—as *Urkunde*), deciding cases (e.g., the ordeal in *Le Roman de Tristan et Iseut*, the trial of Satan or *Belial-Prozess*, the Last Judgment in Walter Map's *Praedicatio Goliae*), and so forth.

17   Mak, J. J. "Het Proces in de Hemel als Strijdgedicht." *Tijdschrift voor Nederlandse Taal- en Letterkunde*, 65 (1948), 241-259.

Speculates on the reasons for the popularity of the "trial in heaven" motif, with a look at other examples of the *Streitgedicht* in literature; notes the crucial place of Truth throughout.

18   Mellinkoff, David. *The Language of the Law*. Boston: Little, Brown, 1963.

In Part Two ("History of the Language of the Law"), the author traces the development of the legal vocabulary in England from Anglo-Saxon days to the present, with separate chapters on "The Law and Latin" and "The Rise and Fall of Law French." The survey represents mainly an abstracting of pertinent material from the standard dictionaries and histories of English.

19   Michaels, Walter Benn. "Against Formalism: The Autonomous Text in Legal and Literary Interpretation." *Poetics Today*, 1 (1979), 23-33.

Employs the analogy between legal and literary interpretation of texts in order to clarify the nature of meaning. The inadequacy of "the parol evidence rule" in the reading of contracts is used to point up the futility of the formalist belief that texts have "some intrinsic, plain, or literal meaning." The use of extrinsic evidence in legal and literary interpretation is inevitable, because "plain meanings are functions not of texts but of the situations in which we read them." [Cf. 1, 12.]

20   Mitteis, Heinrich. "Recht und Dichtung." *Die Rechtsidee in der Geschichte. Gesammelte Abhandlungen und Vorträge von Heinrich Mitteis*. Weimar: Böhlaus, 1957, pp. 681-697.

Elaborates on the many connections, practical and theoretical, between law and literature. Numerous great poets have stressed the idea of justice. Some have borrowed their most effective devices (e.g., court scenes) from law. A few, such as Homer, have even contributed new legal ideas [see items 15, 36, 103]. Because the law demands decisions of the will (Kant), it is itself in a sense an ethical (*sittliche*) idea—the idea of the good, true, and beautiful. Though separate now, literature, law, and religion once constituted a unity. Mitteis's illustrations range over the whole course of literary history: Hesiod, Homer, *Beowulf*, the Icelandic sagas, the *Nibelungenlied*, the *Ackermann aus Böhmen*, Flaubert, Dickens, etc.

21   Myrick, Arthur B. "Feudal Terminology in Mediaeval Religious Poetry." *Romanic Review*, 11 (1920), 1-25.

Cites numerous examples, mostly in Romance poetry, of feudal concepts applied to the relation between God and man. God is described as a great "lord," head of the "manor," a "baron" to whom man as "serf" or "vassal" owes "loyalty," "faith," "homage." "This poetic convention...was undoubtedly an early and natural growth influenced by a highly feudal environment... [and] seems to have lost its life coincidentally with the death of feudalism itself...."

22   Neilson, William Allen. *The Origins and Sources of the Court of Love*. (Harvard) Studies and Notes in Philology and Literature, 6. Boston: Ginn, 1899; rpt. New York: Russell and Russell, 1967.

A rather full survey of medieval allegorical poems in the "court of love" tradition. Neilson calls attention to several works that parody legal procedure (e.g., Martin Le Franc's *Le Champion des Dames*, the anonymous *Die Minneberg,* etc.).

23   Nottarp, Hermann. *Gottesurteilstudien*. Bamberger Abhandlungen und Forschungen, 2. München: Kösel, 1956.

The standard work on ordeals and trial by battle as "Judgments of God" (with some literary examples). There are four sections: 1. the nature and dissemination of the practice; 2. the dynamics; 3. the various forms (ordeal by water, fire, hot iron, combat, etc.); 4. reactions (position of the Church, legislative bans, etc.).

24   Pelikan, Jaroslav. *The Growth of Medieval Theology (600-1300)* (Vol. 3 of his *The Christian Tradition: A History of the Development of Doctrine*). Chicago: University of Chicago Press, 1978.

A splendid history which gives far more attention than most to the role of law and justice in medieval thinking about salvation.

25   Perrow, Eber Carle. "The Last Will and Testament as a Form of Literature." *Transactions of the Wisconsin Academy of Sciences, Arts, and Letters*, 17, Part 1 (1914), 682-753.

Though far from exhaustive, this is the fullest treatment of the last will and testament as a literary genre, extending from its beginnings in antiquity up to the nineteenth century (principally in France and England). The account is neither deep nor well-organized. Its main value is that of a catalogue. Numerous examples from the medieval period are represented, including (from England) the Vernon *Testamentum Christi, Piers Plowman*, Hoccleve's *Le Mal Regle,* Usk's *Testament of Love*, and Lydgate's *Testament*; (from France) the *Testament* of Jean de Meung, Rutebeuf's *Le Testament de l'Âne*, Deguileville's *Pèlerinage de la Vie Humaine*, Villon's *Le Petit Testament* and *Le Grand Testament* (of which numerous imitations); and (from Germany) Walther von der Vogelweide's *Vermächtniss*.

26   Peters, Edward. *The Shadow King: Rex Inutilis in Medieval Law and Literature, 751-1327*. New Haven and London: Yale University Press, 1970.

A model synthesis of legal and literary sources that touch on the problem of the medieval *rex inutilis*, i.e., the weak or ineffectual king. See especially Chapter 2 "The Name of King: Rhetorical and Literary Representations of Royal Inadequacy to 1150" (which discusses *Beowulf, Waltharius,* Geoffrey of Monmouth's *Historia,* and the *chansons de geste*) and Chapter 5 *"Rex Inutilis* in the Arthurian Romances" (Chrétien de Troyes, Wolfram von Eschenbach, the prose Vulgate).

27   Reinhard, J. R. "Setting Adrift in Mediaeval Law and Literature." *PMLA*, 56 (1941), 33-68.

Examines the practice of setting adrift as employed mainly for three classes of persons: 1. non-criminals, 2. persons unwanted in the community, 3. criminals or presumed criminals. In the first class—e.g., Apollonius of Tyre, St. Brandon, Pope Gregory (of Middle English legend), Tristram (*Tristrams saga ok Ísondar*), and Constance (Chaucer's *Man of Law's Tale*)—the sea acts as the arbiter of sin and innocence (guiltless, all survive). In the second—e.g., Mary Magdalene, Emare, King Horn, and Gunnar (*Ólafs saga Tryggvasonar*)—setting adrift "not only salved the conscience of the judges but allowed a chance of escape to the unwanted person." In the case of criminals set adrift—of which nearly all the literary examples are Celtic—the penalty was assigned "in those cases wherein the evidence of guilt was not or could not be conclusive in the eyes of a human judge, or which he was not wholly competent to weigh, or in which it was desirable to temper justice with mercy." Reinhard rejects the opinion that setting adrift is necessarily a kind of ordeal, since "viewed as a legal instrument, [it] tacitly assumes a likelihood of guilt or wrongdoing."

28   _____. "Burning at the Stake in Mediaeval Law and Literature." *Speculum*, 16 (1941), 186-209.

Shows that burning as a penalty for *adultery* is carried out in only three of thirteen cases in romance, in only one of thirteen in Celtic literature, and is not prescribed at all in the Irish laws, the Welsh laws, the Germanic customary law, or Roman law. The penalty does appear, however, in the Old Testament (Gen. 38.24,

Levit. 21.9, Judges 15.6). Thus the author concludes "that in view of the burning penalty provided in the customary laws of Western Europe for some offences [e.g., treason], it was an easy matter for both Romance and Celtic writers to include adultery and fornication among the number of offences so punishable, for they had the authority of the Bible."

29   Schwerin, Kurt. "Rechtssymbole." *Reallexikon der germanischen Altertümskunde*. Ed. Johannes Hoops. Strassburg: Trübner, 1911-1919, 3:469-479.

A lexicon of legal symbols, many of which figure in literature and the visual arts. For example, "foot" is explained as a symbol of power or control: the conqueror puts his foot on the conquered, the bridegroom treads on the foot of the bride, the new owner puts his right foot on the thing possessed, and so on. The following items are treated: foot, mouth, hair, head, hand, glove, shoe, hat, belt, coat, staff, piece of straw, cross, sword, banner, shield, spear, knife, spindle, broom and shears, key, and ring. In a short concluding section, the author discusses the legal significance of certain acts involving the above items, such as throwing, giving, and seizing.

30   Suretsky, Harold. "Search for a Theory: An Annotated Bibliography of Writings on the Relation of Law to Literature and the Humanities." *Rutgers Law Review*, 32 (1979), 727-739.

Annotates thirty-five articles that attempt "to justify the field of law and literature as a whole." Almost all of the items come from legal journals (1866-1979) and show a gradual movement away from the earlier view of literature "as a supplemental tool for the practicing lawyer" to a more expanded vision of the theoretical relationship between the two disciplines.

31   Thompson, Stith. *Motif-Index of Folk Literature*. 6 vols. Bloomington: Indiana University Press, 1955-1958.

Includes a large number of legal motifs (e.g., oaths, judicial combat, trials).

32   Torrance, Robert M. *The Comic Hero*. Cambridge, Mass.: Harvard University Press, 1978.

Chapter 4 deals with the various medieval tales of Reynard the

Fox, "the vicarious comic hero" of an emerging bourgeois class that could identify with the crafty exploits of this "renegade in a world of vassals." Nevertheless, "for all his impudent defiance of feudal institutions Reynard...affirms the necessity of an order that he harasses by repeated outrages but never—in the absence of any considered alternative—calls into serious question." Torrance points out that the tale of Reynard's trial in the *Roman de Renart* is central to the tradition: "The Flemish and German versions from Willem to Goethe are mainly elaborations on this great poem."

33   Traver, Hope. *The Four Daughters of God*. Philadelphia: Winston, 1907.

The standard work in English on the allegory of the Four Daughters of God. Traver shows little sensitivity to the legal aspects of the tradition; however, her comments are still useful in pointing out the works most steeped in legal procedure. Undoubtedly, the best examples from this point of view are the numerous treatments of the "Processus Belial," in which the Devil argues his right to mankind before the court of heaven—e.g., Jacob van Maerlant's *Merlijn*, Bartolus of Saxoferrato's *Questiones ventilate coram domino nostro Jesu Christo inter Virginam Mariam...et dyabolum*, Jean de Justice's *L'Advocacie de Notre Dame*, the *Mascheroen* by Jan Boendale(?), Jacopo da Theramo's *Processus Belial*, and two Provençal cycle plays, *Lo Jutgamen de Jhesus de Nazaret* and *Lo Jutgamen General*. Other pieces of literature in which the debate among the Four Daughters appears—and with it the machinery of the courtroom—are the *Chasteau d'Amour*, Deguileville's *Pèlerinage de l'Ame* and *Le Pèlerinage de Jesucrist,* Mercadé's *Mystère de la Passion*, Greban's *Passion*, the *Castell of Perseverance, Piers Plowman*, the *Court of Sapience*, and numerous other French and English works.

34   _____. "The Four Daughters of God: A Mirror of Changing Doctrine." *PMLA*, 40 (1925), 44-92.

Traver contends that the wide variations in the historical development of the Four Daughters allegory "reflect the changing doctrine of the Church itself." Most of the article is devoted to tracing the rise of the *Processus Belial*, an immensely popular form of literature in which the Devil (or his advocate) brings suit against Christ for His "illegal" recovery of mankind. Among the sources

Traver discusses are the early Jewish and Christian apocalypses; the writings of Tertullian, Irenaeus, Hugh of St. Victor, Stephen of Tournai, et al.; and the cult of Mariolatry. "The versions most expanded and most complete in legal chicanery and dialectic are doubtless also the latest" (e.g., Theramo's *Belial* [1381], *L'Advocacie de Notre Dame*, and the *Questiones* ascribed to Bartolus of Saxoferrato). An extremely useful source of information for study of the genre.

35   Trimpi, Wesley. "The Quality of Fiction: The Rhetorical Transmission of Literary Theory." *Traditio*, 30 (1974) 1-118.

Traces certain characteristics of the rhetorical transmission of literary theory, in particular the concept of quality as found in four of its principal origins: "the logical category of 'quality,' the qualitative attribute of physics and epistemology, the *status qualitatis* of jurisprudence, and the qualitative standard of equity."

36   Ullmann, Walter. *Law and Politics in the Middle Ages*. Ithaca: Cornell University Press, 1975.

The author describes his work as "one of the first attempts to present the principal sources of medieval political ideas in an integrated and coherent manner." Chapter 7 focuses on "Governmental Doctrines in Literary Sources": Ullmann observes that governmental themes appear "in theological tracts, in epistolary communications, in devotional sermons, in dogmatic treatises, in encyclopedic dictionaries, in liturgical arrangements and in instructional monographs—in short, any conceivable literary genre served as a platform from which to propagate the one or the other governmental item" (p. 227). Ullmann's chief examples are Ambrosiaster, Pseudo-Dionysius, Augustine, Orosius, Gregory, Isidore, Alcuin, Smaragdus, Hincmar of Rheims, Honorius of Autun, Gerhoch of Reichersberg, Hugh of St. Victor, Bernard of Clairvaux, John of Salisbury, et al. Of poetry or *belles-lettres* he says nothing. Other chapters are devoted to Roman law, canon law, non-Roman secular law (and the scholarship on each). The book is an indispensable guide to the subject.

37   Van den Bergh, G. C. J. J. *"Auctoritas Poetarum*: The Fortunes of a Legal Argument." *Daube Noster: Essays in Legal History for David Daube*. Ed. Alan Watson. Edinburgh: Scottish Academic Press, 1974, pp. 27-37.

A stimulating history of the authority of poets (primarily Homer and Virgil) in questions of law. The study begins with the glosses of Accursius (on *Inst.* 1.23.2, *Dig.* 1.8.6.5), in which poets are given little authority; then considers several attempts to vindicate poetry (Guillaume Budé, Scipio Gentili, Samuel de Fermat); and ends with a look at Jacob Gothofredus and "the elegant school," which reduced the matter of *auctoritas poetarum* from a legal to a historical topic. The tradition deeply affected not only the nature of legal reasoning but also gave rise to one of the earliest specimens of modern philology, Jacob Grimm's epoch-making "Von der Poesie im Recht" [9], which "can only be understood in the light of the elegant tradition."

38   White, James B. *The Legal Imagination*. Boston: Little, Brown, 1973; rpt. 1981.

An anthology of readings from literary works, intended primarily as a textbook for use in law schools. The readings were chosen to show the connections "between the law and other intellectual activities." A few of the selections are medieval: the story of Burnt Njal, Malory's *Le Morte Darthur*, etc. There are numerous exercises and questions throughout, designed to call attention to the ways in which a lawyer relies on the same resources as the literary artist, e.g., language, figurative speech, ambiguity, labels, narrative structure, imagination, etc.

39   Wolf, Erik. *Vom Wesen des Rechts in deutscher Dichtung*. Frankfurt: Klostermann, 1946.

This book seeks to determine whether literature can offer any binding statements ("etwas Verpflichtendes") on the nature of law. It brings together four of the author's previously published pieces on Hölderlin, Stifter, Hebel, and Droste. Although these figures are relatively late, the medievalist may nevertheless find the legal-philosophical orientation of the work useful.

40   Yunck, John A. "The Venal Tongue: Lawyers and the Medieval
        Satirists." *American Bar Association Journal*, 46 (1960), 267-270.

        A compendium of examples from medieval satire directed
        against lawyers. Their characteristic vice: "venality, flowing from
        avarice." Yunck explains the satire, much of it exaggerated no
        doubt, as "an intensely conservative reaction to social and economic
        changes not wholly intelligible to those who protested." Foremost
        among these changes was the growing importance of money. In
        accepting a fee for his services, the lawyer seemed to violate both the
        Ciceronian ideal of lawyer as public servant and the Christian ideal
        of lawyer as a servant of truth.

41   _____. *The Lineage of Lady Meed: The
        Development of Medieval Venality Satire.* University of Notre Dame
        Publications in Mediaeval Studies, 17. Notre Dame: University of
        Notre Dame Press, 1963.

        The standard work on medieval venality satire (graft, simony,
        and barratry). Yunck traces the sources of the theme in Roman
        literature, Scripture, and exegetical tradition; and provides a rich
        anthology of examples from medieval literature, both Latin and
        vernacular. Many of these complain about the buying and selling of
        justice. The prevalence of venality satire in the later Middle Ages is
        explained as "a conservative reaction to the surprising economic
        developments of the times" and through this literature "one can
        glimpse a prolonged clash between two worlds, the ancient—and
        dying—world of personal loyalties, of feudal obligation and privilege
        on the one hand, and the new world—still developing, not
        understood or even consciously recognized—of cash payment and
        capital investment on the other."

LATIN

General and Miscellaneous

42 Berges, Wilhelm. *Die Fürstenspiegel des hohen und späten Mittelalters.* Schriften des Reichsinstituts für ältere deutsche Geschichtskund. Monumenta Germaniae Historica, 2. Stuttgart: Hiersemann, 1938; rpt. 1952.

A valuable history of the literary genre known as "the mirror for princes," from John of Salisbury's *Policraticus* (1159) to Petrarch's *De re publica optime administranda* (1373). The main issue throughout the tradition is the relation of the king to law. Among other authors treated here are Gerald of Wales, Gilbert of Tournai, the Norse *King's Mirror*, Vincent of Beauvais, Aquinas, Aegidius Romanus, Juan Manuel, Philip of Leyden, and Raoul de Presles. Full bibliographical information is given for numerous other works (pp. 291-356).

43 Chroust, Anton-Hermann. "The Philosophy of Law from St. Augustine to St. Thomas Aquinas." *The New Scholasticism,* 20 (1946), 26-71.

Emphasizes the enormous influence of Augustine on legal philosophy in the Middle Ages, up to and including Aquinas. Despite many references to Aristotle ("a phenomenon which must not be taken too seriously"), "St. Augustine remains the only true and unchallenged authority, that one universal source and inspiration which gives form and substance to this particular period" (p. 71).

44 Curtius, Ernst Robert. *European Literature and the Latin Middle Ages.* Trans. Willard R. Trask. New York: Bollingen Foundation, 1953.

Touches upon the connection between the rhetorical concept of poetry in the Middle Ages and the antique division of the *materia artis* into judicial, political, and epideictic oratory (pp. 154-159).

45   Gaudemet, Jean. "Le droit romain dans la littérature chrétienne
      occidentale du IIIᵉ au Vᵉ siècle." *Ius Romanum Medii Aevi*, Pars. I,
      3, b. Milan: Giuffrè, 1978 (166 pp.).

      A valuable, well-organized survey of references to Roman law in
      the writings of Tertullian, Minucius Felix, Cyprian, Arnobius,
      Lactantius, Ambrose, Ambrosiaster, Jerome, and Augustine. In
      each case Gaudemet tries to show the place of Roman legal concepts
      in the writer's overall thought (e.g., law in the service of theology
      [Tertullian], of ecclesiology [Cyprian, Ambrosiaster], etc.).

46   Ghellinck, J. de. *L'Essor de la littérature latine au XIIᵉ siècle.* 2d ed.
      Brussels: Desclée de Brouwer, 1955.

      The standard guide. In Chapter 1, Ghellinck discusses the rise
      of canon law and its effects on literary production (pp. 102-108); and
      in Chapter 6 he touches on the *débat* or *altercatio*, an antique form
      continued by "les fabulistes et les discussions littéraires des rhéteurs
      et des juristes" (pp. 457-459).

47   Haskins, Charles H. and M. Dorothy George, with introduction by
      R. L. Poole. "Verses on the Exchequer in the Fifteenth Century."
      EHR, 36 (1921), 58-67.

      Includes the text from the earliest of three manuscripts (MS.
      Bodl. 496) along with a modern commentary by M. Dorothy George.
      The poem itself (attributed to John Bell, a customs collector of
      Boston, and dated 1398-1410) describes in 126 lines of rhymed Latin
      verse "all the stages through which an account—that is, a 'foreign
      account'—passes in the exchequer, with a statement of the person
      who has to be bribed at each step." Those requiring bribes include
      the auditor, baron, remembrancer, chancellor, clerk of the pipe
      (roll), controller of the pipe, clerk of the pleas, various clerks of the
      exchequer, sheriff, tellers, usher, chamberlain, writers of the tallies,
      and others.

48   Haskins, Charles H. "Henry II as a Patron of Literature." *Essays in
      Medieval History Presented to Thomas Frederick Tout.* Ed. A. G.
      Little and F. M. Powicke. Manchester: Printed for the Subscribers,
      1925, pp. 71-77.

      Contributes to the study of the close relationship between

administration and literature by providing an annotated list of twenty works dedicated to Henry II.

49   Hilton, R. H. "A Thirteenth-Century Poem on Disputed Villein Services." *EHR,* 56 (1941), 90-97.

Gives the details from legal sources (*Coram Rege Roll* for Michaelmas 4-5 Edward I) of a case described in a late thirteenth-century poem (Bodley MS. 57). The tenants of the abbot and convent of Leicester, desiring greater freedom, decide to present their case in the king's court. Lacking money and power, however, they are defeated and return home weeping. The poet ends with the observation that social advancement for villeins is impossible. The poem, eighty-three lines long, is reproduced in full.

50   Kantorowicz, Hermann, and Beryl Smalley. "An English Theologian's View of Roman Law: Pepo, Irnerius, Ralph Niger." *Mediaeval and Renaissance Studies*, 1 (1941-43), 237-252; rpt. in Kantorowicz's *Rechtshistorische Schriften*. Karlsruhe: Müller, 1970, pp. 231-244.

Reviews the scant evidence concerning the life of "the mysterious Pepo," who was reputed to have revived the study of Roman law. In examining two unprinted works that mention Pepo, the authors incidentallly shed further light on the relation between law and literature. The works are: (1) a history of Siena by Sigismondo Tizio (d. 1528), who describes in detail a lost debate poem or *altercatio* by Gualfredus, Bishop of Siena (1085-1127), on the papal schism; and (2) Ralph Niger's *Moralia Regum*, in which a legal interpretation is given to the story of Absalom: "David signifies justice, in its widest sense, his sons the various kinds of legal procedure. Amnon, who seduced his sister, signifies barbarous old customs; the favourite son, Absalom, signifies Roman Law; as Absalom put to death Amnon (II Reg. XIII) in revenge for his barbarity, so Roman Law supersedes the evil custom of the ordeal," and so on. Niger's commentary on Absalom's conspiracy (II Regum 15.1-6) is edited in full.

51   Lausberg, Heinrich. *Handbuch der literarischen Rhetorik.* 2 vols. München: Hueber, 1960.

A comprehensive guide to the categories and figures of classical rhetoric. The *genus iudiciale* is treated at length (1:85-123). Volume

2 is a glossarial index of terms in Latin, Greek, and French. (Extensive bibliography, 2:605-638.)

52   Lehmann, Paul. *Die Parodie im Mittelalter*. 2d ed. Stuttgart: Hiersemann, 1963.

       The language and procedures of law often served as vehicles for satire (see pp. 113, 155, 199 et passim), and the administration of justice as the object (see pp. 25-68).

53   Lewis, Ewart. *Medieval Political Ideas*. 2 vols. New York: Knopf, 1954; rpt. New York: Cooper Square, 1974.

       An excellent anthology of translated excerpts from the major medieval treatises on law and politics. Among the authors and works presented are Aegidius Romanus, Aquinas, Beaumanoir, Bracton, Dante, *Disputatio inter Clericum et Militem*, Fortescue, James of Viterbo, John of Paris, John of Salisbury, Marsiglio of Padua, the *Somnium Viridarii*, and John Wyclif.

54   Mäder, Eduard Johann. *Der Streit der "Töchter Gottes." Zur Geschichte eines allegorischen Motivs*. Bern and Frankfurt: Lang & Cie, 1971.

       Studies the historical development of the Four Daughters of God theme in medieval Latin and German sources. Especially pertinent is the discussion of the so-called "Satansprozess" (pp. 40-45); the author mentions numerous literary accounts of the Devil's legal maneuvers to retain possession of mankind.

55   Maitland, Frederic William. "A Song on the Death of Simon de Montfort." *EHR*, 11 (1898), 314-318; rpt. in *The Collected Papers of Frederic William Maitland*, ed. H. A. L. Fisher. Cambridge: University Press, 1911, 3:43-49.

       The poem reproduced here (57 rhymed stanzas) is written on a flyleaf of MS. Caius College 85, a volume of treatises on canon law. On the same page there are some tags of jurisprudence, a legal formula, and another short poem about St. Nicholas.

56 Makdisi, George. "The Scholastic Method in Medieval Education:
An Inquiry into Its Origins in Law and Theology." *Speculum*, 49
(1974), 640-661.

Relevant in light of the importance of scholastic method to
literary structure. The article makes three points: 1. The scholastic
method developed first in the Muslim East. 2. In both the West and
the East law supplied the initial impetus for the method
("Furthermore, the role that law played was not simply a formal
one. Law also shares in the inner spirit of scholasticism, a spirit
drawing its strength from two sources: authority and reason"). 3.
Whether, and how, Islamic scholasticism was transmitted to the
West is uncertain.

57 Manitius, Max. *Geschichte der lateinischen Literatur des
Mittelalters*. 3 vols. München: Beck, 1911-31; rpt. 1959.

Monumental guide to writings in Latin from the sixth century
through the twelfth century. Manitius usually describes the content
of individual works, many of which concern law or the abuse of law
(e.g., see his treatment of Walter of Châtillon, 3:920-936).

58 McGovern, John F. "The Documentary Language of Mediaeval
Business, A. D. 1150-1250." *Classical Journal*, 67 (1972), 227-239.

Argues that "the forced clarity and unity of business Latin
constitute its main rhetorical traits and set it apart as a special
language." Based on a close examination of the documents
produced by the Genoese notary Giovanni di Guiberto (between
1200-1211), McGovern exemplifies numerous ways in which clarity
and unity were promoted, e.g., redundancy, amplification,
avoidance of vernacular terminology, copious use of identifiers ("the
same," "aforesaid," etc.) and of conjunctions, adverbs, and
participles (*et, inde, ita, sic, ideo, ut supra, superius, ut infra,* and so
on). The business notary seems to have learned his craft "through
apprenticeship rather than at university, from practical experience
rather than from the reading of handbooks." Though "reckless of
stylistic beauty," the resulting prose "satisfied the contractual world
of the marketplace, and the rigors and vagaries of the law courts."

59   Murphy, James J. *Rhetoric in the Middle Ages: A History of Rhetorical Theory from Saint Augustine to the Renaissance.* Berkeley: University of California Press, 1974.

Includes several notices of the historical connection between law and the study of rhetoric, particularly in the case of the *ars dictaminis* and *ars notariae.*

60   Paetow, Louis John. *The Arts Course at Medieval Universities with Special Reference to Grammar and Rhetoric.* University Studies of the University of Illinois, Vol. 3, No. 7. Champaign: University of Illinois Press, 1910.

Includes a discussion (Chapter 3) of the rise of the *ars dictaminis* and *ars notariae* and their relation to the study of law.

61   Pizzorni, Reginaldo M. "Il diritto naturale nell'alto medioevo e nei decretisti." *Aquinas,* 19 (1976), 237-272.

A chronological guide to statements about natural law in the writings of Isidore, Alcuin, Rabanus Maurus, Ivo of Chartres, Irnerius, Gratian, Paucapalea, Placentinus, Rogerius, Rufinus, Stephen of Tournai, Simon of Bisignano, Huguccio of Pisa, Azo, Johannes Teutonicus, Accursius, and Raymond of Peñafort.

62   Raby, F. J. E. *A History of Secular Latin Poetry in the Middle Ages.* 2 vols. Oxford: Clarendon, 1957.

A standard introduction. Although Raby gives a good summary of debate poems (2:282-308), he says surprisingly little about legal influences on the genre, noting only the curious example *Discussio litis super hereditate Lazari et Marie Magdalene, etc.*: "The point is, of course, that Lazarus had died, and Mary claims the paternal inheritance. Lazarus holds that as he has returned to life, he is not legally to be regarded as dead. This poem is a mere 'juristic school-disputation,' an example of hair-splitting, where rhetoric and the law meet together" (p. 304). [For a more elaborate and sympathetic discussion of the piece, see item 68.]

63   Rashdall, Hastings. *The Universities of Europe in the Middle Ages.* New ed. by F. M. Powicke and A. B. Emden. 3 vols. Oxford: Oxford University Press, 1936.

The standard work on medieval universities. Rashdall treats not only the institutional histories but also the curricula at Paris, Bologna, Oxford, etc. Indispensable for the understanding of the essential relation between law and letters at the time.

64 Stintzing, Roderich. *Geschichte der populären Literatur des römisch-kanonischen Rechts in Deutschland*. Leipzig: Hirzel, 1867.

A compendious survey of medieval commentaries, *summae*, alphabetical handbooks, etc. on civil and canon law. Includes a full discussion of the literary genre known as "the trial of Satan" (pp. 259-279). Stintzing cites numerous versions of the debate attributed to Bartolus, Jacobus de Theramo, et al.

65 Stubbs, William. *Seventeen Lectures on the Study of Mediaeval and Modern History*. 3rd ed. Oxford: Clarendon, 1900.

Lectures VI and VII, "Learning and Literature at the Court of Henry II," constitute still the most comprehensive survey of literary figures directly or indirectly involved in administration at this period. [See also items 66, 158.]

66 Turner, Ralph V. "Clerical Judges in English Secular Courts: The Ideal versus the Reality." *M&H*, N. S. 3 (1972), 75-98.

Despite the advice of St. Paul that "no man that warreth for God entangleth himself in the things of this world," lay rulers throughout the Middle Ages "relied upon members of the clergy to serve them as judges, secretaries, and other administrative agents." Works by literary figures that comment on this discrepancy between the ideal and the reality include *De nugis curialium*, a satire on conditions in the Church and at court, by Walter Map, a clerk of Henry II's household and sometime itinerant justice; *Contra curiales et officiales clericos*, by Nigel Wireker, author also of the popular poem *Speculum stultorum*; and *De Invectionibus*, by Gerald of Wales (Giraldus Cambrensis).

67 Vinogradoff, Paul. *Roman Law in Medieval Europe*. 2d ed. Oxford: Clarendon, 1929; rpt. Cambridge: Speculum Historiale, and New York: Barnes and Noble, 1968.

Includes a discussion (pp. 128-130) of "The Trials of Satan," the name given to a widely diffused literary genre; in which the Redemption is shown to be a matter of justice as well as grace. In the example cited here, attributed to the great doctor Bartolus, Satan's legal claims to mankind are defeated by the Virgin, acting on man's behalf in the tribunal of heaven. The whole procedure is described in strict conformity with Roman law, "evidently with the idea of acquainting beginners with technical terms and fundamental forms of pleading, such as summons, default, equity, possessory and petitory action, exception, replication, count, fraud, etc."

68   Walther, Hans. *Das Streitgedicht in der lateinischen Literatur des Mittelalters.* (Quellen und Untersuchungen zur lateinischen Philologie des Mittelalters, 5.2.) München: Beck, 1920.

The seminal work on literary debates in medieval Latin. Walther cites law as one of the influences on the genre: "The mock trial, which had played such a large role in the rhetorical and juristic instruction of Roman schools, remained alive in the monastic schools and universities of the medieval period" (p. 21). The influence of such instruction is clearly seen in MS. Paris Lat. 3718 (14th cen.), a debate in which the resurrected Lazarus contests Mary Magdalene's right to keep the property she claimed after his death [cf. item 62]. Walther takes the reader through the legal niceties of the argument (pp. 126-129) and in the appendix reproduces the entire text (pp. 234-248). In another debate, the *Altercatio de utroque Johanne Baptista et Evangelista,* the question of which John had the greater dignity is treated in the terms of canon law (pp. 129-134). Jacobus de Theramo's *Belial* or *Processus Luciferi contra Jesum judice Salomone* teaches by example "trial procedure in canon law." Finally, the influence of the Pseudo-Quintilian *Declamationes,* used for teaching juristic eloquence, may be seen in poetic debates by Hildebert of Tours and Peter of Riga (pp. 134-135).

Abelard

69   Gandillac, Maurice de. "Intention et loi dans l'éthique d'Abélard." *Pierre Abélard—Pierre le Vénérable. Les courants philosophiques, littéraires et artistiques en occident au milieu du XIIᵉ siècle.* Ed. René Louis and Jean Jolivet. Paris: Éditions du Centre National de la Recherche Scientifique, 1975, pp. 585-610.

The theme of this essay, says the author, "is the way in which

Abelard defines *intentio*, the cornerstone of his ethical theory, and the relation of this notion to that of *lex*."

Agobard of Lyon

70   Cabaniss, Allen. *Agobard of Lyon, a Ninth-century Ecclesiastic and Critic*. Chicago: University of Chicago Libraries, 1941.

In his two books *Against the Law of Gundobad* and *Against the Judgment of God*, Agobard stresses the need of one law for the empire. He also argues against the judicial ordeal, condemning it as not law but slaughter ("vere hoc non est lex, sed nex"). Guilt and innocence should be decided in a court of justice. On the other hand, in a complaint to his friend Matfred, a court-official, he decries the general corruption of the legal system: "Judges might be bought, sentences remitted, innocent ones suffer." See pp. 115-119. (This is the last chapter of Cabaniss's dissertation, University of Chicago Divinity School, 1939.)

Albertus Magnus

71   Cunningham, Stanley B. "Albertus Magnus on Natural Law." *Journal of the History of Ideas*, 28 (1967), 479-502.

Cunningham argues that Albert's *De bono* (1240-1244) signals an important development in natural law theory. In contrast to previous medieval thinkers, such as Alan of Lille, William of Auxerre, and John of Rupella, Albert defines natural law not as "an exterior norm to which man must conform" but rather as "an interior perfection of reason guiding or inclining man to the just life from within." Where earlier "the principal cause and source of virtue was conformity to prescribed law," for Albert "the direct and immediate cause of natural virtue is not law, but the right human act seen in all of its dynamic complexity."

Alcuin

72   Wallach, Luitpold. *Alcuin and Charlemagne: Studies in Carolingian History and Literature.* Ithaca: Cornell University Press, 1959.

Proposes that "some of [Alcuin's] writings not only are literary products but having been composed either upon the request of Charlemagne or at least with his approval, possess the character of official Frankish documents." In particular, his *Rhetoric* "is here seen as Charlemagne's *via regia* and not merely as a rhetorical textbook." Part One examines the *Rhetoric* as a treatise on kingship and includes a chapter specifically on "Legal Elements in the Rhetoric" (pp. 73-82). Part Two is devoted to "Alcuin's Acquaintance with Procedures of Frankish Law" (pp. 97-140). "References to, and quotations from, Roman and canon law books which are found in his correspondence prove his acquaintance with actual law cases and with Frankish procedures of law." The main issue in these letters is the law of sanctuary. Part Three takes up the question of "Alcuin as the Author and Editor of Official Carolingian Documents"; and Part Four, "The Literary Method of Alcuin."

Aldhelm

73   Cook, Albert S. "Aldhelm's Legal Studies." *JEGP*, 23 (1924), 105-113.

In a letter written in 671, Aldhelm mentions that Roman law was among the studies he was then pursuing at Canterbury under Archbishop Theodore and Abbot Hadrian. Scholars who have touched upon this passage, notes Cook, have not made "any effort to determine with what text or texts he was engaged." Cook offers as a possibility the Breviary of Alaric (506), "the principal, if not the only representative of Roman law in the expansive realm of the Franks [Pollock and Maitland]." An important link in the argument is the inclusion of the Breviary in a manuscript compiled or transcribed by Aldhelm's biographer, William of Malmesbury. Cook speculates that Aldhelm made a copy of the Breviary for himself; that this was later treasured by the monks of Malmesbury "in reverence for their illustrious founder and benefactor"; and that

William "may have made with his own hand a copy of this doubly venerable codex."

Alexander Neckham

74 Kantorowicz, Hermann. "A Medieval Grammarian on the Sources of the Law." *Tijdschrift voor Rechtsgeschiedenis*, 15 (1936), 35-47; rpt. in his *Rechtshistorische Schriften*. Karlsruhe: Müller, 1970, pp. 93-110.

Calls attention to the *Vocabularius* of the English poet and grammarian Alexander Neckham (d. 1217) in Cambr. MS., Gonville and Caius Coll. 385, as an important comment on "the relation between grammar and law in the middle ages." Kantorowicz reproduces the relevant portion of the manuscript (54b-56a) and says: "We can now see what the Law looked like, when stared at through the spectacles of a grammarian for whom the text of the Law was simply a series of isolated Latin words, for whom the question of their accentuation and declension was more interesting than that of their juristic meaning, and for whom the legal signification of a term was of no greater importance than any other signification" (p. 103).

Ambrosiaster

75 Heggelbacher, Othmar. *Vom römischen zum christlichen Recht. Iuristische Elemente in den Schriften des sogenannten Ambrosiaster.* Freiburg/Schweiz: Universitätsverlag, 1959.

Discusses the juristic elements in the writings of the so-called Ambrosiaster. Heggelbacher takes up in order natural law, Roman law, Jewish (Old Testament) law, and church law.

Anselm of Canterbury

76 Dombois, Hans. "Juristische Bemerkungen zur Satisfaktionslehre des Anselm von Canterbury." *Neue Zeitschrift für systematische Theologie und Religionsphilosophie*, 9 (1967), 339-355.

A study of juristic elements in Anselm's theory of the Atonement.

Arnobius

77   Ferrini, Contardo. "Die juristischen Kenntnisse des Arnobius und des Lactantius." *ZRG*, Rom. Abt. 15 (1894), 343-352.

Primarily a listing of excerpts from Arnobius's *Adversus nationes* (with comparisons from Gaius's *Institutes*) and Lactantius's *Institutes* that show the two authors' knowledge of Roman law.

Augustine

78   Campo del Pozo, Fernando. *Filosofía del derecho según San Agustín*. Valladolid: Archivo Agustiniano, 1966.

79   MacQueen, D. J. "St. Augustine's Concept of Property Ownership." *Recherches Augustiniennes*, 8 (1972), 187-229.

Argues that Augustine's doctrine of property ownership "systematizes and incorporates into one coherent unity all the inferences derivable from his basic theorem: a man who possesses goods unjustly usurps another's property: 'omne quod male posidetur, alienum est.'" The idea is introduced by a compact treatment of Augustine's theory of law in general.

80   Ritschl, Dietrich. "Some Comments on the Background and Influence of Augustine's *Lex Aeterna* Doctrine." *Creation, Christ, and Culture: Studies in Honour of T. F. Torrance*. Ed. Richard W. A. McKinney. Edinburgh: Clark, 1976, pp. 63-81.

An attempt to lay bare the contradictions in Augustine's theory of law (both eternal and natural). The crux of the problem is Augustine's concept of God. "In short: had it not been for Augustine's Neo-Platonic understanding of God, which influenced fifteen hundred years of thought in the west, western jurisprudence and political theory, as well as theological ethics, would have been spared a great number of problems."

81   Schubert, P. Alois. "Augustins Lex-Aeterna Lehre nach Inhalt und
      Quellen." *Beiträge zur Geschichte der Philosophie des Mittelalters*,
      24 (1924), 3-61.

          The central discussion of Augustine's theory of Eternal Law. In
      Part I Schubert defines the theory itself; and in Part II he identifies
      the main sources of the idea: Cicero, Plotinus, the Apostle Paul,
      John the Evangelist, the Stoic philosophers, and Heraclitus.

82   Vance, Eugene. "Augustine's Confessions and the Poetics of the
      Law." *MLN*, 93 (1978), 618-634.

          Explores Augustine's use of the metaphor of law (primarily the
      Old vs. the New), based on Paul's exposition in Romans 2. "[S]ince
      the Old Law had come to dominate Augustine through the intimately
      related forms of an idolatrous love of letters, and a passionate
      attachment to the creation..., obviously only through new
      experiences of language and of love may Augustine be redeemed
      from the Letters and the Law of Sin. Accordingly, in his readings of
      St. Paul and St. John, Augustine clings above all to the principle of
      Christ as Word (Verbum)...."

Benedictine Rule

83   Blecker, Michael Paulin. "Roman Law and 'Consilium' in the
      Regula Magistri and the *Rule* of St. Benedict." *Speculum*, 47 (1972),
      1-28.

          Accepting the recent view that the *Rule* of St. Benedict is partly a
      reworking of the earlier *Regula Magistri*, Blecker contrasts the idea
      of *consilium* in both. In the *RM*, the basis of the idea is legal (the
      Roman law of corporations); in the *RB*, it is scriptural (see esp. Acts
      4:32). The change greatly affected the answer to the question: who is
      the owner of monastic property?

Bible moralisée

84   Haussherr, Reiner. "Eine Warnung vor dem Studium von zivilem und kanonischem Recht in der Bible moralisée." *Frühmittelalterliche Studien*, 9 (1975), 390-404.

Finds the contemporary bias against the study of civil and canon law (cf. Pope Honorius III's bull "Super speculum," 1219) reflected in the commentary and illustrations of the *Bible moralisée*.

Boethius

85   Coster, Charles Henry. *The Iudicium Quinquevirale*. Cambridge, Mass.: The Mediaeval Academy of America, 1935.

Discusses the bearing of the *iudicium quinquevirale*—a judiciary committee of the Roman Senate—upon the trial of Boethius (pp. 40-63).

Carmen de Hastingae Proelio

86   Morton, Catherine, and Hope Muntz, eds. *Carmen de Hastingae Proelio of Guy, Bishop of Amiens*. Oxford: Clarendon, 1972.

Edition and translation of the earliest account of the Norman conquest. The introduction (pp. liv-lix) includes a discussion of verses 787-835, "the only detailed contemporary account of the rite by which William the Conqueror was crowned King of the English on 25 December 1066" (p. liv). The notes call attention to plays on the legal meanings of words or phrases (see pp. 16, 354, 465).

Charters of Christ

87   Spalding, Mary Caroline. *The Middle English Charters of Christ*. Bryn Mawr College Monographs, 15. Bryn Mawr: Bryn Mawr College, 1914.

Includes the texts of two Latin "Charters of Christ." [Cited also as 186.]

Commodianus

88   Salvatore, Antonio. *"Lex Secunda* e interpretazione biblica in Commodiano." *Vetera Christianorum*, 5 (1968), 111-130.

A study of the concept of the Old and New Law in the poetic commentaries of Commodianus.

Fulbert of Chartres

89   Behrends, Frederick, ed. and trans. *The Letters and Poems of Fulbert of Chartres*. Oxford: Clarendon, 1976.

Notes that after the Bible and the Latin Fathers, Fulbert's main source of quotations is ecclesiastical and secular law. "His favorite legal sources seem to have been a collection of Carolingian capitularies containing the works of Ansegisus of Fontanelle and Benedictus Levita and another of Pseudo-Isidorian decretals....Fulbert also knew the Theodosian Code..." (pp. xxiii-xxiv). Fulbert's knowledge of how to apply the law to individual cases was probably acquired from his training in rhetoric, which included legal reasoning (pp. xxx-xxxi).

Geoffrey of Monmouth

90   Pähler, Heinrich. "Die 'Leges Molmutinae,' ein Beitrag zum Problem der historischen Wahrheit und politischen Absicht bei Geoffrey von Monmouth." *Anglia*, 73 (1955), 516-518.

Identifies the puzzling "leges Molmutinae" (*Hist. Regum Brit.* 2.17) as the *Leges Wallicae* of Howel the Good (d. 950). The clue comes from the Welsh work "Kulhwch and Olwen" (11th-12th cen.), which states that Howel revised some of the ancient laws of Moelmud Dyvynwal (i.e., Molmutius Dunvallo), a legendary king of about 400 B. C. By renaming a well-known body of law *"leges Molmutinae,"* Geoffrey implied that it originated at the same time as the Twelve Tables of Rome (ca. 450 B. C.). This is consistent with his general purpose, which was to establish a parallel between Britannia and Rome.

91   Williams, Schafer. "Geoffrey of Monmouth and the Canon Law."
       Speculum, 27 (1952), 184-190.

       "To show that Geoffrey had some acquaintance with the canon
       law in one of its great formative periods, that it penetrated into his
       Historia, and, in this wise, to supplement Tatlock's magisterial study
       [*The Legendary History of Britain*, 1950], is the object of this note."
       Williams shows that the terminology which so puzzled Tatlock and
       other researchers in their study of Lucius ("the British king who
       engineered the lightning conversion of himself and his subjects")
       comes from the *False Decretals* of Pseudo-Isidore, specifically, the
       canons *In illis civitatibus* and *Scitote*, which Geoffrey probably knew
       from their reproduction in the *Polycarpus* and Anselm's *Collectio
       Canonum*.

Gregory of Tours

92   Ringel, W. *Das Strafrecht des Gregor von Tours*. Diss. Leipzig 1912.

Guy, Bishop of Amiens (see *Carmen de Hastingae Proelio*)

Henry of Avranches

93   Russell, J. C. and John Paul Heironimus. *The Shorter Latin Poems
       of Master Henry of Avranches Relating to England*. Cambridge,
       Mass.: The Mediaeval Academy of America, 1935; rpt. New York:
       Kraus, 1970.

       Describes the various capacities in which Henry's knowledge of
       law was put to good use (pp. 19-21) and reproduces the texts of his
       poems that contain law—although "such legal poetry constituted
       only a small part of his work."

Jacobus de Voragine

94   Huot-Girard, Giselle. "La Justice immanente dans la 'Légende
      dorée.'" *Épopées, légendes et miracles (Cahiers d'Études
      médiévales, 1).* Montreal, 1974, pp. 135-147.

      The essay seeks to answer three questions: how does immanent
      justice manifest itself in the *Golden Legend*, by what intermediary,
      and against what abuses? The author catalogues numerous examples
      in each case and finds little or no correlation between the gravity of a
      sin and its punishment: an earthquake may swallow up both the
      heresiarch and the man whose only fault is "too great happiness."
      He concludes: "The reign of God maintains itself by fear, terror:
      truth shines out in force. It is the God of the Old Testament, God as
      judge, God as avenger, that reappears in the *Golden Legend.*"

Jerome

95   Violardo, G. *Il pensiero giuridico di San Girolamo.* Milan:
      Pubblicazioni della Università Cattolica del Sacro Cuore, 1937.

      Brings together a number of texts by Jerome that touch upon
      legal questions. Violardo finds twenty-one references to Roman law
      (Gaudemet [45] rejects five of these but adds others, p. 113).

John of Salisbury

96   Dickinson, John. "The Mediaeval Conception of Kingship and
      Some of Its Limitations, as Developed in the *Policraticus* of John of
      Salisbury." *Speculum*, 1 (1926), 308-337.

      A clear exposition of the main lines of thought in the
      Policraticus. John's point of view was dictated not by contemporary
      feudal politics but by the ecclesiastical theory of the state, the heart
      of which was its conception of kingship. He sees the king, whether
      just or unjust, as an agent of the divine will. This leads to a number
      of difficulties. Yet, Dickinson concludes, "It is the very
      inconsistencies in the political thought of the *Policraticus*, and its
      blending of apparently incompatible elements, which give it its
      principal value; for it discloses still in combination a number of

separate strains of thought whose later dissociation was to form the main currents of opposing doctrine for many succeeding centuries" (p. 335).

97   Liebeschütz, Hans. *Mediaeval Humanism in the Life and Writings of John of Salisbury*. Studies of the Warburg Institute, 17. London: The Warburg Institute, 1950.

Touches upon theories of law and the state in discussing the *Policraticus* (see especially Chapter 5). Liebeschütz's treatment elaborates on the following observation: "For John the problem of the State is the problem of the rulers....Therefore the only important task for the political theorist is to develop the feeling of responsibility on the part of the king and his advisers" (p. 46).

98   Rouse, Richard H., and Mary A. "John of Salisbury and the Doctrine of Tyrannicide." *Speculum*, 42 (1967), 693-709.

Tries to show "that John's doctrine of tyrannicide was written as pure theory with a practical purpose." It is theoretical in the sense that John was not proposing it as a plan of action; practical in the sense that he hoped thereby to convince Henry II that "for his own good, he must rule in accordance with the law." By law, John means neither the *Corpus Juris Civilis* nor the *Decretum*, though he quotes from both, but rather custom. Thus, when he defines a tyrant as a king who rules contrary to the law, he means a king "who arrogates to himself powers, prerogatives, or possessions which have not traditionally belonged to the king."

99   Ullmann, Walter. "The Influence of John of Salisbury on Medieval Italian Jurists." *EHR*, 59 (1944), 384-392.

Calls attention to the "absolute authority" of the *Policraticus* among Neapolitan legal scholars, in particular Lucas de Penna [cf. 103].

Lactantius

100   Ferrini, Contardo. *Le cognizioni giuridiche di Lattanzio, Arnobio et Minucio Felice.* Memorie del l'Accademia delle Scienze di Modena, Ser. II, No. 10 (1894).

101   _____. "Su le idee giuridiche contenute nei libri V et VI delle Istituzioni di Lattanzio." *Rivista internazionale di scienze sociali e discipline ausiliarie,* 5 (1894).

102   Loi, V. "L'interpretazione giuridica del *Testamentum* divino nella storia della salvezza." *Augustinianum,* 16 (1976), 41-52.

On Lactantius's interpretation of the word *testamentum* (as used of the Bible and *in* the Bible) to mean a pact, covenant, treaty between God and his people.

Lucas de Penna

103   Ullmann, Walter. *The Medieval Idea of Law, as Represented by Lucas de Penna.* London: Methuen, 1946; rpt. New York: Barnes and Noble, and London: Methuen, 1969.

Ullmann notes in several places Lucas's practice of citing the works of poets in his commentary on the *Tres Libri Codices*: e.g., Virgil, Horace, Terence, Ovid, Plautus, and the poet of his own time "dominus Petrarca laureatus," with whom he corresponded (see pp. 27-33). Lucas also relied heavily on the Bible and early Christian writers (Lactantius, Cyprian, Jerome, Ambrose, Augustine), on Roman thinkers (Cicero, Seneca), and on John of Salisbury's *Policraticus* [99]. The practice is defended in Lucas's preface: "Si etiam describantur inferius alia secundum Isidorum aliosque doctores...vel quid forte poeticum nullus ea tamquam puerilia teneat vel subsannet insidiator, cuius proprium est in malum convertere et in electis ponere maculam" and again "Si pro uberiore expositione auctoritates insertae sunt novi et veteris testamenti, legista nullus irrideat." [On the legal authority of poets, cf. 15, 20, 37.]

Marsilius of Padua

104   Gewirth, Alan. *Marsilius of Padua, the Defender of Peace* (Vol. 1 of
      Marsilius of Padua and Medieval Political Philosophy). New York:
      Columbia University Press, 1951.

      A clear exposition of Marsilius's legal and political thought,
      which diverged sharply from medieval tradition in shifting the focus
      of political discussion from "eternal law" and "right reason" to the
      Aristotelian doctrine of natural desire. See especially Chapter 4
      ("Law: Human and Divine") and Chapter 5 ("The People as
      Legislator").

Novatian

105   Wehofer, Thomas. "Sprachliche Eigenthümlichkeiten des
      classischen Juristenlateins in Novatians Briefen." *Wiener Studien.
      Zeitschrift für classische Philologie*, 23 (1901), 269-275.

      Explains a number of syntactical and lexical peculiarities in the
      letters of Novatian as the result of either a legal education or a close
      familiarity with the writings of such jurists as Gaius and Ulpian.

Placentinus

106   Kantorowicz, Hermann. "The Poetical Sermon of a Mediaeval
      Jurist: Placentinus and his 'Sermo de Legibus.'" *Journal of the
      Warburg Institute*, 2 (1938-39), 22-41; rpt. in his *Rechtshistorische
      Schriften*. Karlsruhe: Müller, 1970, pp. 111-135.

      Claims to have discovered the lost *Sermo de legibus* of
      Placentinus, one of the most influential and renowned jurists of the
      twelfth century. Although structured like a sermon, the work is
      actually a Menippean satire, in which "Ignorantia" and "Legalis
      scientia" debate their respective merits. There are more than fifty
      references to the sources of the Roman law, the *leges*, as well as
      references to Aristotle, Boethius, Horace, Virgil, and the New
      Testament. The text is reproduced in full from Basel MS. C.1.7.

Ranulf de Glanville

107 Russell, Josiah Cox. "Ranulf de Glanville." *Speculum*, 45 (1970), 69-79.

A study of three aspects of the career of Ranulf de Glanville, justiciar under Henry II and reputed author of *De legibus Anglie* and the crusading chronicle *De expugnatione Lyxbonensi.* "The first is his association with Bury St. Edmunds....The second is the length of his career....The third is his association with the authors of his time, his own writings, and his great interest in documents, literacy, and literature."

Ruodlieb

108 Braun, Werner. *Studien zum Ruodlieb*. Berlin: De Gruyter, 1962.

The historical accuracy of the legal elements in the poem, including the marriage contract, is taken up on pages 82-85.

109 Henel, Heinrich. "Die Eheschliessung im *Ruodlieb*." *GR*, 17 (1942), 20-24.

Taking as his point of departure Zallinger's two articles on marriage in the *Nibelungenlied* and *Kudrun* [460, 461], Henel asks, "Is marriage by mutual declaration of the engaged couple identical with the *desponsatio* or *traditio* of Germanic custom? Or does this form of marriage stem from Church law?" Zallinger says no to both questions, "and the *Ruodlieb* proves him correct."

110 Meyer, Herbert. "Die Eheschliessung im 'Ruodlieb' und das Eheschwert." *ZRG*, Germ. Abt. 52 (1932), 276-293.

Reconstructs the ceremonial and legal aspects of the wedding in *Ruodlieb.*

111 Vollmann, Benedikt K. "Der Strafprozess im VIII. Fragment des *Ruodlieb." Befund und Deutung: Zum Verhältnis von Empirie und Interpretation in Sprach- und Literaturwissenschaft.* Ed. Klaus Grubmüller et al. Tübingen: Niemeyer, 1979.

Concludes that the poet's handling of legal process is more idealistic thàn indicative of actual conditions in the eleventh century.

Saxo Grammaticus

112   Haastrup, Niels. "Retorisk analyse af Knud Lavards Forsvarstale på grundlag af laeren om *status*." *Saxostudier*. Copenhagen: Museum Tusculanum, 1975, pp. 107-114.

Analyzes the plea of Kanutus in terms of the rhetorical-juridical strategy of *status*, which Saxo could have taken from either the *Ad Herennium* or Cicero's *De inventione*.

Somnium viridarii (See also French *Songe du Vergier*)

113   Merzbacher, Friedrich. "Das Somnium viridarii von 1376 als Spiegel des gallikanischen Staatskirchenrechts." *ZRG*, Kan. Abt. 42 (1956), 55-72.

Discusses the *Somnium viridarii* (translated into French as *Le Songe du vergier*) as reflecting the policies of Charles V (1364-1380), particularly with respect to the question of *regnum* vs. *sacerdotium*.

Tertullian

114   Barnes, Timothy David. *Tertullian: A Historical and Literary Study*. Oxford: Clarendon, 1971.

Denies that Tertullian the Christian apologist and Tertullian the *iurisconsultus* were the same person (Chapter Four). As for Tertullian's legal knowledge, Barnes notes that, given the place of rhetoric in ancient education, "hardly a single Latin author is free from legal allusions. The line begins with Plautus...[and] continues unbroken, through Apuleius, beyond Tertullian to Cyprian, to Arnobius and Lactantius."

115   Beck, Alexander. *Römisches Recht bei Tertullian und Cyprian.*
       Schriften der Königsberger gelehrten Gesellschaft, Geisteswiss. Kl.
       7/2. Halle: Niemeyer, 1930; rpt. Aalen: Scientia-Verlag, 1967.

116   Bray, Gerald. "The Legal Concept of Ratio in Tertullian." *Vigiliae
       Christianae*, 31 (1977), 94-116.

       Concludes that "*ratio* in Tertullian's usage was a
       well-established legal term uninfluenced by philosophical
       speculation" (in particular, by the Stoic concept of *logos*). In
       common use in the second century A. D. as a juridical term, *ratio*
       meant "method" or "procedure" and referred to the normal means
       for interpreting Roman statute law. "Tertullian borrowed not just
       the word but also the underlying principle of legal interpretation
       from the jurists and applied it to Christianity, using the Scriptures as
       the equivalent of the statute law."

117   Labriolle, P. de. "Tertullien Jurisconsulte." *Nouvelle revue
       historique de droit français et étranger*, 30 (1906), 5-27.

       Seeks to demonstrate that "the chief conceptions of Tertullian,
       those which constitute the framework of his writings, took their form
       from Roman law" (p. 26).

118   Maistre, A.-P. "*Traditio.* Aspects théologiques d'un terme de droit
       chez Tertullien." *Revue des sciences philosophiques et théologiques*,
       51 (1967), 617-643.

       A study of the legal sense of the word *traditio* ("custom") in two
       of Tertullian's works, *De praescriptione haereticorum* and *De
       corona.*

119   Schlossmann, S. "Tertullian im Lichte der Jurisprudenz."
       Zeitschrift für Kirchengeschichte, 27 (1906), 251-275, 407-430.

120   Sider, Robert Dick. *Ancient Rhetoric and the Art of Tertullian.*
       London: Oxford University Press, 1971.

       An analysis of Tertullian's style and form of argument primarily
       in terms of forensic rhetoric (as described by Aristotle, Cicero, and
       Quintilian). Much of the study is given over to the qualitative issue
       or *status qualitatis.* See especially Chapter 5, "The Qualitative Issue
       and 'Legal Questions.'"

121   Stirnamann, Joseph Kaspar. *Die Praescriptio Tertullians im Lichte des römischen Rechts und der Theologie.* Paradosis. Beiträge zur Geschichte der altchristlichen Literatur und Theologie, 3. Freiburg in der Schweiz: Paulusverlag, 1949.

Shows "how deeply the *De praescriptione haereticorum* with its prescriptive rule has been influenced by the Roman legal practice of the *praescriptio*" (Sider). Also an excellent summary of the debate on whether Tertullian was simply advocate or jurisconsult, pp. 2-4.

122   Vitton, Paolo. *I concetti giuridici nelle opere di Tertulliano.* Rome: Tip. della R. Accad. Nazionale dei Lincei, 1924.

Thomas Aquinas

123   Aubert, Jean-Marie. *Le droit romain dans l'oeuvre de saint Thomas.* Bibliothèque Thomiste, 30. Paris: Vrin, 1955.

An important study not only of Thomas's debt to Roman law but also of his philosophy of law in general.

124   Crowe, Michael Bertram. "Synderesis and the Notion of Law in saint Thomas." *L'Homme et son destin. Actes du Premier Congrès International de Philosophie Médiévale* [1958]. Louvain: Éditions Nauwelaerts, and Paris: Béatrice-Nauwelaerts, 1960, pp. 601-609.

Seeks to explain the decline of synderesis and the concomitant rise of legal theory in the *ST.* St. Thomas is anxious to avoid the neo-Platonic doctrine of innate ideas and thus replaces synderesis with the Aristotelian "practical syllogism"—closely associated in his own mind with natural law.

125   _____. "St Thomas and Ulpian's Natural Law: A Puzzling Preference." *St. Thomas Aquinas 1274-1974 Commemorative Studies.* Toronto: Pontifical Institute of Mediaeval Studies, 1974, 1:261-282.

Aquinas's adoption of Ulpian's definition of natural law—"ius naturale est quod natura omnia animalia docuit"—went against the trend of his predecessors and found few followers. Crowe's study includes a brief history of the definition from Ulpian to St. Thomas.

126   Harding, Alan. "The Reflection of Thirteenth-Century Legal
       Growth in Saint Thomas's Writings." *Aquinas and Problems of His
       Time*. Ed. G. Verbeke and D. Verhelst. The Hague: Leuven
       University Press, 1976, pp. 18-37.

       Although many of the points made in the sections devoted to law
       in the *ST* suggest the legal and political situation in contemporary
       France, they are all traceable to conventional authorities such as
       Aristotle and Cicero. "I can only conclude," says Harding, "that
       Thomas's discussion of law is so profound as a synthesis of juristic
       ideas that it is nearly useless as an indication of the influence on
       Thomas of contemporary facts."

127   Kulmann, B. C. *Der Gesetzbegriff beim hl. Thomas von Aquin im
       Lichte des Rechtsstudium seiner Zeit*. Bonn: Peter Hanstein, 1912.

128   Lottin, Odon. *Le droit naturel chez saint Thomas d'Aquin et ses
       prédécesseurs*. 2d ed. Bruges: Beyaert, [1913].

       The standard introduction to natural law in Aquinas. Lottin
       traces the development of natural law theory (mainly in the twelfth
       and thirteenth centuries) under three headings: the Decretists
       (Roman law, Isidore of Seville, Gratian, et al.), the pre-Thomist
       theologians (Anselm of Laon, William of Auxerre, Albertus
       Magnus, Bonaventure, Alexander of Hales, et al.), and Aquinas.
       Throughout Lottin stresses the importance of Anselm of Laon and
       his school, which reduced the natural law to certain primordial
       principles ("do good and avoid evil"), defined it as an "inbred
       habit," and identified it with the divine law. The influence of these
       ideas on Thomas is considered. But "his true merit, which assured
       the durability of his doctrine, is to have put in full light the intrinsic
       character of natural law. The natural law is nothing other than
       human nature expressing itself *rationally*" (p. 103).

129   McIlwain, Charles Howard. *The Growth of Political Thought in the
       West*. New York: Macmillan, 1932.

       On St. Thomas's legal thought see pp. 323-335. McIlwain's
       perspective may be inferred from the following: "St. Thomas was a
       man of his time, and it was the habit of thought at that time to
       conceive of the state primarily in terms of law, not law in terms of the
       state. The foundations of his political theory must therefore be
       sought in his conception of the nature and source of law..." (p. 326).

130   O'Connor, D. J. *Aquinas and Natural Law*. London: Macmillan, 1967.

      A short, very readable introduction to Aquinas's thinking on natural law, which is "basic to [his] moral philosophy...." O'Connor treats Aquinas more as philosopher than theologian and views his work in the light of modern, as well as medieval, philosophical assumptions.

Valla

131   Stevens, Henry J., Jr. "Lorenzo Valla's *Elegantiae*: A Humanistic View of the Latin Language." Diss. Bryn Mawr 1973.

      One of Lorenzo's main targets in *De linguae latiniae elegantiis* (1435-1439) is the study of law as practiced in the Middle Ages. In an effort to bring legal usage into conformity with Ciceronian standards of meaning, Valla "composes two books of *differentiae* (Books IV and V) and thus seeks to revise material contained in the medieval lexica..., whose source is often Isidore's *Etymologiae*."

Walter of Châtillon

132   Strecker, Karl. *Moralisch-satirische Gedichte Walters von Chatillon*. Heidelberg: Winter, 1929.

      The poems edited here include many criticisms of the legal establishment. Of particular interest is the poem beginning "In domino confido" (pp. 33-57), Walter's satire on the ideal university, which he claims to have read before the Faculties of Law and Arts at Bologna; part 2 (pp. 44-46) describes the "ideal" faculty of law.

Wulfstan *Cantor*

133   Whitelock, Dorothy. "Wulfstan *Cantor* and Anglo-Saxon Law." *Nordica et Anglica: Studies in Honor of Stefan Einarsson*. Ed. Allan H. Orrick. The Hague: Mouton, 1968, pp. 83-92.

      Makes two inferences about law from the poem *Narratio Metrica de Sancto Swithumo*, composed between 992 and 994 by Wulfstan

Cantor: first, that the poem "affords evidence of a lost edict of Edgar," and second, that a reeve "was expected to keep as his own property the composition paid to him in the course of his exercise of justice."

Wyclif

134 Daly, L. J. *The Political Theory of John Wyclif*. Chicago: Loyola University Press, 1962.

Chapter 1 traces Wyclif's intellectual heritage (Augustine and the "Oxford school") and the political thought of his contemporaries John of Paris, Giles of Rome, Marsilius of Padua, and William of Ockham. Chapter 2 relates his thought to the fourteenth-century historical background. In Chapter 3 Daly stresses that Wyclif's ideas concerning civil society are more those of a theologian than a philosopher, an Augustinian than an Aristotelian. He "heartily despised the Roman civil law" and constantly advocated the law of the gospel instead. Chapter 4, "The Monarchial Form of Government," has much to say about the role of law in Christian society and its relation to the king. Finally, in Chapter 5, Daly summarizes Wyclif's contribution to the growth of centralized government.

135 Farr, William. *John Wyclif as Legal Reformer*. Leiden: Brill, 1974.

Studies Wyclif's construction of "a legal artifice that would subject the whole of the English clergy to lay regulation and ultimately ecclesiastical reform through the dispossession of the clergy's temporality." Wyclif supports his argument on two levels: "theologically, based on the Fathers and the canon law and legally within the framework of English feudal law and practice" (p. 165).

136 Maitland, Frederic William. "Wyclif on English and Roman Law." *Law Quarterly Review*, 1896; rpt. *The Collected Papers of Frederic William Maitland*. Ed. H. A. L. Fisher. Cambridge: University Press, 1911, 3:50-53.

Notes the contrast made between civil and English law in Wyclif's *De officio regis*. Wyclif "has a feud with the bishops who have been fostering the study of 'civil law' in the universities. Thus they have been withdrawing men and means from theology. Of the two, the clergy of England had better read English than Roman law" (p. 51).

OLD AND MIDDLE ENGLISH

General and Miscellaneous

137 Alford, John A. "Literature and Law in Medieval England." *PMLA*, 92 (1977), 941-951.

Analyzes examples of the legal metaphor in the Anglo-Norman *Château d'Amour, Piers Plowman*, the so-called "Charters of Christ," *Pearl*, and the lyric poem "Quia Amore Langueo." The author suggests that the metaphor drew its power from the medieval belief in the unity of all law—divine, natural, and human—and that the later separation of these various kinds of law resulted necessarily in its downfall.

138 Barnie, John. *War in Medieval Society: Social Values and the Hundred Years War 1337-99*. London: Weidenfeld and Nicolson, 1974.

The aim of this study is two-fold: to trace the changing responses of Englishmen to the Hundred Years War and to examine the effect of the war on the ideas of chivalry and nationalism. What distinguishes his approach, says Barnie, is the extensive use of literary sources, material that is "partially or totally neglected by historians of the period." These sources are mainly the works of Chaucer, Erghome, Froissart, Gower, Minot, Walsingham, and the anonymous *Morte Arthure* and *Mum and the Sothsegger*. At various points the discussion includes the literary response to such abuses as purveyance, maintenance, and other crimes aggravated by the war.

139 Bartels, Arthur. "Rechtsaltertümer in der angelsächsischen Dichtung." Diss. Kiel 1913.

140 Baum, Richard H. "The Medieval Outlaw: A Study in Protest." Diss. University of Utah 1972.

Attempts a more rigorous definition of the outlaw than merely "an individual who has been placed outside the law." Concentrating on "the romance of England's Greenwood Forest," Baum also seeks to establish which outlaws were historical figures and which (like Robin Hood, in his view) were not.

141   Bennett, Josephine Waters. "The Mediaeval Loveday." *Speculum*, 33 (1958), 351-370.

Believes that Spargo [231] "was misled by his initial assumption that the loveday was originally or primarily a 'legal institution' and that the word was a technical legal term." In an extremely thorough examination of the actual usage of the word, Bennett shows that any meeting of contending parties for the purpose of settling their dispute might be called a loveday, that "love" in this case means concord (not leave or permission), and that the court, though it might allow a private settlement, had nothing to do with appointing the day. She rejects also the idea that *loveday* is a translation of *dies amoris*; on the contrary, "it seems reasonable to suppose that Middle English *loveday* was formed on the analogy of *lawday*, and that the English is the older form, of which *dies amoris* and *jour d'amour* were translations."

142   Bethurum, Dorothy. "Stylistic Features of the Old English Laws." *MLR*, 27 (1932), 263-279.

In this admirable study, packed with information about the literary aspects not only of Anglo-Saxon but also of other Germanic legal codes, Bethurum explores the early connection between law and poetry. Although numerous scholars have agreed on the poetic nature of early Germanic laws, "no very definite statement has been made about the kind of verse the laws illustrate." One feature in particular that stands out is alliteration. The alliterative formulas so characteristic of Germanic law do not conform, however, to the customary five-type line. These illustrate another metrical form "less dignified, slightly less regular"—to use Sievers' term, *Sagvers*. Originating in a time when the laws were published by oral declaration, the alliteration of *Sagvers* was primarily a mnemonic device. Yet not all of the alliterative phrases in the Anglo-Saxon laws can be traced to this early period. Some of them show the influence of the Bible. It is this combination—the "influences of the sophisticated Latin writing of the first six centuries on crude, fresh Germanic material"—that chiefly interests Bethurum.

143   Chaney, William A. *The Cult of Kingship in Anglo-Saxon England.*
      Berkeley: University of California Press, 1970.

      A superbly documented study of sacral kingship, emphasizing
      the continuity of pagan elements in the Christian era. Chaney draws
      upon every kind of available evidence but most extensively upon law
      and literature (including the Icelandic sagas).

144   Culbert, Taylor. "The Single Combat in Medieval Heroic
      Narrative." Diss. University of Michigan 1957.

      Shows the development of single combat as a literary motif from
      Beowulf to *The Wallace.* Gradually, vengeance as the primary
      motive is replaced by religion and patriotism; in this larger setting,
      however, the single combat is unable to provide more than a merely
      symbolic resolution.

145   Fisher, John H. "Chancery and the Emergence of Standard Written
      English in the Fifteenth Century." *Speculum,* 52 (1977), 870-899.

      Argues that during the crucial period between 1420 and 1460,
      before printers and educators decided the "approved" forms and
      idioms of written English, "the essential characteristics of Modern
      Written English were determined by the practice of the clerks in
      Chancery."

146   Green, A. Wigfall. *The Inns of Court and Early English Drama.*
      New Haven: Yale University Press, 1931.

      Although this book focuses on the sixteenth and seventeenth
      centuries, it is not without interest to students of an earlier period.
      Chapter 1 provides a general survey of the numerous writers from
      Chaucer to Dickens associated with the Inns. Chapter 2 discusses the
      rise of the Inns and their internal organization. The remaining six
      chapters deal with various kinds of dramatic performances
      connected with the Inns—revels, masques, plays.

147   Hallmundsson, May N. "A Collection of Materials for a Study of
      the Literary Scene at the End of the Fourteenth Century." Diss. New
      York University 1970.

      Brings together documentary evidence (grants, petitions, wills,
      muniments of real estate or financial transactions, much of it
      concerning "literary" civil servants, such as Scogan, Clanvowe, Usk,

and Hoccleve) in order to create "a fully documented picture of the
literary community of London in the last quarter of the fourteenth
century, a community composed of aristocrats and commoners,
revolving about the royal palace, Chancery, and the government
offices of Westminster and the Inns of Court."

148   Hilton, R. H. "The Origins of Robin Hood." *Past and Present,* 14
       (1958), 30-44.

       Argues that Robin Hood never existed but still has historical
       significance as the reflection of peasant aspirations in the face of
       legal and social oppression. The conditions described in the earliest
       tales indicate "a thirteenth or at the latest fourteenth-century
       origin." Included in the article is a brief discussion of the changing
       nature of outlawry in the thirteenth century.

149   Holt, J. C. "The Origins and Audience of the Ballads of Robin
       Hood." *Past and Present*, 18 (1960), 89-110.

       In response to Hilton [148], Holt emphasizes that Robin Hood,
       as a "prude" and "curteyse" outlaw, was a hero "not of a
       discontented peasantry, but of the gentry."

150   Kelly, Henry Ansgar. *Love and Marriage in the Age of Chaucer.*
       Ithaca and London: Cornell University Press, 1975.

       Demonstrates—in opposition to C. S. Lewis and other
       proponents of "courtly love"—that love and marriage were
       intimately linked in medieval thought and practice. "Marriage was
       considered the most desirable conclusion to serious love. There was
       no tradition of incompatibility between love and marriage, except in
       the literature of satire and complaint; and in such literature neither
       love nor marriage was taken seriously or sympathetically. The
       practical founder and main preceptor of the romance of marriage
       was Ovid, and his lessons were inescapable in the Middle Ages." The
       book is a judicious blending of literary analysis (mainly of Chaucer
       and Gower) and historical research (with evidence concerning sex
       and marriage drawn chiefly from canon law and its commentators).
       [Cf. 212.]

151   Lange, Joost de. *The Relation and Development of English and Icelandic Outlaw Traditions.* Haarlem: Tjeenk Willink & Zoon, 1935.

Hypothesizes a common ancestry (Norwegian) for both the English and Icelandic outlaw traditions. Similarities between the two are noted on the basis of six literary examples: (English) Hereward, Gamelyn, Robin Hood, and (Icelandic) the *Gísli-saga, Horðr-saga, Grettir-saga.* One major difference, however, is that the Icelandic hero is an individual; the English, a social type.

152   Lyall, R. J. "Politics and Poetry in Fifteenth and Sixteenth Century Scotland." *Scottish Literary Journal,* 3 (1976), 5-29.

Argues that the complaints of injustice in Middle Scots poems are more conventional than reflective of specific abuses under James III (and therefore of little help in dating the poems). Among the works shown to have legal interest are *The Thre Prestis of Peblis, Lancelot of the Laik, The Talis of the Fyve Bestes, The Buke of Gud Counsale,* Henryson's *Fabillis,* and Dunbar's *The Thrissill and the Rois.*

153   Reed, Thomas Lloyd, Jr. "Middle English Debate Poetry: A Study in Form and Function." Diss. University of Virginia 1978.

Devotes a chapter to possible influences of legal training on the genre of literary debate.

154   Scattergood, V. J. *Politics and Poetry in the Fifteenth Century.* New York: Barnes and Noble, 1972.

Concerned principally "with ideas, attitudes and opinion about fifteenth-century politics and society as they are expressed in contemporary verses." The book begins with an overview of political poetry—its authors, patrons, audience—and then moves into a discussion of poems on foreign affairs (Chapter 3) and poems on domestic affairs (Chapters 4-6). There is a brief look at verses on religion and the clergy (Chapter 7). Three concluding chapters deal with literary reflections of English society: the theoretical basis, e.g., the breakup of the tenurial system (Chapter 9), and protest and revolt (Chapter 10). Treating the poetry primarily as historical record (and thus somewhat superficially from a literary point of view), Scattergood shows how firmly grounded it was in the contemporary scene, including the issues of law and abuses of law.

155   Schoeck, R. J. "Rhetoric and Law in Sixteenth-Century England." *SP,* 50 (1953), 110-127.

   Although this article explores the relation between rhetoric and law in the sixteenth century, it takes a preliminary look at the Middle Ages. Schoeck observes, for example, that "the resurgence of legal studies (that is, of Roman law) in the early Middle Ages was closely affiliated with rhetoric, and only with Irnerius did law cease to be a sub-division of rhetoric and become a subject in its own right." He also notes that elementary legal procedure was taught along with rhetoric at Oxford in the fifteenth century—but to what extent and to whom is unclear.

156   Stenton, F. M. *The Latin Charters of the Anglo-Saxon Period.* Oxford: Clarendon, 1955.

   Although concerned primarily with Anglo-Saxon charters (and only royal grants at that), this study nevertheless describes a class of documents that for "vividness of detail...entitles them to rank as literature" (p. 44). Characterized by one source as a *talu,* i.e., the statement or narrative record of a case, these documents "are remarkable as pieces of free composition in English prose and they have unique interest as illustrations of the way in which the fortunes of individuals were affected by the salient events of history."

157   Taylor, Rupert. *The Political Prophecy in England.* New York: Columbia University Press, 1911.

   Besides elaborating on the close connection between prophecy and politics, Taylor notes specific laws against the dissemination of prophecies (the first in 1402, another in 1406).

158   Tout, Thomas Frederick. "Literature and Learning in the English Civil Service in the Fourteenth Century." *Speculum,* 4 (1929), 365-389.

   In this important article, Tout seeks to demonstrate "that an appreciable proportion of fourteenth-century English literature came from the civil servants of the state." After considering the contributions of such minor literary figures as Richard of Bury,

Thomas Bradwardine, John Froissart, and the anonymous Chandos Herald, Tout turns to Geoffrey Chaucer, Thomas Usk, and Thomas Hoccleve. He rejects Manly's theory that Chaucer was educated at the Temple: "Households, royal and baronial, were the usual training ground for officials...." Of Usk, the author of *The Testament of Love,* he says, "He was..., if not quite a civil servant, engaged in official work." In Hoccleve, finally, we obtain a glimpse of the mentality and career of an ordinary civil service clerk of the later Middle Ages. [Cf. 65, 66.]

159   Whitelock, Dorothy. "Anglo-Saxon Poetry and the Historian." *Transactions of the Royal Historical Society,* Ser. IV, 31 (1949), 75-94.

Although "Old English poetry will not let us into the secrets of contemporary politics," it will enable us to look at Anglo-Saxon society "through a contemporary's eyes." Whitelock cites a few passages in *Juliana, The Gifts of Men,* and *Genesis,* from which information on the law may be inferred. "But it does not get us very far."

160   _____. *The Beginnings of English Society.* Harmondsworth: Penguin Books, 1952; rpt. 1964.

A standard introduction to Anglo-Saxon history and culture. In her discussion of legal and quasi-legal institutions, Whitelock draws consistently on the evidence of Old English poetry, e.g., in chapters on "The Bonds of Society," "The King and His Court," "The Classes of Society," and "The Law."

161   Woodbine, George E. "The Language of English Law." *Speculum,* 18 (1943), 395-436.

Argues that the rise of French as the language of English law occurred not after the Conquest but rather after the French "invasion" of the thirteenth century. Woodbine cites a multitude of interesting legal texts, some literary texts (Jocelin of Brakelond's *Chronicle,* Walter Map's *De nugis curialium,* Ralph de Coggeshall's *Chronicle,* the works of Giraldus Cambrensis), but hardly any scholarship by modern linguists.

162   York, Ernest C. "Isolt's Ordeal: English Legal Customs in the Medieval Tristan Legend." *SP*, 68 (1971), 1-9.

Argues that in their treatment of Isolt's ordeal, the *Tristan* of Gottfried von Strassburg, the Norse *Tristram saga,* and the English *Sir Tristrem* all reflect legal customs that are distinctly Anglo-Saxon or English. Three characteristically English features are noted: the order of the procedure, the place of the trial (either a bishop's see or a place appointed by the bishop), and the fact that the choice of ordeal (hot iron or water) belongs to the accuser rather than to the accused.

Aelfric

163   Jost, Karl."The Legal Maxim in Aelfric's Homilies." *ES*, 36 (1955), 204-205.

The legal maxim in Aelfric's *Catholic Homilies* (I.212.6), advising complete submission to the rule of a king, was apparently borrowed from Atto, Bishop of Vercelli (d. 961), who in turn got it from John Chrysostom. However, Aelfric gives the legal maxim a theological application, and the "strikingly original parallel between the tyrannical King and the devil" seems to be his own idea.

Amis and Amiloun

164   Baldwin, Dean R. "*Amis and Amiloun*: The Testing of Treuþe." *PLL*, 16 (1980), 353-365.

Sees a distinction in the tale between genuine and merely technical *treuþe,* "a distinction analogous to the Christian differentiation between the 'spirit' and the 'letter' of the law." As an example of "test literature" *Amis and Amiloun* "shows the value of unswerving loyalty to a sworn oath while insisting that adherence to the spirit of the vow is more important than mere fidelity to the letter."

165   Leach, MacEdward, ed. *Amis and Amiloun.* EETS, 203 (for 1935). London: Oxford University Press, 1937.

    Contains in the introduction a brief discussion of the judicial combat and the "tricked ordeal" (lxxix-lxxxvii).

The Battle of Brunanburh

166   Baran, Kazimierz. "Stosunek wasalny w świetle praw i literatury anglosaskiej Brytanii." *Czasopismo Prawno-Historyczne,* 22, part 2 (1970), 1-29 [Summary in French].

    Makes use of the *Battle of Brunanburh* and the *Battle of Maldon,* in addition to certain legal writings (especially Athelstan's laws), in order to clarify the nature of a vassal's duties to his lord.

The Battle of Maldon

167   Gordon, E. V. "The Date of Aethelred's Treaty with the Vikings: Olaf Tryggvason and the Battle of Maldon." *MLR,* 32 (1937), 24-32.

    Questions the assumption that Anlaf (Olaf Tryggvason) was the leader of the Viking forces at Maldon. The assumption is based on the identification of the treaty between Aethelred and Anlaf (ed. Liebermann, *Die Gesetze der Angelsachsen,* 1:220 f.) with the one made in 991 after the Battle of Maldon. Gordon identifies it with a treaty made in 994, however, and cites the account of Anlaf's movements in the *Ólafsdrápa* (996) and later sagas as evidence that he probably was not present at Maldon.

168   Thundyil, Zacharias. "A Study of the Anglo-Saxon Concept of Covenant and Its Sources with Special Reference to Anglo-Saxon Laws and the Old English Poems: *The Battle of Maldon* and *Guthlac.*" Diss. University of Notre Dame 1969.

    A study of the covenant motif in *The Battle of Maldon* and *Guthlac* in the light of Anglo-Saxon political, legal, cultural, and intellectual history. Chapter 1 deals with the relation between human and divine covenants, and Chapter 2 with the legal and political matrix of the concept. The rest of the study is more theologically oriented: *The Battle of Maldon* is analyzed in terms of the New

Covenant doctrine of salvation, and *Guthlac* in terms of the monastic ideal of social and spiritual harmony (*koinonia*).

Beowulf

169   Anderson, Earl R. "Treasure Trove in *Beowulf*: A Legal View of the Dragon's Hoard." *Mediaevalia,* 3 (1977), 141-164.

"My basic thesis in this paper is that in his various descriptions and allusions to the dragon's treasure, the *Beowulf* poet develops a submerged legal theme which affirms the Germanic principle of treasure-regality (the ruler's right to all treasure trove), which in turn encourages the belief that Beowulf has a right to the treasure." The passages treated are lines 2214b-43a, 2275b-93a, 2401-13a, 2764b-66, 3051-57, and 3069-75.

170   Baird, Joseph L. "Grendel the Exile." *NM,* 67 (1966), 375-381.

Argues that Grendel had a powerful effect on the *Beowulf* audience not only because he is a monster but also because he is an exile, "an outlaw who refuses to settle the feud with compensation."

171   Bloomfield, Morton W. "Beowulf, Byrhtnoth, and the Judgment of God: Trial by Combat in Anglo-Saxon England." *Speculum,* 44 (1969), 545-559.

Tentatively suggests that Beowulf's victory over Grendel and Byrhtnoth's defeat in *The Battle of Maldon* are both instances of the *judicium Dei.* Most of the article is taken up by a history of trial by combat—"the general legal proceeding of ordeal which seems to have been confined to the Germanic peoples." Acknowledging the lack of evidence for this form of trial in England before the Conquest, Bloomfield says that if the two literary passages do not prove trial by combat at an earlier date, they at least show "something very close to it."

172   Chaney, William A. "Grendel and the *Gifstol*: A Legal View of Monsters." *PMLA,* 77 (1962), 513-520.

Focuses on the problems of Grendel's relation to the *gifstol* (presumably the throne of Hrothgar) in *Beowulf* line 168. Citing numerous Anglo-Saxon laws, particularly those concerned with royal asylum, the author concludes that Grendel is prevented by God from approaching the *gifstol* because he is polluted "both ritually and legally, as *Godes andsaca* and as the uncleansed murderer of thirty of Hrothgar's *comitatus*."

173   Donahue, Charles. "*Beowulf* and Christian Tradition: A Reconsideration from a Celtic Stance." *Traditio,* 21 (1965), 55-116.

Interprets the poem in light of the author's belief in a *tempus legis naturae,* a concept partly indebted to Irish saga-tellers and jurists (as illustrated by the legal treatise *Corus Bescna*).

174   Garbáty, Thomas Jay. "Feudal Linkage in *Beowulf.*" *N&Q*, N. S. 6 (1959), 11-12.

Sees in Wiglaf's references to the *comitatus*' oath to support Beowulf (lines 2633-38, 2864-72) a link to the feudal theme in later English literature.

175   Golden, John Thomas. "Societal Bonds in Old English Heroic Poetry: A Legal and Typological Study." Diss. Cornell University 1970.

After discussing the reliability of various sources of information on early Germanic institutions (Tacitus' *Germania,* Old Norse literature, the continental Germanic law-codes), the author turns to an evaluation of the vernacular Old English laws for insight into the heroic concept of community. The study focuses on two institutions in particular: kingship and land tenure. Golden finds a theory of kingship in the *Beowulf*-poet's treatment of Hrothgar's *gifstol,* a symbol of lawful rule and thus unapproachable by Grendel. Legal principles of land tenure are applied to three instances of gifts of land in the poem: the folkshare which Hrothgar reserves for his warriors, the land which Higelac gives to Beowulf, and the land of the Waegmundings, which Beowulf presents to Wiglaf. Throughout the study, emphasis is placed on the intermingling of legal and Christian elements.

176   Grinsell, L. V. "Barrow Treasure, in Fact, Tradition, and Legislation." *Folklore,* 78 (1967), 1-38.

A summary of the evidence related to barrow treasure, depending in part on *Beowulf* ("the only substantial poem that has survived" on the subject) and early legislation in Scandinavia and England.

177   Murray, Alexander C. "The Lending of Hrunting and the Anglo-Saxon Laws." *N&Q,* N. S. 17 (1970), 83-84.

Citing several Anglo-Saxon laws, Murray explains the legal ramifications of the lending of Hrunting. "In the eyes of the law and, we may suppose, of the audience of *Beowulf,* a man was held partly responsible for a slaying committed with his sword, even though he himself may not take part physically in the actual deed. In lending Hrunting, Unferth is offering to take a part in the killing of Grendel's mother. To be sure, this might mean a share in the glory of the slaying but it also means a share in the responsibility for the killing, that is, a willingness to share the feud, if one resulted from the slaying of Grendel's mother."

178   Reynolds, R. L. "An Echo of *Beowulf* in Athelstan's Charters of 931-933 A.D.?" *Medium Aevum,* 24 (1955), 101-103.

Translates with an admittedly "Beowulfian slant" the Latin proems of Athelstan's charters of 931-933 in order to show the possible influence of the poem.

179   Riley, Samuel M. "Bede, *Beowulf,* and the Law: Some Evidence for Dating the Poem." *Old English Newsletter,* 11, No. 2 (1978), 20.

Argues that the poet uses the terms *gesiðcund* and *cyninges þegn* in the same sense as Wihtraed's laws and Bede's *Historia* (translating *gesið* as "comes," and *þegn* as "miles"), thus indicating a *terminus a quo* of 695.

180   Seebohm, Frederic. *Tribal Custom in Anglo-Saxon Law.* London: Longmans, Green, and Co., 1911.

Attempts to describe, primarily on the basis of wergild amounts, the division of classes and their holdings in Anglo-Saxon society. Chapter 3 considers the evidence provided by *Beowulf,* in particular, the evidence concerning kinship. Three inferences (much elaborated) are drawn: 1. There is no feud within the kindred when one kinsman slays another; 2. Marriage between two kindreds is a common means of ending feuds between them; 3. The wife does not pass entirely out of her own kindred into her husband's; and her son may even become the chieftain of his maternal kindred on failure of direct male succession. [Cf. 332.]

181   Stanley, E. G. "Did Beowulf Commit 'Feaxfeng' against Grendel's Mother?" *N&Q*, N. S. 23 (1976), 339-340.

Suggests that *eaxle* "shoulder" in *Beowulf* line 1537 be emended (following Rieger, 1876, and Holthausen, 1942) to *feaxe* "hair." Both the meter and the sense of the line are improved by reading that Beowulf pulled Grendel's mother to the ground *by her hair*—"an indignity well attested by the Laws of the Anglo-Saxons and Frisians."

182   Taylor, A. R. "Two Notes on *Beowulf*." *Leeds Studies in English and Kindred Languages,* 7-8 (1952), 5-13.

Finds Whitelock's reading of the lines [183] unsatisfactory and develops further the suggestion made by H. M. Chadwick (*The Cult of Othin*, 1899). That is, that the lines "may contain a reminiscence of the Oðinn cult and...that in heathen times the bodies of the princely dead may have been hung on the gallows." The hanging of the old man's son, therefore, need not imply that he was executed as a criminal.

183   Whitelock, Dorothy. "*Beowulf* 2444-2471." *Medium Aevum,* 8 (1939), 198-204.

Points out that Hrethel, unable legally to avenge the slaying of his son Herebeald by his other son Haethcyn, is in the same position as a father unable to avenge the death of a son executed as a lawbreaker.

184   _____. *The Audience of Beowulf.* Oxford: Clarendon, 1951.

Reiterates her earlier view [above] that the Hrethel passage in *Beowulf* "became clear enough if one looked for its interpretation to Anglo-Saxon law instead of to remote legends" and adds a further supporting example from the Finn story (pp. 17-19).

185   Williams, David Eliot. "Cain and *Beowulf*." Diss. University of
      Toronto 1970.

      Seeks to recover the intellectual background of *Beowulf* through
      an examination of 1. the Anglo-Saxon laws concerning homicide and
      fratricide, and 2. the exegetical tradition concerning the archetypal
      fratricide, Cain. Under the influence of Christianity, Anglo-Saxon
      law not only shifted its position on vengeance against non-kinsmen
      from approval to condemnation (for all men are kinsmen through
      Christ) but it did so in language replete with Cain imagery. *Beowulf*
      may be seen as a record of this shift, "a poem of Christian apology in
      a semi-converted society where the lingering pagan values of
      vengeance and bloodshed are identified with the original fratricidal
      act of Cain."

Charters of Christ

186   Spalding, Mary Caroline. *The Middle English Charters of Christ*.
      Bryn Mawr College Monographs, 15. Bryn Mawr: Bryn Mawr
      College, 1914.

      This is the basic study of a type of allegorical literature using the
      language and structure of a legal grant or charter, the "Charter of
      Christ," which "purports to be a grant of Heaven's bliss, made to
      mankind by the Saviour, upon condition that man give, in return, his
      love to God and to his neighbor." Spalding provides not only a
      history of the genre, a genealogy of manuscripts, and a commentary
      on the language, but also the complete texts of the so-called *Short
      Charter, Long Charter,* and four other examples. [Cited also as 87.]

Chaucer

187   Baird, Joseph L. "The 'Secte' of the Wife of Bath." *ChauR*, 2
      (1968), 188-190.

      Taking as his point of departure Howard Schless's argument
      [229] that "secte" in the *Legend of Good Women* (line 1382) refers
      to *secta curiae* or "suit at law," Baird makes a similar case for the
      Clerk's comment on the Wife of Bath, "whos lyf and al hire secte
      God mayntene." Since "to maintain a 'secte' could hardly avoid
      suggesting a 'legal' debate," the line furnishes "the clearest support

for Kittredge's view that the Clerk acknowledged, and replied to, the suit of the good Dame Alisoun.''

188 _____. "Law and the *Reeve's Tale.*" *NM*, 70 (1969), 679-683.

A note on "the legalism in the background of the *Tale*, both overt and implied." Contains little not suggested already by Olson [220].

189 _____. "*Secte* and *Suit* Again: Chaucer and Langland." *ChauR,* 6 (1971), 117-119.

Rejects Lillian Hornstein's definition of *secte* (*Clerk's Tale* 1171) as "oath-helpers" or "compurgators" [209] and reaffirms, with additional evidence, his earlier argument for "legal suit or action." The clearest evidence is *Piers Plowman*, B.5.98, "But in owre secte was the sorwe and thi sone it ladde," where a legal interpretation is likely for both *secte* and *ladde* (cf. "to lead" in OED: "To bring forward, adduce [testimony]; to bring [an action]").

190 Baugh, A. C. "Chaucer's Serjeant of the Law and the Year Books." *Mélanges de langue et de littérature du moyen âge et de la Renaissance offerts à Jean Frappier.* Geneva: Droz, 1970, pp. 65-76.

Baugh explains the lines concerning the Serjeant of the Law—

In termes hadde he caas and doomes alle
That from the tyme of kyng William were falle—

as meaning not that "he had in terms, knew how to express in proper terms, was well acquainted with" (Skeat) or that he could quote or remember all the judgments from "the tyme of kyng William" (Manly) but rather (as proposed by A. W. Reed in 1928) that he had a collection of Year Books containing them, arranged in Terms, i.e., Hilary, Easter, Trinity, and Michaelmas. Quite aside from the main issue, the article is useful for its bibliography on the history of the Year Books themselves.

191 Beichner, Paul. "Chaucer's Man of Law and *Disparitas Cultus.*" *Speculum,* 23 (1948), 70-75.

Sees the wording of the impediment to marriage of Constance and the Sultan—"swich diversitee/ Betwene hir bothe lawes" (B 220-221)—as an echo of the legal term *disparitas cultus.* Instead of following Trivet's life of Constance, in which the Roman emperor Tiberius requires the Sultan's baptism as a condition of marriage to a Christian, Chaucer has the whole matter of *disparitas cultus* brought up first in the Sultan's council and thus allows "the legal profession [to] display its knowledge of canon law." As for Chaucer's own knowledge of canon law, Beichner believes, it was "common knowledge improved by his reading in works similar to the *Summa* of Raymond of Pennafort...."

192   _____. "Confrontation, Contempt of Court, and Chaucer's Cecilia." *ChauR,* 8 (1974), 198-204.

In his redaction of the St. Cecilia legend, Chaucer shifted the high point from her martyrdom to the trial scene. A comparison of his Latin source and the corresponding part in the *Second Nun's Tale* shows how "he sharpened the conflict and heightened the dialogue in small ways."

193   Bland, D. S. "Chaucer and the Inns of Court: A Re-Examination." *ES,* 33 (1952), 145-155.

Reviews the evidence for the theory that Chaucer was a student at the Inner Temple [215, 224] and finds it insufficient.

194   Blenner-Hassett, Roland. "Autobiographical Aspects of Chaucer's Franklin." *Speculum*, 28 (1953), 791-800.

Suggests that Cecilia Chaumpaigne's "release" of Chaucer may be echoed in Aurelius's release of Dorigen from her promise.

195   Braddy, Haldeen. "Chaucer, Alice Perrers, and Cecily Chaumpaigne." *Speculum*, 52 (1977), 906-911.

Speculates that the stepmother of Cecilia Chaumpaigne was Alice Perrers, notorious mistress of Edward III; that the oft-mated stepmother was also the prototype for the oft-married Alice of Bath; and that one "Geoffrey Perrers" mentioned in the Calendar of the Patent Rolls (1374) might have been the illegitimate son of Alice and Chaucer. The connections proposed are all extremely hypothetical.

196 Breslin, Carol Ann. "Justice and Law in Chaucer's *Canterbury Tales.*" Diss. Temple University 1978.

Offers the concept of justice and law as a way of unifying the *Tales*. Many of the pilgrims are associated directly or indirectly with the administration of law; moreover, the tales told by the Man of Law, the Wife of Bath, and the Physician contain fully-developed trial scenes, "which reflect in numerous ways the current practices and procedures of medieval courts."

197 Carruthers, Mary. "The Wife of Bath and the Painting of Lions." *PMLA*, 94 (1979), 209-222.

Touches upon the Wife's property rights. Despite the restrictions of the common law, the customs of the bourgeoisie would have allowed her to own property in fee simple and to trade in her own name whether she was married or not.

198 Cook, A. S. "Chaucer's 'Linian.'" *RR*, 8 (1917), 353-382.

Provides a full account of the life of Lignano, the great Bolognese lawyer mentioned in the Prologue of the *Clerk's Tale*, and a partial list of his writings.

199 Cowgill, Bruce Kent. "Chaucer and the Just Society: Conceptions of Natural Law and the Nobility in the *Parliament of Fowls*, the *Knight's Tale*, and the Portraits of Miller and Reeve." Diss. University of Nebraska 1970.

Explores Chaucer's use of natural law as the standard of human society. The *Parliament* can be understood "as an allegory of the terrestrial paradise and the lawlessness which corrupts it." In the *Knight's Tale*, "the two young Thebans' misunderstanding of law is played off against Theseus' insight." The tournament by which the conflict is resolved is not realistic, though it does resemble the fourteenth-century judicial duel and also a tournament form no longer current in Chaucer's day, the mass melee.

200 _____. "The *Parlement of Foules* and the Body Politic." *JEGP*, 74 (1975), 315-335.

Interprets the *Parlement of Foules* as political allegory. Scipio the guide is seen as a traditional figure of wise temporal leadership; the garden, as the image of the earthly commonwealth; the tercel eagle, as a law-breaker, "whose perversion of Nature's injunction to choose a 'fere' precipitates the sudden disharmony."

201   Dunleavy, Gareth W. "Natural Law as Chaucer's Ethical Absolute." *Transactions of the Wisconsin Academy of Sciences, Arts and Letters*, 52 (1963), 177-187.

Looks for evidence of natural law theory in Chaucer's works, a theory assimilated perhaps from his reading of Aristotle and English lawbooks (e.g., Bracton, *Fleta, Britton*) and from his familiarity with the law merchant. Echoes of natural law are noted in the *Book of the Duchess, Parliament of Fowls*, and the Prologue to the *Canterbury Tales*.

202   Frost, George L. "Chaucer's Man of Law at the Parvis." *MLN*, 44 (1929), 496-501.

Rejects Manly's suggestion that "at the parvys" refers either to the court of the Exchequer at Westminster or to the moots of students in the inns of court, and argues for the traditional association of the phrase with St. Paul's Cathedral.

203   Gaylord, Alan T. "The Promises in *The Franklin's Tale*." *ELH*, 31 (1964), 331-365.

Includes a good discussion of the conditions under which promises and contracts need not be kept, with evidence from scriptural commentary (on the rash promises of Jepthah and Herod) and from canon law (see esp. p. 365).

204   Gerould, Gordon Hall. "The Social Status of Chaucer's Franklin." *PMLA*, 41 (1926), 262-279.

In arguing against the OED's definition of "franklin" as a freeholder "ranking next below the gentry"—and thus against the literary interpretations of Chaucer's Franklin based upon it (e.g., Root's, Kittredge's)—Gerould draws on a large variety of legal sources: charters, statutes, patent and close rolls, parliamentary writs, and legal treatises such as *Fleta*, Bracton's *De legibus et consuetudinibus Angliae* and Fortescue's *De laudibus legum Angliae*. Along with "franklin," he examines the meaning of other words also applied to this pilgrim by Chaucer, namely, sheriff, countour, and vavasour. He concludes that far from being a parvenu, "Chaucer's Franklin was a member of that class of landed gentry which was already old in the fourteenth century and which has never felt the lack of any higher title than gentleman...." [Cf. 233.]

205   Goffin, R. C. "Chaucer and 'Reason.'" *MLR*, 21 (1926), 13-18.

By the word "reason" in the Prologue of the *Canterbury Tales* (line 37), Chaucer means *ordo* in its old rhetorical sense. Goffin notes in passing, however, that *ratio* was a term originally applied to oratory and the pleading of cases. Chaucer uses "reason" in this sense in the *Parliament of Fowls* (line 534) and in the *House of Fame* (line 707).

206   _____. "Chaucer and Elocution." *Medium Aevum*, 4 (1935), 127-142.

Contrasts Chaucer's distrust of "termes of phisyk" and the inclination of "contemporary French courtly poetry to grow 'metaphysical' with borrowed technical terms of all kinds, especially perhaps ecclesiastical and legal jargon," e.g., Froissart's *Plaidoirie de la rose et de la violette* or, to name a Middle English poem, *Fortune*.

207   Hamel, Mary. "The Wife of Bath and a Contemporary Murder." *ChauR*, 14 (1979), 132-139.

Suggests that in referring to wives that "han slayn hir housbondes in hir bed," Jankyn is alluding not to some dark deed in Dame Alisoun's past (*pace* Rowland, Palomo) but to a scandalous murder of 1387 or 1388, reported in the continuation of Higden's *Polychronicon* (IX.173).

208   Haselmayer, Louis A. "The Apparitor and Chaucer's Summoner." *Speculum*, 12 (1937), 43-57.

Examines ecclesiastical records of the thirteenth and fourteenth centuries in order to answer questions about the summoners in the General Prologue and in the Friar's Tale—questions "concerning this class of officers as a whole, the scope of its activities, the amount of corruption, the social standing of the office, and the universality or particularization of the Chaucerian portraits." Although the documentary evidence points to widespread abuse of the office,

Chaucer's portraits seem to be "more violent than necessary" and may be based on an actual prototype.

209 Hornstein, Lillian Herlands. "The Wyf of Bathe and the Merchant: From Sex to 'Secte.'" *ChauR*, 3 (1968), 65-67.

Adds to the interpretation of "al hire secte" (*Clerk's Tale* E 1171) as "sex," "her kind of person," and "a suit of law" another definition drawn from legal sources: "secte" as *secta*, the oath-helpers or compurgators required in order to maintain a law suit. Since the Merchant echoes the Wife's sentiments on the woe that is in marriage, he may be regarded, in a legal sense, as one of her *secte*. [Response in 189.]

210 Jeffrey, David Lyle. "The Friar's Rent." *JEGP*, 70 (1971), 600-606.

Replaces the usual interpretation of the Friar's "rente" (Gen. Prol. 256) as "permanent income from investment or land" with "the concept of rente as *homage* service." Thus, "to say that the Friar's *purchase* is better than his *rente* is to say in no uncertain terms that he has reneged on his spiritual and prelatical homage responsibilities...."

211 Johnson, Lynn Staley. "The Prince and His People: A Study of the Two Covenants in the *Clerk's Tale*." *ChauR*, 10 (1975), 17-29.

Contrasts the behavior of Walter's subjects and that of his wife: "The people provide the outstanding negative response to adversity and are best approached in terms of the Old Covenant, as Griselda is through the New Covenant." In general, the people are guided by the "letter" and Griselda by the "spirit" of the law. The implications of this contrast are developed in the light of covenant theory both in the Bible and in medieval political writings.

212 Kelly, Henry Ansgar. "Clandestine Marriage and Chaucer's 'Troilus.'" *Viator*, 4 (1973), 435-457.

Describes the relation between Troilus and Criseyde as a clandestine marriage. Canon law tried to discourage such unions, but a search of consistory court records shows that they were extremely common in Chaucer's day. (The article is a shorter version of several chapters from Kelly's book [150].)

213   Lambkin, Martha Dampf. "Chaucer's Man of Law as a Purchasour." *Comitatus*, 1 (1970), 81-84.

This note attempts to uncover the implications of the word "purchase" in Chaucer's description of the Man of Law ("So greet a purchasour was nowher noon," Prol. 318). The author reviews the unsavory connotations of the word in other Middle English contexts, the widespread use of purchase ("the possession of land by means other than descent") as a means, often unprincipled, of piling up wealth, and Manly's identification of the upstart Thomas Pynchbeck as Chaucer's model [215]. She concludes that, among other things, "Chaucer's probable Serjeant-at-Law model, and the portrait of the Man of Laws in the *Canterbury Tales* as a *purchasour*, cast a strong suspicion that the Man of Laws is indeed akin to a crook, albeit a socially and professionally prominent one."

214   Lindahl, Carl. "Chaucer the Storyteller: Folkloric Patterns in the Canterbury Tales." Diss. Indiana University 1980.

A survey of civil and gild court records concerning slander (Chapter 4) "reveals that Chaucer's pilgrims observe insult taboos identical to those observed in medieval England." Status was all. Successful plaintiffs were nearly always socially above the defendant. Thus the principle: "If you must slander someone, slander a social equal or social inferior who does not hold a position in government." This and similar principles drawn from the legal records are corroborated by the patterns of behavior in the *Canterbury Tales.*

215   Manly, John Matthews. *Some New Light on Chaucer.* New York: Holt, 1926.

Attempts to shed new light on two areas: first, the background of Chaucer, and second, the historical reality of his characters in the *Canterbury Tales.* As for Chaucer himself, Manly supports the theory of a legal education at the Inner Temple; indeed, he argues, such training would have been desirable if not necessary for some of the offices held by the poet—controller of the customs, justice of the peace, clerk of the king's works, subforester of the king's park, and so on. As for the *Canterbury Tales*, Manly draws heavily on legal sources in order to identify the historical models for some fifteen or more of his portraits.

216   McGuire, John B. "The Clandestine Marriage of Troilus and Criseyde." *ChauR*, 8 (1974), 262-278.

Argues that Chaucer "might have been implicitly suggesting that his audience view the affair between Troilus and Criseyde as a clandestine marriage rather than as an illicit love affair." [Cf. 212.]

217   Montgomery, Franz. "A Note on the Reeve's Prologue." *PQ*, 10 (1931), 404-405.

Connects line 3912 of the Reeve's Prologue ("For leveful is with force force of-showve") and the scribal sidenote *vim vi repellere* with the *Digesta*, IX.2,45,4; but concludes that the line, because it repeats a well-known maxim of the law of England, "throws no light on the question of Chaucer's legal training."

218   Myers, Louis McCorry. "A Line in the Reeve's Prologue." *MLN*, 49 (1934), 222-226.

Rejects Montgomery's suggestion [217] that line 3912 of the Reeve's Tale shows Chaucer's familiarity with the *Digesta* of Justinian, and gives other possible sources in which the phrase *vim vi repellere* occurs, including Bracton and *Fleta*. However, "the doctrine has never been fully adopted in English law."

219   O'Connor, Clive Patrick. "A Study of *Troilus and Criseyde* in the Light of Medieval Legalistic Fictions." Diss. State University of New York at Buffalo 1968.

Proposes that certain legal metaphors (illustrated from Ernst Kantorowicz's *The King's Two Bodies* [15]), may form part of the reader's response to *Troilus*. "The argument is that when a reader of the *Troilus* experiences a fiction his memory of other fictions with similar patterns and configurations, such as medieval legalistic fictions, will evoke these fictions in such a way as to control and reinforce his response."

220   Olson, Paul A. "The *Reeve's Tale*: Chaucer's *Measure for Measure*." *SP*, 59 (1962), 1-17.

The Reeve, who "occupied a quasi-judicial position" in the medieval system, bases his revenge against the Miller on the legal maxim of *vim vi repellere* ("Leveful is with force force of-showve"). A similar maxim underlies the revenge in his tale: "Gif a man in a point be agreved,/...in another he sal be releved" ("Qui in uno gravatur in alio debet relevari"). By comparison with its probable sources, the tale seems "deliberately stylized to embody the principle of measure for measure," a principle interpreted not in the mechanical eye-for-an-eye fashion of the Old Law, however, but in the light of the New Testament idea that "with the *will* in which you do evil, with that *will* you will be punished." Ironically, this principle works against the vengeful Reeve, "the *guilor* who is ultimately beguiled and beguiled in the profound sense that he does not recognize his own liability to the justice which he asserts for others."

221   Plucknett, T. F. T. "Chaucer's Escapade." *Law Quarterly Review*, 64 (1948), 33-36.

Rejects the view of Watts [234] that Goodchild and Grove were Chaucer's accomplices in *raptus*. "To me it seems more likely that they were loyal friends who lent their financial credit to get the poet out of a scrape." As for the more difficult question of Cecilia's rights in the matter, the terms of her release seem to show that "she had a civil remedy for rape, and that her release was effectual to bar it." Although Plucknett accepts the interpretation of *raptus* as "rape," he cautiously advises that Cecilia's use of the word does not constitute evidence.

222   Reisner, Thomas Andrew. "The Wife of Bath's Dower: A Legal Interpretation." *MP*, 71 (1974), 301-302.

Argues that in his remark on the Wife of Bath, "Housbondes at chirche dore she hadde fyve," Chaucer is alluding to the nature of the Wife's dower. In contrast to the common-law rule that "the wife was not entitled to any particular land but had to wait until it was assigned to her," dower *ad ostium ecclesiae*, falling under the jurisdiction of the canon law, "was granted at the time of the marriage by the husband and it might consist of any amount of land." Thus, the phrase is more evidence of the Wife's shrewdness in marriage.

223   Revard, Carter. "The Tow On Absalom's Distaff and the Punishment of Lechers in Medieval England." *ELN*, 17 (1980), 168-170.

Revard cites a regulation in the *Liber Albus* (Book III, Part IV) as a gloss on the following passage in the *Miller's Tale* (Absalom, after the humiliation of the misplaced kiss, has just been greeted by Gerveys the smith):

> ...no word agayne he yaf;
> He hadde moore tow on his distaff
> Than Gervyes knew...

Although editors have taken the phrase "to have tow on one's distaff" as meaning generally "to have business at hand," Revard connects it more precisely with the punishment of lechers as prescribed by city law.

224   Rickert, Edith. "Was Chaucer a Student at the Inner Temple?" *The Manly Anniversary Studies in Language and Literature.* Chicago: University of Chicago Press, 1923; rpt. Freeport, New York: Books for Libraries, 1968, pp. 20-31.

This is the seminal article on the subject of Chaucer's legal training [see also 193, 215]. Rickert identifies William Buckley, chief butler of the Inner Temple, as the Master Buckley quoted by Speght (1598) as having seen in a Temple record that "Geoffrey Chaucer was fined two shillings for beating a Franciscan fryer in Fleetstreete." On the basis of this identification and other circumstantial evidence, Rickert is convinced "that Chaucer belongs among the poets who went into literature by way of the law."

225   Robertson, D. W., Jr. "Some Disputed Chaucerian Terminology." *Speculum*, 52 (1977), 571-581.

Exposes "the difficulties involved in evaluating Chaucer's portraits of humbler folk" (the Reeve, Plowman, Yeoman, the cottagers of the *Nun's Priest's Tale, Friar's Tale*), with much information drawn from legal-historical sources.

226   _____. "'And For My Land Thus Hastow Mordred Me?': Land Tenure, the Cloth Industry, and the Wife of Bath." *ChauR*, 14 (1980), 403-420.

Suggests that "Chaucer meant his audience to think of the Wife of Bath as a rural clothier from the west country and quite possibly as a bondwoman." How the wife was able to accumulate her wealth—and thus her husbands—is explained in the light of English land law (in great, and sometimes gratuitous, detail). Part of the discussion turns on the interesting and illustrative case of Margery Hayne (d. 1455), who, like Dame Alisoun, was a remarried widow, a cloth-maker, a land-holder from near Bath and—despite her bondwoman status—a singularly wealthy woman.

227   Rowland, Beryl. "The Physician's 'Historial Thyng Notable' and the Man of Law." *ELH*, 40 (1973), 165-178.

Surveys the traditional arguments on the superiority of law over medicine, and then suggests that the *Physician's Tale* constitutes a rebuttal.

228   Sadler, Lynn Veach. "Chaucer's *The Book of the Duchess* and the 'Law of Kinde.'" *AnM*, 11 (1970), 51-64.

Suggests that the Law of Nature is the framework in which the two major approaches to the poem—as a "consolation" for the knight (or Gaunt) and as a "lesson" for the Dreamer—may be reconciled. Sadler's use of the term "law of nature" is very imprecise, however, and has little to do with the medieval understanding of the phrase.

229   Schless, Howard. "Chaucer and Dante." *Critical Approaches to Medieval Literature.* Ed. Dorothy Bethurum. Selected Papers from the English Institute, 1958-59. New York: Columbia University Press, 1960, pp. 134-154.

Includes a legal interpretation of the following lines from the *Legend of Good Women* (1381-83):

> Yif that I live, thy name shal be shove
> In English, that thy sekte shall be knowe!
> Have at thee, Jason! now thyn horn is blowe!

Here Chaucer is said to be issuing a legal challenge ("Have at thee!") against Jason, who has committed a felony by deserting (and causing the deaths of) Hypsipyle and Medea. "Sekte" refers to the suit against Jason, and "thyn horn is blowe" to the usual method of proclaiming outlawry or of raising the hue and cry.

230   Schoeck, R. J. "A Legal Reading of Chaucer's *Hous of Fame.*" *University of Toronto Quarterly*, 23 (1954), 185-192.

Schoeck proposes that *The Hous of Fame* is an occasional poem, written for the Christmas revels at the Inner Temple. He has two main purposes: to establish the early existence of such revels, arguing primarily from Gerard Legh's account in the *Accedence of Armorie* (1562), and to show the suitability of such an occasion to the poem.

231   Spargo, John Webster. "Chaucer's Love-Days." *Speculum,* 15 (1940), 36-56.

An attempt to construct a history of the medieval loveday leads Spargo to the phrase *dies amoris* in English, Roman, and canon law; *jour d'amour* in French law; and *minne* in German law. Legal writings shed little light on the practice, however, and Spargo thus turns to etymology for help. On the basis of Scandinavian *lof* (permission, license), which he thinks influenced the "love" in ME "loveday," he defines the term as "a day appointed by the express license or permission of a court for settling a case amicably out of court, with the reservation that the court did not abandon its claim to fees." (The argument is rejected by Bennett [141].)

232   _____. "Questio quid iuris." *MLN,* 62 (1947), 119-122.

Spargo identifies the Summoner's words *questio quid iuris* as the ill-understood mimicking of the opening of a common writ, *quid iuris clamat,* "used to summon before a court that man who had refused to comply with a decision concerning title."

233   Specht, Henrik. *Chaucer's Franklin in the Canterbury Tales: The Social and Literary Background of a Chaucerian Character.* Publications of the Department of English, University of Copenhagen, 10. Copenhagen: Akademisk Forlag, 1981.

Uses legal records, in part, to fill out Gerould's study [204] of the Franklin's social status (especially in Chapter 4, "The Legal and Manorial Background").

234   Watts, P. R. "The Strange Case of Geoffrey Chaucer and Cecilia Chaumpaigne." *Law Quarterly Review,* 63 (1947), 491-515.

Affirms that the charge of *raptus* brought against Chaucer by Cecilia Chaumpaigne was, indeed, that of "rape"; and suggests that his agents Goodchild and Grove, though not accessories to the act itself, had exposed themselves to civil action for assault, battery, etc. and hence "expected to be indemnified by Chaucer against Cecilia's demands." The pertinent documents are reproduced. [For a legal historian's criticism of the argument, see 221.]

235 Wentersdorf, Karl P. "Some Observations on the Concept of Clandestine Marriage in *Troilus and Criseyde.*" *ChauR,* 15 (1980), 101-126.

Tries to show that Chaucer's implication of a clandestine marriage between Troilus and Criseyde "not only raises the story above the level of an amorous intrigue but also heightens the poignancy of Criseyde's faithlessness in granting her favors to Diomede." That clandestine marriages were commonplace is illustrated both by canon law (here treated in depth) and by other literary representations (*Handlyng Synne,* Boccaccio's *Decameron* and *Il Filocolo,* Marguerite de Navarre's *Heptameron,* and Gower's *Confessio Amantis*). [Cf. 212, 216.]

236 Yunck, John A. "'Lucre of Vileynye': Chaucer's Prioress and the Canonists." *N&Q,* N. S. 7 (1960), 165-167.

Yunck observes that Chaucer's use of the phrase "lucre of vileynye" (*Prioress's Tale* 490) "correctly interpreted by the medieval glossator of the Ellesmere Manuscript as a translation of 'turpe lucrum,' is not merely a biblical reminiscence [of I Tim. 3.8] but a technical legal term, polished and sharpened by centuries of medieval canon law."

Cleanness

237 Twomey, Michael William. "The Anatomy of Sin: Violations of *'Kynde'* and *'Trawþe'* in *Cleanness.*" Diss. Cornell University 1979.

In the course of explaining the metaphorical identity of idolatry and homosexuality in *Cleanness,* Twomey discusses the poet's understanding of the law of nature "as the historical period before the Law, as the primary moral guide underlying all law, and as innate, sexual desire leading to the procreation of children."

Cynewulf

238   Abraham, Lenore MacGaffey. "Cynewulf's *Juliana*: A Case at
       Law." *Allegorica*, 3 (1978), 172-189.

       Explains the difference between Cynewulf's *Juliana* and the
authorized legend of the saint in Latin as the poet's deliberate
attempt to make the story "conform to the social and legal customs
of his own society, for the cogent reason that he would thereby give
Juliana's trial, and its outcome, the persuasive force of established
law." As a corollary of this thesis, the poem must have been written
in the late tenth century "because only at that time did all the legal
conditions exist to which the poem conforms." Abraham's
argument is very systematic and covers a great number of legal terms
and concepts in the poem, e.g., *gerefa* (steward, *praefectus*),
ealdorman, mundbyrd (guardianship), *sceapa* (thief), *hlop* (robber
troop of not more than thirty-four men), *gafol* (collection of taxes),
anefang (formal attempt by the claimant at physical seizure of the
object under dispute), *wite* (legal penalty), etc.

Drama

239   Brockman, Bennett A. "The Law of Man and the Peace of God:
       Judicial Process as Satiric Theme in the Wakefield *Mactatio Abel*."
       Speculum, 49 (1974), 699-707.

       Argues that certain scenes (lines 330-470) "strongly criticize
fifteenth-century England by associating aspects of its
administration of criminal justice with the ethos of Cain's City of
Man." In his proclamation of "the king's peace," Cain echoes two
legal instruments, often abused—the royal letter patent,
corresponding to "the biblical mark which shields Cain from
vengeance," and the royal letter patent of pardon. His comment
"Here will I lig this fourty dayes" alludes to the criminal's right to
sanctuary. However, his invitation for anyone to kill him, although
consonant with his despair, looks back to an earlier practice ("wolf's
head") rather than to the contemporary "more tractable difficulties
of the outlawed condition." Finally, his invocation of the king's
peace must have seemed to the audience in pointed contrast to the
peace of God, which by murder he has forfeited.

240   Chandler, Arthur Bayard. "The Concept of Justice in Early English Drama." Diss. University of Illinois 1973.

Traces the development of the concept of justice in English drama from the twelfth through the first half of the sixteenth century. The cycle plays are examined for their use of current legal procedures and language. The morality plays are shown to develop justice "as an operative force in man's quest for salvation." Toward the end of the period, the emphasis shifts from divine to human justice.

241   Conley, John. "*Everyman* 29: 'Lawe' or 'Love'?" *N&Q*, N. S. 27 (1980), 298-299.

Rejects the usual emendation of *lawe* to *love* in the following speech by God:

> My lawe that I shewed whan I for them dyed
> They forgete clene and shedynge of my blode rede.

Lawe here is meant as a translation of *geloef* in the playwright's source, the Dutch *Elckerlijc*, the neglect of which by ME scholars "and the sentimental reduction of the Gospel to love have fostered the persistence of the emendation."

242   De Smet, Imogene L. "A Study of the Roles of Mercy and Justice in the Morality Plays, *Everyman, The Castle of Perseverance*, and *Mankind*." Diss. University of Toronto 1969.

Studies vernacular religious works in England (sermons, penitentials, pastorals, devotional works) in order to determine what in popular theology might account for the differing roles of mercy and justice in three English moralities. The heavily juridical emphasis in the religious works is reflected most fully in *Everyman*.

243   Hanks, Dorrel Thomas, Jr. "Social Satire in the Medieval English Cycle Plays." Diss. University of Minnesota 1976.

Examines the villains of the cycle plays (Pilate, Herod, Annas and Caiaphas, et al.) as types of medieval secular and ecclesiastical lords, who use the law primarily to persecute the poor and the weak. The plays "mirror the disturbing social conditions" that caused the revolts of 1381 and 1450.

244   Knight, W. Nicholas. "Equity and Mercy in English Law and
       Drama (1405-1641)." *Comparative Drama*, 6 (1972), 51-67.

       Includes a discussion of equity ("that which legally recognizes
       the exception to the law in the name of higher or natural justice") in
       two medieval morality plays, *The Castle of Perseverance* (1405) and
       Mankind (1475). In the first, which dramatizes the divine court,
       "one can witness the equation (in the popular mind) of God's justice
       with common law, and God's mercy and grace with the
       extraordinary relief furnished by equity" [cf. 248, 291, 292]. In the
       second—written shortly after the Chancellor assumed the power of
       dispensing equity independent of the King—one can see that Mercy's
       actions, though still representing divine justice, take effect in the
       secular realm during Mankind's life-time and "are similar to the
       operations of a Chancellor, who is also an ecclesiast, and able to seek
       out and offer remedy to those oppressed by a Common court in
       which law has been misused, or become corrupt."

245   McCutchan, J. Wilson. "Justice and Equity in the English Morality
       Play." *Journal of the History of Ideas*, 19 (1958), 405-410.

       Justice appears as an allegorical character in eleven English plays
       before 1617. This article traces "the progress of Justice from the role
       of a strictly theological virtue or grace in *The Castle of Perseverance*
       to the position of legal judge in *Respublica*, and on to that of
       chancellor combining the concepts of literal justice with equity in the
       moralities and interludes of the 1560's."

246   Riggio, Milla B. "The Allegory of Feudal Acquisition in *The Castle
       of Perseverance*." *Allegory, Myth, and Symbol*. Harvard English
       Studies, 9. Ed. by Morton Bloomfield. Cambridge, Mass.: Harvard
       University Press, 1981, pp. 187-208.

       Finds that the religious allegory of the play is supported by "a
       consistent substructure of allusions that associate economic and
       social abuse with feudal patronage." Many of these allusions are
       legal. For example, included in the terminology of feudal vassalage
       and possession, which "takes on abstract moral meaning" in the
       play, are the following: *seised, feffe, entail, assize, enprise, trust,
       ure, owse, good entent*. Riggio points also to the contrast in the play
       between God's law and "the legal processes of Mundus, which foster
       only dissension and disorder."

247   Squires, Lynn B. "Legal and Political Aspects of Late Medieval
       English Drama." Diss. University of Washington 1977.

       Comments on late medieval and early Tudor drama in the
       context of fifteenth-century law. The *Ludus Coventriae* passion
       sequence is said to reflect English legal practice; the Towneley cycle,
       social and political disorder of the period; and the Coventry
       Shearman and Taylors' Play and the Digby *Conversion of St. Paul*,
       contemporary theories about just and unjust kingship. A continuous
       theme of the study is the conscious parallel between the New Law of
       Christ and the rise of equity.

248   _____. "Law and Disorder in *Ludus Coventriae*."
       Comparative Drama, 12, (1978), 200-213.

       Sees in the plays a reflection of many contemporary legal abuses
       and an implicit call for reform. Like other scholars [241, 291, 292],
       the author identifies English common law with the Old Law of
       Moses, and the emerging rule of equity with the New Law of Christ.
       Although Squires tends to overstate her case, subordinating
       theological to legal concerns, she does show that law is a pervasive
       theme.

Erkenwald

249   Faigley, Lester L. "Typology and Justice in *St. Erkenwald*."
       American Benedictine Review, 29 (1978), 381-390.

       Sees the two types of justice represented in the poem—on the one
       hand the rulings of the pagan judge, issued "ne mechefe, ne routhe,"
       and on the other the merciful attitude of Bishop Erkenwald—as
       corresponding to the Old and the New Law.

Exeter Book

250   Anderson, James Edward. "Strange, Sad Voices: The Portraits of
       Germanic Women in the Old English *Exeter Book*." Diss. University
       of Kansas 1978.

       Argues that the points of view expressed in four poems of *The
       Exeter Book—Deor, The Husband's Message, The Wife's Lament*,

and *Wulf and Eadwacer*—reflect the status of women as *property* under Germanic law. The first two represent statements by men, the other two by women. Behind *Deor* and *Wulf and Eadwacer* lies a story of heroic abduction, apparently connected with the Norse *Hjaðningavíg*. *The Wife's Lament* contains unique information on women as legal victims of heroic feuding. *The Husband's Message* is based on a legal theme also—the solemn promise sealed with an oath. Anderson's analysis of the poems depends heavily on legal terms and concepts therein, many identified as such for the first time.

Fortescue

251   Keaney, Winifred Gleeson. *"The Governance of England*: Fifteenth-Century Prose Style in Sir John Fortescue's Treatise on Kingship and Law." Diss. University of Maryland 1975.

Sees "Fortescue's habits of associative thinking, developed over years of training and experience in law," as contributing to his remarkably controlled prose style in *The Governance of England*, the first constitutional treatise written in English (1470-1475).

Gower

252   Fisher, John H. "A Calendar of Documents Relating to the Life of John Gower the Poet." *JEGP*, 58 (1959), 1-23.

Collects the documents relevant "in any attempt to reconstruct Gower's biography." To those cited previously by Nicolas and Macaulay, Fisher adds fifty-four, bringing the total to more than eighty-three references. Most are legal in nature.

253   _____. *John Gower: Moral Philosopher and Friend of Chaucer*. New York: New York University Press, 1964.

Discusses in passing a number of legal questions concerning Gower's life and work: the Leland tradition of a legal education (pp. 55-58); his associations with officials of the law (pp. 58-63); the pervasiveness of law and justice as themes in his writings (pp. 154-203); and the possibility that he was the model for Chaucer's Man of Law (pp. 287-292).

254   Olsson, Kurt. "Natural Law and John Gower's *Confessio Amantis*." *M & H*, N. S. 11 (1982), 229-261.

"John Gower's frequent use of the concept of natural law in the *Confessio Amantis* provides a rich example of the adaptation of legal topoi to the literary concerns of writers in late medieval England." According to Olsson, Gower found in five different meanings of the term *jus naturae* "a means to organize material he [had] gathered for this vast encyclopedic work."

Henryson

255   Carruthers, Ian Robert. "A Critical Commentary on Robert Henryson's *Morall Fabillis*." Diss. University of British Columbia 1977.

Approaching the *Fabillis* by way of Henryson's own background, the author attempts a re-evaluation of the work. For example, "If we accept that Henryson was a university graduate in Arts and Canon Law, a reading of Aristotle, penitential handbooks and encyclopedias will help us to appreciate the polysemous allusiveness of his figural poetry, in which animal physiology, moral psychology and legal expertise are delightfully and subtly blended."

256   McDonald, J. C. "Law and the Poetic Imagination: the Poetry of Robert Henryson." Diss. University of York 1980.

A thorough investigation of legal terminology, procedure, and thought in Henryson's work. The poet uses the law primarily in two ways—"to comment on moral frailty on the personal level, and to explore the social ills of Henryson's own day."

257   _____. "The Perversion of Law in Robert Henryson's Fable of the *Fox, the Wolf, and the Husbandman*." *Medium Aevum*, 49 (1980), 244-253.

Discusses legal doctrines touching the motif of the rash promise, which is at the heart of Henryson's fable (two-thirds of the narrative is concerned with the wolf's attempt to collect on the husbandman's unintentional offer of his unruly oxen). McDonald summarizes the conditions under which oaths were of no force—"when they were made imprudently, without consideration of their effects; when they were made under stress; and when they necessitated an immoral course of action"—and he goes on to suggest that "at the heart of the conflict between the wolf and the labourer is the question of equity." Henryson's concern with justice and equity, the author concludes, grew out of the current situation in Scotland.

258   MacQueen, John. *Robert Henryson: A Study of the Major Narrative Poems*. Oxford: Clarendon, 1967.

Accepts the evidence of Henryson's own legal training in Aesop's speech (Prologue to *The Lion and the Mouse*):

> My native land is Rome withoutin nay;
> And in that Towne first to the Sculis I yude,
> In Civile Law studyit full money ane day.

"[A]s I do not know any other author who says that Aesop studied law at Rome," MacQueen comments, "it is conceivable that Henryson intended the description of Aesop to have some relevance to himself." The *Morall Fabillis* contain other evidence as well. MacQueen calls attention to—but does not discuss in depth—the legal elements in several of the tales.

259   Rowlands, Mary E. "Robert Henryson and the Scottish Courts of Law." *Aberdeen University Review*, 39 (1962), 219-226.

Rowlands accepts the view that Henryson was trained in the law. Focusing on *The Morall Fabillis*, in particular "The Taill of the Scheip and the Doig," she explains certain points directed against abuses in the court system. For example, despite the sheep's legally correct protests—"Heir I declyne the Juge, the tyme, the place"—he is tried anyway and found guilty. This travesty of justice is an indictment of both the consistory and the sheriff courts. Though historically inaccurate, Henryson's treatment of the two courts together was "quite deliberate." (Among the terms mentioned: *contumax*, feriat, borchs or borrows, and certain officials, e.g., apparitors, assessors, crownars.)

260   Stearns, Marshall W. "A Note on Robert Henryson's Allusions to Religion and Law." *MLN*, 59 (1944), 257-264.

A superficial look at some of Henryson's allusions to law, based almost entirely on the notes furnished by editors of his work. The focus is on Henryson's criticism of the civil and ecclesiastical courts in "The Sheep and the Dog."

261 _____. *Robert Henryson*. New York: Columbia University Press, 1949.

In Chapter 2 ("Politics, Religion, and Law"), Stearns uses the fable of "The Sheep and the Dog" to illustrate Henryson's detailed knowledge of law. The discussion adds little to the same author's earlier study [above].

Hoccleve

262 Reeves, A. C. "The World of Thomas Hoccleve." *Fifteenth Century Studies*, 2 (1979), 187-201.

Organizes by topic Hoccleve's references to contemporary life, including his complaints about the administration of law and justice.

Langland (See *Piers Plowman*)

Lyrics

263 Bowers, R. H. "A Middle-English Poem on Lovedays." *MLR*, 47 (1952), 374-375.

Brief excerpt from Cambridge Univ. Lib. MS. Dd. 1.1, part of the author's unsuccessful search for "a contemporary account of the actual procedure of holding a loveday." [For the complete text, with commentary, see next item.]

264 Heffernan, Thomas J. "A Middle English Poem on Lovedays." *ChauR*, 10 (1975), 172-185.

Edits, with commentary, Cambridge Univ. Lib. MS. Dd. 1.1. fols. 300v-302v, a 218-line poem in ME and Latin on the duties of arbitrators and litigants who take part in lovedays. The poem contains many legal terms, some of which are glossed by the editor (*domys man, questmen, asseth*). Heffernan follows Bennett [141] rather than Spargo [231] in defining *loveday* as "the meeting or time of meeting at which a dispute is settled amicably." [The poem was first noted by Bowers, above.]

265   Revard, Carter. "The Lecher, the Legal Eagle, and the Papelard Priest: Middle English Confessional Satires in MS. Harley 2253 and Elsewhere." *His Firm Estate: Essays in Honor of Franklin James Eikenberry.* Ed. Donald E. Hayden. Tulsa: University of Tulsa Press, 1967, pp. 54-71.

Of the three poems discussed—"The Man in the Moon," "A Satire on the Consistory Courts" (both Harley 2253), and "The Papelard Priest" (Additional 45896)—the first two require some knowledge of medieval legal practice. In the first poem, the fine points of law seem to be these: "(1) It was possible for the manorial bailiff to allow an out-of-court settlement of a case which had not yet been presented in court...; (2) it was sometimes legal for the hayward to collect a 'fee' for keeping the case out of court." The second poem requires a knowledge of procedure in the ecclesiastical courts. The *boc* to which the defendant refers (line 12) is "the famous 'Archdeacon's book' in which were inscribed the names of all sinners brought into one of the ecclesiastical courts...." "Lines 15-16 ('of scathe y wol me skere,/ ant fleo from my fere') are apparently the speaker's version of an oath which the court-officials forced him to swear"—probably, as extant records suggest, an oath to abjure not only the sin but also the sinner, the *fere.* By the end of his complaint, however, the speaker has unwittingly proved the truth of the accusation against him.

266   Robbins, Rossell Hope. "Middle English Poems of Protest." *Anglia*, 78 (1960), 193-203.

Makes the important point that most protest literature came from and was addressed to the middle and upper classes. This is especially true of complaints about legal abuses: "villeins who were not allowed to plead in the law courts would hardly be concerned with corruption of the law." In general, what this body of literature calls for is support of law and order, not reform or rebellion.

Malory

267 Baugh, A. C. "Documenting Sir Thomas Malory." *Speculum*, 8 (1933), 3-29.

Accepting Kittredge's identification of Malory as Sir Thomas Malory, knight, of Winwick (Northamptonshire) and Newbold Revell (Warwickshire), Baugh reproduces, with comment, a number of newly-discovered items from the Coram rege and Controlment Rolls in an effort to fill in the record of Malory's scrapes with the law.

268 Hicks, Edward. *Sir Thomas Malory*. Cambridge: Harvard University Press, 1928.

A biographical account of Sir Thomas Malory of Newbold Revell, based largely on the Patent Rolls and other types of legal evidence. That the Warwickshire knight was the same Malory who wrote the *Morte d'Arthur* is argued in Chapter 15.

269 York, Ernest C. "Legal Punishment in Malory's *Le Morte Darthur*." *ELN*, 11 (1973), 14-21.

Finds Malory's depiction of legal practices to be historically sound. Where French law is different from English, Malory follows —as one would expect in view of his French sources—the French tradition. In two cases, where his source simply recommends death, he specifies the legally appropriate punishment.

270 _____. "The Duel of Chivalry in Malory's Book XIX." *PQ*, 48 (1969), 186-191.

Argues convincingly that the judicial battle depicted in Malory's Book XIX is a duel of chivalry rather than a duel of law. In the former the contest is initiated by a bill rather than by an oral accusation; the combatants fight in full armor on horseback rather than on foot with non-lethal weapons; the battle is begun by a herald's cry "Lessez les alier...et faire lour devoire" and, in contrast to the duel of law, may be halted by the cry "Hoo" from the king. Malory's treatment of these details, however, seems to owe more to English legal practice than to French.

271   Whitteridge, Gweneth. "The Identity of Sir Thomas Malory,
       Knight-Prisoner." *RES*, 24 (1973), 257-265.

       Rejects the identification of Sir Thomas Malory of Newbold
       Revell and the notorious felon Sir Thomas Malory of Fenny
       Newbold. A thorough search of the extant legal documents "points
       to two men of different age-groups and different political opinions,
       adherents of the opposing sides in the Wars of the Roses."

Mum and the Sothsegger

272   Mohl, Ruth. "Theories of Monarchy in *Mum and the Sothsegger.*"
       PMLA, 59 (1944), 26-44.

       Identifies the poet's views on monarchy with "those of the
       medieval theorists who looked forward to the modern democratic
       state rather than backward to the days of feudal and monarchial
       tyranny." As a "practical legist," the author deals with some of the
       major conflicts of his day (early fifteenth century): "the doctrine of
       monarchy as opposed to that of feudalism; the doctrine of monarchy
       instituted by popular sovereignty and maintained by due process of
       law as opposed to lawless absolutism; the theory of passive obedience
       as opposed to that of resistance and even tyrannicide; and finally the
       distinctive and sometimes divergent claims of Positive and Natural
       Law." Using the poem as illustration, the article is an excellent
       summary of the various kinds of law recognized in medieval England
       —common law, civil (Roman) law, canon law, and natural law.

The Owl and the Nightingale

273   Atkins, J. W. H., ed. *The Owl and the Nightingale.* Cambridge
       Cambridge University Press, 1922.

       Although Wilhelm Gadow was the first to point out the
       correspondence between the debate here and the structure of a
       thirteenth-century lawsuit, Atkins was the first to develop the idea in
       detail. The introduction to his edition (pp. lii-lv) and the comments
       scattered throughout his footnotes remain one of the best sources of
       information on the legal character of the poem.

274   Huganir, Kathryn. *The Owl and the Nightingale: Sources, Dates, Author*. Philadelphia: n. p. [Univ. of Pennsylvania diss.], 1931.

This study makes extensive use of legal documents and writings in addressing a variety of problems. First, Huganir assigns a date of 1182-83 partly on the basis of the poet's discussion of "this peace" (lines 1730-34), a reference to "the peace established by the momentous legislation of the years 1176-81" (pp. 72-139). Next she demonstrates the close correspondence between the form of the debate and contemporary court procedure (pp. 154-162). Finally, she proposes as author of the poem Nicholas, son of Thorald, an itinerant justice of the peace (pp. 162-182).

275   _____. "Equine Quartering in *The Owl and the Nightingale*." *PMLA*, 52 (1937), 935-945.

Seeks to justify the harsh punishment—outlawry, mutilation, and a fine of one hundred pounds—given the knight who had a nightingale quartered by horses (lines 1061-62, 1093-1101). In the absence of much strictly legal evidence, Huganir argues from a number of romances (*La Chanson de Roland, Roman de Troie, Roman d'Alexandre, Renaus de Montaubon, Cligés, La Chevalerie Ogier de Danemarche*) that equine quartering was a punishment of lese majesty, a special prerogative of kings. This prerogative the knight has usurped, and his punishment is appropriately that of a traitor.

276   Lampe, David Elwood. "Middle English Debate Poems: A Genre Study." Diss. University of Nebraska 1969.

Uses canon law procedure to suggest the sequence and nature of argument in *The Owl and the Nightingale*.

277   Russell, J. C. "The Patrons of *The Owl and the Nightingale*." *PQ*, 48 (1969), 178-185.

The allusions to canon law in the poem play a small role in Russell's conjecture that the implied patron was a bishop, perhaps Geoffrey, natural son of Henry II and, after his father's death, Archbishop of York.

278   Stanley, Eric Gerald, ed. *The Owl and the Nightingale*. Manchester: Manchester University Press, and New York: Barnes and Noble, 1972.

   Pp. 27-30 provide a convenient summary of the legal elements in the poem, most of which seem to be based "on the practice of the ecclesiastical courts and not of the lay courts." Terms cited are speche, tale, mid riȝte dome, fals dom, bare worde, bicloped, forbonne, niþ and onde, fordeme lif an lime, rem, skere, sake, at bedde and at borde, utheste, pes, griþbruche.

279   Wilson, R. M. *Early Middle English Literature*. London: Methuen, 1939, rpt. 1968.

   Includes a discussion of the technical legal vocabulary developed during the Old English period (Chapter 4) and its survival in early ME literature, particularly in the *O&N* (Chapter 7): "Probably the most characteristic feature of the poem is its legal background. A vague legal flavour was characteristic of most of the vernacular debates but it does not, as a rule, go beyond that. The dispute in the *Owl and the Nightingale*, however, is modelled on the form of a twelfth-century law-suit, and the author consistently uses legal terminology...many of the technical legal terms being derived from the pre-Conquest legal vocabulary."

Pearl

280   Carson, Sister M. Angela. "A Study of the Technical Language in the Fourteenth-Century *Pearl*." Diss. Fordham University 1968.

   Finds that the metaphors of law and hunting "are sustained for the length of the poem and are congruent at every point with the literal action of the narrative." The legal process at the heart of *Pearl* is that of replevin, an action initiated for the purpose of regaining a personal possession which has been lost or stolen. The narrator is in the position of one who brings suit to recover his loss; the Pearl "is both the possession lost and the one who speaks for the defendant (Christ), and it is His verdict which she finally pronounces."

281   Everett, Dorothy, and Naomi D. Hurnard. "Legal Phraseology in a
       Passage in *Pearl*." *Medium Aevum*, 16 (1947), 9-15.

       The purpose of this note is to explain the legal procedure behind
       Pearl, lines 701-704:

> Forþy to corte quen þou schal com,
> Þer alle oure causeȝ schal be tryed,
> Alegge þe riȝt þou may be innome
> By þys ilke spech I have asspyed.

       The authors translate as follows: "Therefore, when you shall come
       to court where all our cases shall be tried, if you plead right (or
       righteousness), you may be trapped by (or refuted in argument by)
       this same speech that I have seen." Much of the discussion centers
       on the terms *alegge* (derived from OF *esligier*, "to bring forward as a
       legal ground or plea, to plead"), *riȝt*, and especially *innome*, the past
       participle of *nimen*, which is the English equivalent (it is argued) of
       the technical legal term *excipere*, "to take exception to, to refute a
       plea, etc." (Cf. the *Owl and the Nightingale* line 541.)

282   Horgan, A. D. "Justice in *The Pearl*." *RES*, N. S. 32 (1981),
       173-180.

       Distinguishes two kinds of justice in the *Pearl*: the classical view
       of human justice, i.e., what each owes to another; and the Hebrew
       idea of God's justice (*sedeq*), i.e., what God owes himself. The
       Dreamer can think only in terms of the first. From this point of view,
       Pearl's high status in heaven cannot be justified; but, as she explains,
       she has been rewarded not for her own righteousness but for the
       trawthe of God. Her argument is shown to parallel Paul's discussion
       of the law in Romans 2 and 3.

283   Reisner, Thomas Andrew. "The 'Cortaysye' Sequence in *Pearl*: A
       Legal Interpretation." *MP*, 72 (1975), 400-403.

       Argues that the poet's use of the word 'cortaysye' (lines 409 ff.)
       has legal connotations, implying coparcenary tenure. "Unlike joint
       tenancies in our own times, coparcenary estates, though complete
       and entire from the outset, could thus perpetually admit new
       co-owners *in loco decedentis*—an essential point, for this is precisely
       why Pearl herself, only lately arrived to claim her share of the
       heavenly kingdom, can justly assert her right to possession." [For an
       opposing view, see 137.]

Piers Plowman

284   Alford, John A. "Some Unidentified Quotations in *Piers Plowman*.
       MP, 72 (1975), 390-399.

       Among the three dozen quotations here identified for the first
       time are several legal maxims, e.g., "Qui agit contra conscientiam,
       edificat ad iehennam," "Consentientes et agentes pari pena
       punientur," "Audi alteram partem," etc.

285   _____. "The Grammatical Metaphor: A Survey of
       Its Use in the Middle Ages." *Speculum*, 87 (1982), 728-760.

       Notes the connection between law and grammar in *Piers* C.4.
       335-409, where the terms of both overlap (e.g., case, parties,
       number, accord). Because both law and grammar are seen by
       Langland as grounded in the very nature of things, they "function as
       virtually interchangeable concepts in his exposition of truth."

286   _____. "More Unidentified Quotations in *Piers
       Plowman*. *MP* [forthcoming].

       The sequel to Alford's earlier piece [284]. Additional phrases
       and quotations with legal significance include the following from
       canon and Roman law: "Intentio iudicat hominem," "infamis,"
       "ad pristinum statum ire," "ingratus," "clamare," and "pre
       manibus."

287   Baldwin, Anna P. "The Double Duel in *Piers Plowman* B XVIII
       and C XXI." *Medium Aevum*, 50 (1981), 64-78.

       Argues that Christ's two battles with Lucifer—first on the cross
       and then in Hell—are patterned, respectively, after the "civil duel of
       law" and the "chivalric duel of treason." Numerous parallels are
       noted.

288   _____. *The Theme of Government in Piers
       Plowman*. Cambridge: D. S. Brewer, 1981.

       The most extensive treatment of the legal elements in *Piers
       Plowman*. Baldwin interprets the *Visio* as an analogy not only for
       English society but also for the society of the Church (king:
       subjects::Christ:Christians). In the context of this analogy, many
       legal ideas take on added significance. Baldwin discusses in detail the

problem of political authority, Lady Meed's threat to law and social order, the trial of Wrong, and the extended legal metaphor of Redemption in C. Passus 18-20. (Legal terms and devices treated include the following: bail, mainprise, surety [wage or borwe], charter, lètter patent, seal, feoffment, trial by battle, pardon, felony, appeal [accuse], subpoena, maintenance.)

289 _____. "A Reference in *Piers Plowman* to the Westminster Sanctuary." *N&Q*, N. S. 29 (1982), 106-108.

Explains the comparison in B.20.281-289 between sinners who confess to friars and debtors who abuse the sanctuary offered them by Westminster Abbey. Both are trying to avoid paying what they owe. Parliament specifically addressed the problem of the Westminster Sanctuary in two statutes in 1377 and 1378—probably the inspiration behind Langland's comparison and further evidence for dating the B-text after 1377.

290 Barratt, Alexandra. "Civil and Theology in *Piers Plowman*." *Traditio*, 38 (1982).

Explains the opposition between Civil and Theology in Passus 2 by defining them, respectively, as the academic study of civil (Roman) law and theology. The traditional enmity between the two disciplines is traced in various authors: Pope Honorius III (who forbade the teaching of civil law at Paris in 1219), Roger Bacon, John Wyclif, and certain Wycliffite writers. Langland's treatment of Civil in an ecclesiastical context is also appropriate, Barratt points out, since the study of civil law was normally the foundation of a training in the canon law. [Cf. 297.]

291 Birnes, William J. "Patterns of Legality in *Piers Plowman*." Diss. New York University 1974.

Explores the patterns of legality implicit in the poem's central concept of Christ as the embodiment of law. The first pattern consists of a conventional attack upon the venality of lawyers, magistrates, and justices; the second, of legal terms and references to actual statutes; the third, of an equation between English common law/chancery law (equity) and the Old Law/New Law. These patterns are summarized and completed in the Harrowing of Hell episode, where Christ establishes his claim to man on the principles of law. In an appendix, the author provides an analytical list of the legal references in the poem.

292   _____. "Christ as Advocate: The Legal Metaphor of *Piers Plowman.*" *AnM*, 16 (1975), 71-93.

This article summarizes a large part of Birnes's dissertation. Specifically it argues that the medieval concept of universal law, embodied in the figure of Christ, is the framework in which Langland develops his theological ideas. The main focus is on the debate of the Four Daughters of God (a futile exercise under the Old Law), which prefigures the Harrowing of Hell episode (the triumph of Christ under the New Law). The contrast between the Old and New Law is developed, according to Birnes, in the legal terms, respectively, of English common law ("rigid and inflexible") and the emerging equity law of the Chancery. The implied fusion of divine and human law places Langland's earlier references to the law in a new and broader context.

293   Bowers, R. H. "'Foleuyles Lawes' (*Piers Plowman,* C.XXII.247)." *N&Q*, N. S. 8 (1961), 327-328.

Suggests that the "Foleuyles lawes" by which the Holy Spirit charges some "to ryde and rekevere that unryghtfulliche was wonne" is an allusion to the five notorious Folville brothers of Ashby-Folville, Leicestershire, and Teigh, Rutland (prominent in court records between 1326-1347). Bowers shows that "while men such as the Folvilles were criminals according to modern standards, some of their contemporaries thought of them as performing a kind of rough justice, like Robin Hood." Hence, the expression, as used by Langland, points to a popular doctrine of "justifiable redress."

294   Burton, Dorothy Jean. "The Compact with the Devil in the Middle English *Vision of Piers the Plowman*, B.II." *California Folklore Quarterly*, 5 (1946), 179-184.

Burton suggests that the marriage contract in *Piers Plowman* B.2.74-88 is based, in part, on the folk motif of the compact with the Devil. Langland is unique, she says, in "combining this traditional compact motif with the conception of a marriage contract, complete to its dowry agreement in due legal form." Burton's approach is too narrowly folklorist, however, and takes little notice of earlier literary treatments of the theme.

295 Coleman, Janet. *Piers Plowman and the Moderni*. Rome: Edizioni di Storia e Letteratura, 1981.

Although this book is chiefly concerned with the relation between *Piers* and the Ockhamist, terminist, voluntarist atmosphere of fourteenth century scholasticism, it says a great deal in passing about natural, civil and common law.

296 Donaldson, E. Talbot. *Piers Plowman: The C-Text and Its Poet*. Yale Studies in English, 113. New Haven: Yale University Press, 1949.

In Chapter 4 ("The Politics of the C-Reviser"), the author touches upon certain legal commonplaces in the course of arguing that the political views expressed in B and C, far from differing, show the same "middle-of-the-road tendency." The discussion focuses on the king's relation to law, the precise meaning of the term *comunes*, and the debt of Langland's political thought to the coronation oath.

297 Gilbert, Beverly Brian. "'Civil' and the Notaries in *Piers Plowman*." *Medium Aevum*, 50 (1981), 49-63.

Seeks to explain the close association of Civil and Simony (in Will's vision of Meed), and the reason for including notaries in the satire. Rejecting the interpretation of Civil as a "representative of the English secular courts," Gilbert notes the importance of civil (Roman) law both in the study of canon law and in church administration. In order to show that Langland's audience was "prepared to regard Civil as a vehicle of satire on the ecclesiastical courts," he quotes several writers who see the study of civil law as a danger to the law of the Gospel (e.g., Bernard, Bacon, Wyclif). Like the civilian, the notary was a functionary of Roman law, and his chief occupation was in ecclesiastical business. Although notaries sometimes falsified documents, Langland's reason for including them here was probably to satirize "the sheer expense of legal processes which required payments to personnel of the courts at every step of the way...." [Cf. 290.]

298 Jones, Florence. "Dickens and Langland in Adjudication upon Meed." *The Victorian Newsletter*, 33 (1968), 53-56.

Imagines how Dickens might have narrated the *Visio*.

299   Kean, P. M. "Love, Law, and *Lewte* in *Piers Plowman*." *RES*, N. S. 15 (1964), 241-261.

Suggests that Langland is deeply concerned in the *Visio* (B-text) with the Aristotelian virtue of justice (i.e., *lewte*); that this virtue necessarily involves the idea of law; and that the two are part of a triad with love, without which in Langland's view "no moral action is conceivable." Kean's discussion of law and justice focuses on the relation between the king and the "comunes" and is based almost entirely on the writings of Thomas Aquinas.

300   _____. "Justice, Kingship and the Good Life in the Second Part of *Piers Plowman*." *Piers Plowman: Critical Approaches*. Ed. S. S. Hussey. London: Methuen, 1969, pp. 76-110.

In this sequel to her article above on the *Visio*, Kean argues for a correspondence between the triads (1) of law, *lewte*, love and (2) of Dowel, Dobet, Dobest, both of which give rise to a fourth and competing term—kingship. However, there is little discussion of the law as such.

301   Kirk, Rudolf. "References to the Law in *Piers the Plowman*." *PMLA*, 48 (1933), 322-327.

Suggests that the references to law that occur in the three texts of the poem "reveal a significant increase in legal knowledge from the A-text to the later texts." Kirk finds "about thirteen legal words" in the A-text; "at least forty-five" in the B-text; and an additional half dozen or so in the C-text. However, the basis of selection is very arbitrary (e.g., summoner and beadle are considered "legal words," while bailiff, legistre, and juror are not); and, as Kirk admits, the figures are roughly proportional to the differing lengths of the three texts themselves.

302   Mathew, Gervase. "Justice and Charity in *The Vision of Piers Plowman*." *Dominican Studies*, 1 (1948), 360-366.

Behind all Langland's social doctrine lies the medieval definition of justice as "the unswerving determination to give to each man that which is his due." However, the motive force behind justice is charity, that is, love of God and man.

303 Pritchard, Gretchen Wolff. "Law, Love and Incarnation: An Interpretation of *Piers Plowman*." Diss. Yale University 1976.

Presents a close reading of the B-text "in order to point out the crucial function of the dialectic of law and love and its rhetorical and structural projections." Love does not destroy the law but fulfills it; the movement is one not of replacement but of reconciliation.

304 Roush, George Jonathan. "The Political Plowman: The Expression of Political Ideals in *Piers Plowman* and Its Successors." Diss. University of California at Berkeley 1966.

Finds the roots of the poem in conventional political theory, in which the modern distinction between "political" and "religious" ideas has little meaning. Like other political poets, Langland invokes both divine law and sacred history as guides for his own society. Moreover, he seems "relatively familiar with contemporary political and legal thought."

Pilgrimage of the Soul

305 McGerr, Rosemarie. "'The Judgment of the Soul': A Critical Edition of the Middle English Pilgrimage of the Soul, Book I." Diss. Yale University 1981.

This anonymous adaptation (ca. 1413) of Deguileville's *Pèlerinage de l'âme* adds a great deal of legal material to Book I, the account of the pilgrim soul's trial and judgment at the court of the Archangel Michael, provost of heaven. Arguments are made by the Four Daughters of God (here Justice, Reason, Truth, and Mercy). McGerr observes that the presentation of heavenly judgment as a medieval court scene makes the abstract theology more accessible, sometimes even humorous, at the same time that it emphasizes the superiority of heavenly law (the pilgrim soul runs amok when he tries to apply temporal values during the trial [cf. 449]). The scene concludes with the soul's pardon and Satan's vow to appeal the sentence.

Romances

306   Boone, Lalia Phipps. "Criminal Law and the Matter of England."
       Boston University Studies in English, 2 (1956), 2-16.

       This article attempts to show that in the Matter of England,
       crime and punishment "are realistically portrayed [and]... reflect
       with a fair degree of accuracy the workaday criminal law of twelfth-
       and thirteenth-century England." The romances treated are *Guy of*
       Warwick (trial by compurgation and judicial combat), *Athelston*
       (trial by ordeal), *Havelock the Dane* and *Beves of Hamtoun* (trial
       before the king's council), and *Gamelyn* (trial before the shire moot).

307   Davis, Robert Evan, Jr. "Justice in the Middle English Metrical
       Romances." Diss. The Pennsylvania State University 1979.

       Although they picture widespread corruption among officers of
       the law, the ME metrical romances all "advocate support of, and
       obedience to, the legal structure as the best means of preserving order
       and justice." Moreover, they endorse the English system of common
       law and trial by a jury of one's peers as consistent with reason and
       justice. Thus, the outlook is conservative. All who commit crimes in
       the romances, even minor crimes, are with few exceptions *punished*.

308   Delany, Sheila, and Vahan Ishkanian. "Theocratic and Contractual
       Kingship in *Havelok the Dane*." *Zeitschrift für Anglistik und*
       Amerikanistik, 22 (1974), 290-302.

       Reflecting the thirteenth-century English view of kingship (e.g.,
       Bracton's *De legibus et consuetudinibus Angliae)*, *Havelok the Dane*
       presents a hero "who functions in the romance both as theocratically
       ordained monarch, and as socially responsible leader of a nation
       united under law." The omission of a coronation ceremony is
       especially significant. Havelok's "secular coronation" emphasizes
       the rights of *regnum* over those of *sacerdotium* and pointedly recalls
       the   manner   of   Edward's   own   accession   to   the   throne
       (1272-1307)—"the first time that full legal recognition had been
       extended to an heir before coronation."

309   Gist, Margaret Adlum. *Love and War in the Middle English*
       Romances. Philadelphia: University of Pennsylvania Press, 1947.

       Seeks to determine to what extent the ME romances faithfully reflect actual conditions in the areas of love (i.e., sex and marriage) and war. Although the romances are certainly true "in picturing the troubled and disordered environment in which women moved, and in showing that they had no adequate protection against the violence of the lustful male" and also true "in representing the lawlessness, the violence, the brutality of warfare and warriors," they are "not accurate in their presentation of aspects of civil and ecclesiastical law. Authors seem almost stupidly unaware of legal and ecclesiastical provisions that would have solved the problems of their characters. Too often the penalty exacted for misconduct is not a fourteenth-century penalty but a more severe provision of a much earlier period chosen to fit the didactic purpose of the author."

310   Heffernan, Carol Falvo. "*Raptus*: A Note on Crime and Punishment in *Le Bone Florence of Rome.*" *Medieval Studies in Honor of Lillian Herlands Hornstein.* Ed. Jess B. Bessinger, Jr. and Robert Raymo. New York: New York University Press, 1976, pp. 173-179.

Suggests that the poet's treatment of *raptus* (Florence's detention by Mylys) does not reflect late fifteenth-century canon law but rather looks forward to the policies instituted by the Council of Trent (1545).

311   Keen, Maurice. *The Outlaws of Medieval England.* Toronto: University of Toronto Press, 1961; rpt. 1977.

Focuses on the outlaws of the "Greenwood"—Hereward, Wallace, Robin Hood, Gamelyn, etc. The background of the legends is historical, and yet the stories themselves are only partly historical. "They are born of historical situations in which justice and the law have, by some irony of fate, found themselves in opposite camps" (p. 215).

312   _____. "Robin Hood: A Peasant Hero." *History Today*, 8 (1958), 684-689.

Explains the popularity of Robin Hood, "the first hero of the common people of England," as primarily a reaction against oppressive laws and corrupt officers. Like Gamelyn, however, his role is "not to destroy, but to right the wrongs of the old system....At heart, he is as loyal a subject of his King as any man alive."

313   Kratins, Ojars. "Treason in Middle English Metrical Romances." *PQ*, 45 (1966), 668-687.

Shows that the handling of treason in ME romances "conformed, on the whole, to legal practice." Nevertheless, "it would be unreasonable to expect a poet to pay close attention to a great number of details of purely legal interest when what matters to him most is the moral lesson of the tale." In particular, the belief that God has an active interest in bringing about justice explains why the *iudicium Dei* plays a much greater role in the romances than in contemporary legal practice. Among the romances treated are *Kyng Alisaunder, Generydes, Sir Launfal, The Erl of Toulous, Amis and Amiloun, The Seven Sages of Rome, Athelston, Havelock the Dane, Syr Tryamore, Partonope of Blois, Guy of Warwick.*

314   Murphy, Gratia H. "Arthur as King: A Reading of the Alliterative *Morte Arthure* in the Light of the *Fürstenspiegel* Tradition." Diss. Kent State University 1976.

Among other things, connects Arthur's final battle with the idea in *Fürstenspiegel* tradition that the king is under the law.

315   Shannon, Edgar F., Jr. "Mediaeval Law in *The Tale of Gamelyn*." *Speculum*, 26 (1951), 458-464.

Shows that "the author was well versed in the law of his day and that the poem mirrors accurately and in some detail the uncertain, though gradually developing, processes of justice in the fourteenth century." Topics covered include Gamelyn's father's will, which though legal is contrary to the rule of primogeniture; Gamelyn's outlawry (he is "cryed and maad" a "wolves-heed"); his imprisonment and bail or mainprise; his trial by a stacked jury; his overturning the unjust sentence by force, hanging both judge and jury himself; and finally his winning the king's pardon and the return of all his property. Shannon's main purpose is to explain the finer points of law along the way.

316   Tamanini, Mary E. Mulqueen. "*The Tale of Beryn* (An Edition with Introduction, Notes, and Glossary)." Diss. New York University 1969.

Notes in the introduction how the English translator has enlarged the legal machinery of the tale. "This suggests that it may have been written for audiences with a special interest in law, such as those at the Inns of Court.''

317   Vale, Juliet. "Law and Diplomacy in the Alliterative *Morte Arthure*." *NMS*, 23 (1979), 31-46.

Tries to demonstrate "that the poet's expertise in the legal and diplomatic aspects of current military practice is an indication of the milieu in which we should seek him." This expertise included a technical knowledge of letters of safe-conduct, diplomatic exchanges and protocol, the law of arms, etc. The precise use of terms points to a period just after the middle of the fourteenth century as the date of composition, and to someone with a legal and administrative background as the poet. [Item repeated 670.]

Sir Gawain and the Green Knight

318   Barron, W. R. J. *"Trawthe" and Treason: The Sin of Gawain Reconsidered.* Manchester: Manchester University Press, 1980.

Treats the hunting scenes, Gawain's contracts, and his battle with the Green Knight in the context of medieval law. Barron focuses particularly on the concept of treason.

319   Burrow, John A. *A Reading of Sir Gawain and the Green Knight.* London: Routledge and Kegan Paul, 1965; rpt. 1977.

Includes a brief discussion of the legal terminology in Gawain's contracts with the Green Knight (pp. 21-23, 66-70 et passim), e.g., "quit-clayme," "diȝt me þe dom," give "respite," "a twelmonyth and a day," "in hyȝe and in loȝe," etc.

320   Lester, G. A. "Gawain's Fault in Terms of Contemporary Law of Arms." *N&Q*, N. S. 23 (1976), 392-393.

Gawain's accepting and concealing the green girdle shows not only a lack of faith in the Virgin but also a disregard for the contemporary law of arms. According to *The Ordenaunce and Fourme of Fightyng within Listes*, promulgated by Thomas Woodstock, Duke of Gloucester and Constable of England under Richard II, the constable is to administer the following oath to combatants: "...thou swerest that thou ne havest...ne stone of vertue, ne herbe of vertue, ne charme, ne experiment, ne carocte [talisman], ne othir inchauntment by the...ne that thou trustith in noon othir thynge, but oonly in god and thi body...."

321   Spendal, R. J. "The Fifth Pentad in 'Sir Gawain and the Green Knight.'" *N&Q*, N. S. 23 (1976), 147-148.

Posits an equivalence between the five virtues of Gawain's shield and the parts of justice defined by Aquinas, that is, *fraunchyse* (liberalitas), *felaȝschyp* (amicitia), *clannes* (religio), *cortaysye* (observantia or amicitia), and *pite* (pietas and amicitia). "The climactic position of these virtues suggests that the pentangle as a whole may be broadly emblematic of justice....We may conclude, then, that Gawain's ethic seems to be founded primarily upon the virtue of justice." Indeed, both the Beheading Game and Temptation "turn on Gawain's giving a man his just due" and both represent bargains "couched in legalistic terminology that gives them the weight of formal contracts." After breaking the compact with his host, therefore, "Gawain can no longer claim the pentangle as his spiritual emblem."

Usk

322   Bressie, Ramona. "The Date of Thomas Usk's *Testament of Love.*" *MP*, 26 (1928), 17-29.

Uncovers new evidence in the Issue Rolls of the Exchequer for July, 1385, of still another imprisonment (besides those in 1384 and 1387) during which Usk might have written the *Testament*. Bressie rejects the view of the work as religious allegory. It is Usk's defense of himself for having appealed Norhampton, More, and Norbury and "a reminder to his patrons that he languishes in prison."

323   Hallmundsson, May Newman. "The Community of Law and Letters: Some Notes on Thomas Usk's Audience." *Viator,* 9 (1978), 357-365.

Sees the *Testament* as a "plea," in the legal sense, directed to the clerks, lawyers, and judges of Chancery, in an effort to expedite a review of his case and release from Newgate prison. Hallmundsson's main purpose is to identify the Chancery personnel known or likely to have been known by Usk.

Wulfstan

324   Bethurum, Dorothy. "Six Anonymous Old English Codes." *JEGP*, 49 (1950), 449-463.

    Arguing primarily on the basis of stylistic features in his *Homilies*, such as "the habit of arranging lists in alliterating and rhyming pairs," Bethurum identifies Archbishop Wulfstan as the author of six anonymous OE codes printed in Liebermann's *Die Gesetze der Angelsachsen*.

325   _____. "Wulfstan." *Continuations and Beginnings: Studies in Old English Literature*. Ed. Eric Gerald Stanley. London: Nelson, 1966, pp. 210-246.

    Like Whitelock's earlier article, this chapter is primarily a survey of Wulfstan's career and writings, especially the homilies and laws.

326   Cummings, Michael Joseph. "Social History in Wulfstan's Authentic Homilies: Based on Terminology." Diss. University of Toronto 1971.

    Generalizes about Anglo-Saxon institutions and social organizations on the basis of lexical items in Wulfstan's homilies. Besides his references to economic life, kin and kinship, and the relation between Church and State, Wulfstan has a great deal to say about law. Cummings' discussion centers on three terms: *dom, lagu,* and *riht*. He argues that the distinction between *dom* (judicial act) and *lagu* (legislative act) represents a "terminological revolution in English that undoubtedly owes its origin to lexical contrasts in the language of the Danelaw." *Riht* functions chiefly as the abstract principle (divine justice) from which *dom* and *lagu* receive their sanction. The fact that they can exist apart from *riht*, however, is perhaps further reflection of the separateness of the religious and the secular kingdoms in Wulfstan's thought.

327   Whitelock, Dorothy. "Wulfstan and the so-called Laws of Edward and Guthrum." *EHR*, 221 (1941), 1-21.

    Questions the early dating of "the Laws of Edward and Guthrum" (921-939) by Liebermann, proposing instead a date "not much before 1008." Much of Whitelock's evidence is based on similarities of style between the Laws and Wulfstan's

Homilies—such as "the excessive use of certain intensives," "formulae common in late laws and in Wulfstan's homilies, but absent from tenth-century laws," certain striking agreements of vocabulary, etc.

328 _____. "Archbishop Wulfstan, Homilist and Statesman." *Transactions of the Royal Historical Society*. Ser. IV, 24 (1942), 25-45.

A summary of scholarship on Wulfstan, with much discussion of the relationship between his sermons and the legal codes in which he is presumed to have had a hand.

Wynnere and Wastour

329 Moran, Dennis V. "*Wynnere and Wastoure:* An Extended Footnote." *NM*, 73 (1972), 683-685.

Sees the St. Hilary Parliament of 1352 as "the motive for the poem." The poet: 1. alludes to William de Shareshull, Chief Justice (line 317), who in this parliament attacked the civil disturbances personified by Wastoure; 2. elaborates upon the complaints brought before this same parliament (forestalling, maintenance, unauthorized bearing of arms, fraud, exorbitant tithes); 3. mentions the year as the twenty-fifth of Edward's reign, i.e., 1352; and 4. describes the action, a debate, as occurring before Edward III and his eldest son, the Black Prince, both of whom were present at the parliament. Finally, Moran notes the legal connotation of "wastour"—a tenant who destroys or injures the property in his care—as appropriate to both the parliament and the poem.

GERMAN

General and Miscellaneous

330 Amira, Karl von. "Recht." Paul's *Grundriss der germanischen Philologie*. Strassburg: Trübner, 1900, 3:51-222.

    A basic survey of the sources and character of early Germanic law (i.e., German and Scandinavian), much indebted to Jacob Grimm's philological approach in *Deutsche Rechtsaltertümer* [348] and elsewhere.

331 Bader, Karl S. "Deutsches Recht." *Deutsche Philologie im Aufriss*. 3 vols. Ed. Wolfgang Stammler. Berlin: Schmidt, 1962, 3:1971-2024.

    A valuable description of the sources available to the legal historian. Includes a brief discussion of the documentary value of literature, with particular mention of Hartmann von Aue, the *Heliand*, and the *Nibelungenlied*.

332 Bell, Clair Hayden. "The Sister's Son in the Medieval German Epic." *University of California Publications in Modern Philology*, 10 (1922), 67-182.

    Concludes that the close association of the uncle and the sister's son in medieval German epics represents the survival of matriliny [cf. 180].

333 Blank, Walter. *Die deutsche Minneallegorie. Gestaltung und Funktion einer Spätmittelalterlichen Dichtungsform*. Stuttgart: Metzler, 1970.

    Discusses at various points (pp. 65 ff., 78-87, 181-183) the judgment theme in *minne*-allegories (e.g., *Der Minne Gericht, Bestraften Untreue, Minne vor Gericht, Die Mörin* and *Der Spiegel* of Hermann von Sachsenheim).

334   Borchling, Conrad. "Poesie und Humor im friesischen Recht."
       Abhandlungen und Vorträge zur Geschichte Ostfrieslands, 10 (1908),
       1-59.

335   Bumke, Joachim. *Studien zum Ritterbegriff im 12. und 13.*
       Jahrhundert. Beihefte zum Euphorion. Zeitschrift für
       Literaturgeschichte (Heft 1). Heidelberg: Winter, 1964. Trans. as
       The Concept of Knighthood in the Middle Ages. W. T. H. and Erika
       Jackson. New York: AMS Press, 1982.

       An exhaustive analysis of such words as *Ritter* and *Dienestmann*,
       as found in the major literary works of the twelfth and thirteenth
       centuries. Among other things, the author concludes that *Ritter*
       stands for two different concepts, one social, the other ethical.

336   Burdach, Konrad. "Der juristische Rahmen des altdeutschen
       Streitgesprächs." *SBAW*, 1913 (No. 29).

337   Dohse, Jutta. "Zu 'helfe' und 'rât.' Der Lehenseid in der
       mittelhochdeutschen Dichtung." *'Getempert und gemischet' für*
       Wolfgang Mohr zum 65. Geburtstag von seinen Tübinger Schülern.
       Göppingen: Kümmerle, 1972, pp. 219-229.

       Observes that because of the audience's familiarity with the
       ritual, investiture in MHG literature is reduced to a symbolic gesture
       (*inmixtio manum*) or to the vernacular formula "zu helfe und rât"
       (Latin *auxilium et consilium*). The formula may describe a contract
       not only between vassal and lord, however, but also between man
       and God (e.g., *Parzival*) and—to emphasize love's legal
       nature—between man and woman (especially in Minnesang).

338   Ehrismann, Gustav. *Geschichte der deutschen Literatur bis zum*
       Ausgang des Mittelalters. München: Beck, 1918-1935.

       A standard history of medieval German literature. Ehrismann is
       very sensitive to legal elements (see 1:130 [*Hildebrandslied*]; 3:456
       [Hermann von Sachsenheim], 507 [*Der Minne Gericht*], 605
       [*Satansprozess*], et passim).

339 Faber, B. M. "Eheschliessung in mittelalterliches Dichtung vom Ende des 12. bis zum Ende des 15. Jahrhunderts." Diss. Bonn 1973.

Finds no single type of betrothal predominant. Canon law prevails in epics derived from French models, but traditional forms prevail in works with a peasant milieu. Although poets are generally faithful in their handling of marriage law, they insist, at the same time, on the greater validity of personal commitments.

340 Fehr, Hans. *Kunst und Recht.* 3 vols. (1. *Das Recht im Bilde.* Erlenbach-Zürich, München, Leipzig: Eugen Rentsch, 1913. 2. *Das Recht in der Dichtung.* Bern: Francke, [1931] 3. *Die Dichtung im Recht.* Bern: Francke, 1936).

This monumental survey must be the centerpiece in any bibliography of German literature and law. In Volume 1, Fehr looks at representations of the law (trials, punishments, commercial transactions, etc.) in the visual arts, especially in medieval miniatures (222 illustrations). In Volume 2, he devotes individual essays to the legal elements in nearly 200 literary works (Norse and German) from the *Edda* and *Hildebrandslied* up to the twentieth century (over 75 examples are medieval). In Volume 3, he concentrates on legal documents and treatises that show the influence of literary skill (rhyme, alliteration, symbolism, dramatization, proverbs, etc.). The volume of greatest interest to the literary historian, of course, is the second one. Typical of Fehr's procedure is his treatment of Gottfried von Strassburg's *Tristan.* He reproduces with commentary excerpts that illustrate the ordeal, trial by battle, lawful marriage, illegitimacy, dowry, etc. A glossary of legal terms and phrases in *Tristan* follows. Throughout the volume Fehr's point of view is mainly that of a legal historian; he is less interested in how a knowledge of law illuminates the literature than in how the literature clarifies or confirms points of law. There is a long summary of his findings at the end (pp. 519-562).

341 _____. "Die Dichtung des Mittelalters als Quelle des Rechts." *Festschrift für Karl Haff.* Innsbruck, 1950, pp. 62-66.

342 _____. "Tod und Teufel im alten Recht." *ZRG,* Germ. Abt. 67 (1950), 50-75.

For a true understanding of the medieval conception of law, which often involved such "extra-legal and irrational" elements as death and the devil, one must rely not on the "official" sources of law but on popular forms of literature. The intimate connection between death and justice may be seen in the motif of the *Bahrprobe* (e.g., *Nibelungenlied*), in treatments of the Last Judgment, and most explicitly in the *Ackermann aus Böhmen*. Theology and jurisprudence come together in the literary genre known as "the trial of Satan," of which Fehr cites several examples (Bartolus de Saxoferrato, Jacobus de Theramo, Petrus Meckel, et al.). Eventually the *Satansprozess* fuses with the "debate of the Four Daughters of God." [Cf. 385.]

343   Freudenthal, Karl Fredrik. *Arnulfingisch-karolingische Rechtswörter. Eine Studie in der juristischen Terminologie der ältesten germanischen Dialekte.* Göteborg: Elanders, 1949.

A study of early Germanic legal terms and their geographical diffusion. The investigation focuses on three fields of meaning: 1. *Testis-testimonium-testari*, 2. *Judicium-judicare-judex,* 3. *Accusatio-accusare*. In addition to legal texts, Freudenthal relies on the *Heliand*, the Gothic Bible, Otfrid's *Evangelienbuch*, Notker of St. Gall's glosses and numerous other scriptural commentaries.

344   Frölich, Karl. "Die Eheschliessung des deutschen Frümittelalters im Lichte der neueren rechtsgeschichtlichen Forschung, Ergebnisse und Ausblicke." *Hessische Blätter für Volkskunde*, 27 (1928), 144-194.

A summary of work by legal historians on the subject of early medieval marriage (Ferdinand Frensdorff, Otto Zallinger, Ernst Hoyer, Karl Eckhardt, Herbert Meyer, et al.). The success of Zallinger [460, 461] and Meyer [370] in their studies of *Kudrun* and the *Nibelungenlied* leads Frölich to urge greater cooperation between legal and literary historians.

345   Gaisser, Erich. "Minne und Recht in den Schöffensprüchen des Mittelalters." Diss. Tübingen 1955.

346   Gellinek, Christian. "Marriage by Consent in Literary Sources of Medieval Germany." *Studia Gratiana*, 12 (1967), 557-579.

Tries to show "that marriages by deliberate consent of the marrying partners (the so-called *Friedelehe* or *Neigungsehe*) were practiced at least in Southern Germany, and probably elsewhere in Europe, during the eleventh and twelfth centuries." Gellinek relies chiefly on the *Ruodlieb* and *König Rother* (with additional illustrations from *Die Hochzeit, Der Arme Heinrich,* and *Parzival*). He insists that poetry can be a source of information about contemporary customs "if the results of generally accepted legal scholarship on the same period also are consulted." (The article contains a useful explanation of MHG marriage-law terminology as well.)

347 Gerstein, Mary Roche. "Warg: The Outlaw as Werwolf in Germanic Myth, Law, and Medicine." Diss. University of California at Los Angeles 1972.

Uses the evidence of Germanic myth, law and medicine to illuminate the relationship between the berserk warrior and the *warg* (the "werwolf-outlaw" expelled as a wild beast by the community). The argument turns on the word *warg* itself, which has "a wide range of disease meanings." It is concluded that "the relationship between the frenzied warrior, the raging *warg*, and the terrible grain-disease, *ergot*, is fundamental to Gmc. custom, belief, and medical lore."

348 Grimm, Jacob. *Deutsche Rechtsaltertümer.* 4th ed., 2 vols. Leipzig: Theodor Weicher, 1899.

First published in 1828, this was a landmark study in which the new "scientific" philology was put to the service of legal history. In a long introduction (1:1-310) Grimm illustrates the literary characteristics of early Germanic law (alliteration, rhyme, tautology, etc.). Thousands of examples are given. The work is divided into six books on the following topics: I. Status and the divisions of society, II. The household, III. Property, IV. Things (movables), V. Crime, VI. Judgment. Illustrations from literature are used freely throughout.

349 Grosse, Rudolf. "Zur sprachgeschichtlichen Untersuchung der spätmittelalterlichen deutschen Rechtsdenkmäler." *Forschungen und Fortschritte*, 38 (1964), 56-60.

Emphasizes the value of legal documents and treatises (e.g., *Sachsenspiegel, Schwabenspiegel*) for philological research. The notes constitute a good bibliography of linguistic approaches to legal texts.

350   Gruenter, Rainer. "Über den Einfluss des Genus Iudicale [sic] auf den höfischen Redestil." *DVLG*, 26 (1952), 49-57.

Notes the importance of judicial rhetoric in the education of medieval writers. The study of the *genus iudiciale* helped to form not only their literary style and sense of structure but also their treatment of psychological problems. Although its influence can be traced as far back as Notker of St. Gall, the early works of Hartmann von Aue are among the best illustrations of its use. However, a poet's delight in the formal interplay of *pro* and *con* may lead him to sacrifice the deeper logic of ethical judgment (as happens, Gruenter believes, in the conversation between Laudine and Lunette in *Iwein*). Long after Hartmann, the form of argumentation prescribed by legal rhetoric continues to be an extremely popular *Erzählmotiv*, but it often degenerates into a merely mechanical exercise.

351   Harms, Wolfgang. *Der Kampf mit dem Freund oder Verwandten in der deutschen Literatur bis um 1300*. München: Eidos, 1963.

Surveys the theme of combat among friends and relatives in numerous medieval German works. Legal aspects both of the combat itself (*Gerichtskampf, Feldkampf*, etc.) and of the terms describing the combatants' relationship (*sippe, mâc, friunt, geselle, man*) are discussed. Thus, for example, *sippe*. The word means, according to the *Sachsenspiegel*, relatives to the seventh degree. The *Prose Lancelot* uses it in this rather strict sense and sees combat between relatives as a way of restoring the equilibrium of justice. Wolfram von Eschenbach, however, has a larger vision of its meaning: an offense against any member of the family is an offense against mankind in general and thus against God.

352   Hattenhauer, Hans. "'Minne und recht' als Ordnungsprinzipien des mittelalterlichen Rechts." *ZRG*, Germ. Abt. 80 (1963), 325-344.

Explains the formula "minne und recht," a commonplace in MHG literature, from a strictly legal point of view ("minne und recht" = canon law "consilio vel iudicio," "secundum amorem vel iustitiam," etc.). *Minne*, which has its source in the Christian Church, is close to but not identical with the concept of *aequitas*. Hattenhauer sees a tension, an "antithetische Spannung," between *minne* and *recht* and yet at the same time a reciprocity. Each "corrects" and takes its meaning from the other.

353   Jacoby, Michael. *wargus, vargr, "Verbrecher," "Wolf." eine sprach- und rechtsgeschichtliche Untersuchung.* Studia Germanistica Upsaliensia, 12. Uppsala: University of Uppsala, 1974.

    Traces the semantic development of the word *wulf* (wolf, outlaw) in Germanic texts, both legal and literary, up to the year 1200.

354   Jones, George Fenwick. *Honor in German Literature.* University of North Carolina Studies in the Germanic Languages and Literature, 25. Chapel Hill: University of North Carolina Press, 1959.

    Investigates the transformation of the idea of honor in German literature from an *external* quality (old Germanic love of fame, fear of shame) to an *internal* quality (as defined by Christianity). Since the shift occurred during the medieval period, most of the study deals with Old and Middle High German texts, focusing on the writers' use of such terms as *êre, triuwe, schande*, etc. The concept of law plays an important role throughout the work.

355   _____. "Was Germanic *Blutrache* a Sacred Duty?" *Studia Neophilologica*, 32 (1960), 218-227.

    Finds no evidence in early Germanic literature that blood revenge was ever considered a sacred duty. "In every case reference is made to the social disgrace that will plague the offended until he gets revenge."

356   Kanzog, Klaus. "Literatur und Recht." *Reallexikon der deutschen Literaturgeschichte.* Berlin: de Gruyter, 1965, 2:164-195.

    INDISPENSABLE. A comprehensive survey of the historical relationship between literature (Norse and German) and law, from the beginnings to the present. The medieval period is especially well represented: virtually every major work dealing with law or showing the direct influence of law is mentioned. Kanzog's order of treatment is meant to suggest a parallelism between literary and legal history: he organizes the works into groups that seem to reflect major shifts in legal attitudes or policies (e.g., the tension between Adelsherrschaft and Königtum in the twelfth century, the conflict between Church and State, the Reception of Roman law, and so forth). The discussion of each group is followed by an extensive

bibliography of secondary materials by both legal and literary
scholars.

357   Kettler, Wilfried. *Das Jüngste Gericht. Philologische Studien zu
den Eschatologie-Vorstellungen in den alt- und frühmittel-
hochdeutschen Denkmälern.* Berlin: de Gruyter, 1977.

358   Kisch, Guido. "Über Reimvorreden deutscher Rechtsbücher."
Niederdeutsche Mitteilungen, 6 (1950), 61-83.

Takes as his point of departure the work of Fehr [340], Grimm
[9, 348], and especially Künssberg [366]. Kisch notes that rhymed
prologues are common in German lawbooks, e.g, Johann von Buch's
gloss on the *Sachsenspiegel* (1325), the work of Ruprecht von
Freising (1328), the *Berliner Stadtbuch* (1397). Ten of the twelve
books in the legal compilations of Johannes Rothe and Purgoldt
have rhymed introductions. And rhymed epilogues are found in the
Freisinger Rechtsbuch, the *Cautela* of Hermann von Oesfeld
(mid-fourteenth cen.), and the *Meissener Rechtsbuch* (betw.
1357-1387). Kisch reproduces for discussion two rhymed prologues,
one attached to the *Sachsenspiegel* (from a MS. in the Hamburger
Staats- und Universitätsbibliothek, ca. 1314), and another from a
Schöffenspruchsammlung of 1474. Comparing the outlook of the
prologues with that of the poems "Vom Recht" and "Die
Hochzeit," Kisch stresses the importance of biblical and theological
influences.

359   Klibansky, Erich. *Gerichtsszene und Prozessform in erzählenden
deutschen Dichtungen des 12.-14. Jahrhunderts.* Germanische
Studien, 40. Berlin: Ebering, 1925.

This important study of trials and court scenes in medieval
German literature is divided into two parts: religious works and
secular works. Under the first heading Klibansky takes up
representations of the trial of Jesus (*Diu Urstende* of Konrad von
Heimesfurt, the *Evangelium Nicodemi* of Heinrich von Hesler, and
Gundacker von Judenburg's *Christi Hort*); the Last Judgment (as
described by the Hamburger *Jüngste Gericht,* the *Linzer Antichrist,*
Frau Ava, Hugo von Langenstein, Heinrich von Neustadt, et al.);
and finally the trial of Archbishop Udo von Magdeburg, as reported
in his legend (14th cen.). Because of the nature of their material,
Klibansky observes, these authors could not depart radically from

their sources but did revise portions that might have offended their audiences' "legal sensitivity." Under the heading of secular works, Klibansky discusses *Reinhart Fuchs* (the first instance in literature of the term *Landfried*); the *Schwanrittersage* of Konrad von Würzburg; *Meier Helmbrecht* and the *Rolandslied*. All reflect a high degree of legal knowledge on the part of their authors.

360 Knapp, Fritz Peter. *Der Selbstmord in der abendländischen Epik des Hochmittelalters*. Heidelberg: Winter, 1979.

An analysis of suicide as a literary motif in medieval German, French, and English works (e.g., Chrétien de Troyes, Hartmann von Aue, Konrad von Würzburg, Wolfram von Eschenbach). The study traces ideological shifts in literary treatments of the theme. Especially important was the influence of Christian ethics. Unlike early Germanic custom, church law condemned suicide as a sin.

361 Knappe, Karl-Bernhard. *Repräsentation und Herrschaftszeichen. Zur Herrscherdarstellung in der vorhöfischen Epik*. Münchener Beiträge zur Mediävistik und Renaissance-Forschung, 17. München: Arbeo-Gesellschaft, 1974.

Surveys the representations of rulership and the symbols thereof (e.g., sword, lance, banner, scepter, crown, throne, etc.) in early Germanic epics, such as *Graf Rudolf, Herzog Ernst, König Rother, Ludwigslied, Münchener Oswald, Orendel, Rolandslied, Salman und Morolf, Strassburger Alexander, Vorauer Alexander, Waltharius,* and *Wiener Oswald*.

362 Köbler, Gerhard. *Das Recht im frühen Mittelalter*. Köln: Böhlau, 1971.

Takes issue with F. Kern's famous dictum that medieval law must be "old" and "good." Köbler concludes, "In den gesamten frühmittelalterlichen Quellen des untersuchten Gebiets findet sich nämlich kein einziger Beleg für den Sachinhalts gutes altes Recht." The investigation centers on four concepts and the words attached to them in early medieval law: *ius, lex, mos, consuetudo*. Literary sources such as the *Heliand* and Otfrid's *Evangelium* are drawn upon occasionally but are relatively unimportant to the argument.

363   Krause, Hermann. "Mittelalterliche Anschauungen vom Gericht im
       Lichte der Formel: iustitiam facere et recipere, Recht geben und
       nehmen." *SBAW*, 1974 (Heft 11).

       Follows the historical continuity of the formula in both legal and
       literary texts (including the *Schwabenspiegel, Sachsenspiegel,
       Parzival, Tristan und Isolde, Willehalm,* the *Schachgedicht* of
       Heinrich von Berlingen, and medieval folksong).

364   Künssberg, Eberhard Freiherr von. "Die deutsche Rechtssprache."
       Zeitschrift für Deutschkunde, 44 (1930), 379-389.

       A study of the reciprocal relationship of law and language. The
       histories of both are seen to have parallel development.

365   _____. *Rechtsgeschichte und Volkskunde.* Rev. by
       Pavlos Tzermias. Köln: Böhlau, 1965. Revision of Künssberg's
       paper which appeared in *Jahrbuch für historische Volkskunde*, 1
       (1925).

       Argues the value of folklore for legal-historical research
       (Chapter 1). Folk songs, fairy tales, legends, proverbs, riddles—all
       provide insight into legal terminology and practices. Numerous
       examples are given.

366   _____. "Rechtsverse." *Neue Heidelberger
       Jahrbücher.* N. F. 1933, 89-167.

       An influential survey of *Rechtsverse,* illustrated by 117
       examples, all reproduced at the end of the article (pp. 109-167).
       Künssberg distinguishes three classes: 1. religious *Rechtsverse* (oaths,
       courtroom formulas invoking God's justice, etc.), 2. verses
       regulating social behavior (e.g., *Kellerordnungen*), and 3. verses
       whose main object is the elucidation of law itself (e.g., the rhymed
       prologues to legal treatises such as the *Sachsenspiegel*).

367   Lofmark, Carl. "The Advisor's Guilt in Courtly Literature."
       German Life and Letters, 24 (1970), 3-13.

       Illustrates the medieval emphasis on the advisor's guilt (often
       considered to be greater than the perpetrator's) with numerous
       examples (e.g., Lunete in *Iwein*; Arofel in *Willehalm*; the wicked
       barons in *Tristan*). Lofmark observes, "Courtly poets find it
       convenient to use the advisor's responsibility as an alibi for a king or

hero whose conduct must be presented in a favorable light." The literary motive, however, is supported by both theological and legal traditions. Medieval interpretations of the Fall laid heavier responsibility on the devil as tempter than on Adam and Eve; and Germanic law generally provided for punishment of the advisor as well as of the doer (according to the *Kulmisches Recht* and *Schwabenspiegel* evil advice might cost a man his tongue).

368 Loudner, M. "Eheschliessung und Darstellung der Frau in der spätmittelalterlichen Märendichtung. Eine Untersuchung auf der Grundlage rechtlichsozialer und theologischer Voraussetzungen." Diss. Freie Universität Berlin 1973.

A comparison of the man-woman relationship in medieval law and fairy-tale literature. Under the influence of social change and economic rivalry between man and woman, the literary sources reveal a more liberalized view of marriage than is found in Germanic tradition.

369 Maurer, Friedrich. *Leid. Studien zur Bedeutungs- und Problemgeschichte, besonders in den grossen Epen der staufischen Zeit.* Bern und München: Francke, 1951; rpt. 1961.

Maurer's purpose in this important study is three-fold: 1. to establish the meaning of the word *leid* (*leit*) in MHG literature (i.e., the *Nibelungenlied, Der Arme Heinrich, Erec, Gregorius, Iwein, Heliand, Rolandslied, Parzival, Willehalm, Tristan,* and the works of Heinrich von Veldeke); 2. to show how the meaning of the word is affected by different contexts; and 3. to determine the function of *leid* in the various works. In works that represent a pre-Christian milieu (e.g., the *Nibelungenlied*), *leid* is caused by an injustice such as slander and inevitably elicits revenge. However, in works with a more Christian orientation (under the influence especially of the Augustinian doctrine of evil), the perspective from which *leid* is viewed is more theological than legal (e.g., the cause is sin; the reaction, penance).

370 Meyer, Herbert. "Friedelehe und Mutterrecht." *ZRG,* Germ. Abt. 47 (1927), 198-286.

This study of the controversy regarding the priority of patriliny or matriliny takes as its point of departure Zallinger's use of literary sources in his work on marriage law. Meyer looks closely at four works in particular: *Kudrun, Nibelungenlied, Meier Helmbrecht,* and *Ruodlieb.*

371 _____. "Das Mühlhäuser Reichsrechtsbuch und die deutsche Stadtrechtsgeschichte." *Hansische Geschichtsblätter,* 59 (1934), 3-27.

   Considers briefly the question of poetic influence on the style (especially the alliteration) of early Germanic lawbooks (pp. 7 ff.). Meyer minimizes such influence: "In Wahrheit sind diese poetischen Formen in der Rechtssprache älter als in der Dichtung."

372 Munske, Horst Haider. *Der germanische Rechtswortschatz im Bereich der Missetaten. Philologische und sprachgeographische Untersuchungen. I. Die Terminologie der älteren westgermanischen Rechtsquellen.* Studia Linguistica Germanica, 8/1. Berlin: de Gruyter, 1973.

   A study of Anglo-Saxon, Old Frisian, and Old High German legal terminology, which makes occasional use of literature to verify the meanings of certain words.

373 Pfütze, Max. "'Burg' und 'Stadt' in der deutschen Literatur des Mittelalters. *Die Entwicklung im mittelfrk. Sprachgebiet vom Annolied bis zu Gotfrid Hagens Reimchronik* (ca. 1100-1300)." *BGDSL* (Halle), 80 (1958), 272-320.

   Shows how *stat* gradually displaced *burc* as the general term for "town" (a process influenced mainly by the rise of the bourgeoisie and the civic communes). Pfütze says that the earliest proof is not in legal but rather in poetic writings. The study is based on the *Annolied, Servatius, Vorauer Alexander, Strassburger Alexander, Basler Alexander, Eneide, Morant und Galie, König Rother, Münchener Oswald, Wiener Oswald, Herzog Ernst, Gotfrid Hagen,* and Eilhart's *Tristant.*

374 Ponert, Dietmar Jürgen. *Deutsch und Latein in deutscher Literatur und Geschichtsschreibung des Mittelalters.* Stuttgart: Kohlhammer, 1975.

   Chapter 10 ("Recht und Urkunde") treats the rise of German as the language of legal treatises and documents.

375 Reiffenstein, Ingo. *Rechtsfragen in der deutschen Dichtung des Mittelalters.* Salzburger Universitätsreden (Heft 12). Salzburg, München: Pustet, 1966.

376 Rosenau, Peter Udo. "Wehrverfassung und Kriegsrecht in der mittelhochdeutschen Epik. Wolfram von Eschenbach, Hartmann von Aue, Gottfried von Strassburg, *Der Nibelungen Not, Kudrunepos, Wolfdietrichbruchstück A, König Rother, Salman und Morolf.*" Diss. Bonn 1959.

377 Schäfer, Dietrich. "Consilio vel judicio = mit minne oder mit rechte." *Sitzungsberichte der königlich preussischen Akademie der Wissenschaften,* 1913, 719-733.

The purpose of this article is to distinguish two concepts that appear in the phrase "consilio vel judicio" and its translation "mit minne oder mit rechte" (*Österreichische Reimschronik, Sachsenspiegel*). Numerous early medieval legal documents are consulted. [Cf. 352, 446.]

378 Schlesinger, Walter. "Herrschaft und Gefolgschaft in der germanisch-deutschen Verfassungsgeschichte." *Beiträge zur deutschen Verfassungsgeschichte des Mittelalters.* Göttingen: Vandenhoeck & Ruprecht, 1963, 1:9-52.

In addition to legal codes, Schlesinger draws on literary works, in particular, *Heliand* and the Anglo-Saxon *Genesis*.

379 Schmidt-Wiegand, Ruth. "Eid und Gelöbnis, Formel und Formular im mittelalterlichen Recht." *Recht und Schrift im Mittelalter.* Ed. Peter Classen. Vorträge und Forschungen/ Konstanzer Arbeitskreis für mittelalterliche Geschichte, 23. Sigmaringen: Thorbecke, 1977.

Addresses the question of how the structure of legal oaths, essentially oral in character, is affected when they are recast in written form. The discussion relies primarily on five examples: "die Strassburger Eide, der althochdeutsche Priestereid, das Schwäbische Verlöbnis, ein Gottesurteilsritual mit deutschen Formeln und der Erfurter Judeneid." The form of the Priestereid is compared with Laudine's promise in Hartmann's *Iwein*; the form of the Judeneid with that of a song by Walther von der Vogelweide, the *Kindheit Jesu* by Konrad von Fussesbrunnen, and other pieces.

380   Schröder, Edward. "'Herzog' und 'Fürst.'" *ZRG*, Rom. Abt. 44 (1924), 1-29.

Follows the semantic development of *Herzog* "duke" and *Fürst* "prince" through *Vom Recht, Die Hochzeit, Wiener Genesis, Rolandslied, Kaiserchronik, König Rother, Kudrun,* and works by Heinrich von Veldeke, Herbort von Fritzlar, Hartmann von Aue, Wirnt von Gravenberc, Gottfried von Strassburg, and Wolfram von Eschenbach.

381   Schroeder, Richard. "Beiträge zur Kunde des deutschen Rechts aus deutschen Dichtern." *ZDA*, N. F. 1 (1867), 139-175.

An influential article that stresses the mutual concerns of legal and literary historians. Schroeder's illustrations concern mainly inheritance litigation (*possessorische Verfahren*) in *Der Schwanenritter, Parzival, Lohengrin, Jüngerer Titurel*, Berthold von Holle's *Der Crane*, and the *Chevalier au Cygne*, but he also touches upon the topics of judicial combat (*Der Schwanenritter, Sachsenspiegel,* the *Nibelungenlied*) and marriage customs (*Lohengrin*). In his conclusion, Schroeder envisions a *corpus iuris poeticum*, "which would significantly advance our research and serve as a lasting monument to the close relationship between legal science and philology" [cf. 444]. An appendix almost as long as the article itself provides a history of the law of possession in Germany, with special reference to Swabian law as seen in *Der Schwanenritter*.

382   Schubert, Fritz. *Sprachstruktur und Rechtsfunktion. Untersuchung zur deutschsprachigen Urkunde des 13. Jahrhunderts.* Göppinger Arbeiten zur Germanistik, 251. Göppingen: Kümmerle, 1979.

Notes briefly (p. 38) that the language of the earliest legal documents tends toward the poetic. (Other approaches to Urkundensprache are noted in the bibliography, pp. 87-95.)

383   Schwartz, Stephen. "Comparative Legal Reconstruction in Germanic." *Myth and Law Among the Indo-Europeans.* Ed. Jaan Puhvel. Berkeley: University of California Press, 1970, pp. 39-53.

Calls for a new approach to the study of Germanic law, based on the model of comparative linguistics, in order to reconstruct a Proto-Germanic law or "Urrecht." The chief impediment to a determination of "what constitutes Germanic law" is the lingering influence of Romantic ideas, in particular the unfounded (and improbable) notion that outlawry was the basis for all Germanic customary law ("one is unlikely to have punishment territorial in nature before the establishment of clearly demarcated territories"). Schwartz is critical of the sometimes careless methodology of the study of "law in literature" (his term) and of languages for the purpose of identifying "petrified items of legal vocabulary." The evidence resulting from these approaches "should be placed in the framework of Germanic law and not used to build up its structure."

384 Siebs, Theodore. Review article of Rudolf Kögel's *Geschichte der deutschen litteratur*. *ZDP*, 29 (1897), 394-414.

Speaks at some length on the formal relationship between Germanic law and literature (especially on the question of the source of alliteration [cf. 9, 348]).

385 Strothmann, Friedrich Wilhelm. *Die Gerichtsverhandlung als literarisches Motiv in der deutschen Literatur des ausgehenden Mittelalters.* Deutsche Arbeiten der Universität Köln. Jena: Diederichs, 1930; rpt. Darmstadt: Wissenschaftliche Buchgesellschaft, 1969.

An important survey of trial process as a literary theme. The subject is treated under two headings: 1. Legal process as "a stylistic medium" in secular literature (*Fastnachtspiele, Ackermann aus Böhmen,* Jacob Anrer's *Prozess wider der Königin Podagra Tyrannei, Morin, Reineke Fuchs*); 2. Legal action as an ideological problem in religious literature (the *Satansprozess,* the debate among the Four Daughters of God, and fusions of the two in Jacobus de Theramo's *Belial*). In his conclusion Strothmann observes that the juristic kernel of Christian dogma "predestined" the literary treatment of salvation as a legal problem.

386 Willson, H. B. *Love and Order in the Medieval German Courtly Epic.* Inaugural Lecture, University of Leicester, 9 November 1971. Leicester: Leicester University Press, 1973.

A convenient summary of Willson's main ideas, with illustrations drawn primarily from his previous articles [e.g., 398, 414, 489]. Although he says nothing about law as such, his explanation of *ordo* provides a good basis for understanding the place of law in medieval thought.

387   Zacharias, Rainer. "Die Blutrache im deutschen Mittelalter." *ZDA*, 91 (1962), 167-201.

        Draws heavily on literary examples (*Parzival, Willehalm, Nibelungenlied, Song of Roland*, etc.). The author makes an important distinction between *Blutrache* (revenge), the duty of a murdered man's kinsmen, and *Fehde* (feud, *bellum privatum*), the legal prerogative of nobility only.

388   Zallinger, Otto. "Die Ringgaben bei der Heirat und das Zusammengeben im mittelalterlichdeutschen Recht." *SBAW*, 212, Abh. 4 (1931), 3-65.

        An important article on the legal significance of ring-giving in medieval marriage, with illustrations drawn from *Ruodlieb, Tristan, Helmbrecht, Lohengrin, Wigalois, Nibelungenlied*, Hartmann von Aue and Konrad von Würzburg.

Albrecht von Johansdorf

389   Schirmer, Karl-Heinz. "Rhetorisches im Kreuzlied Albrechts von Johansdorf: Die hinnen varn, die sagen durch got (MF 89, 21)." *Mediaevalia litteraria. Festschrift für Helmut de Boor zum 80. Geburtstag.* Ed. Ursula Hennig and Herbert Kolb. München: Beck, 1971, pp. 229-253.

        Argues that the rhetorical pattern of the song came not from the *genus iudiciale* but rather from the *genus deliberativum* (as described by Quintilian). The end of the song could be interpreted in a rhetorical-juridical sense as the poet's self-defense.

Benediktinerregel

390   Ibach, H. "Zu Wortschatz und Begriffswelt der althochdeutschen Benediktinerregel. 3." *BGDSL* (Halle), 80 (1958), 190-271.

        Part of a series published in volumes 78-82, this article includes a full investigation of the OHG vocabulary used to translate Latin words concerning law and justice in the *Benedictine Rule* (see pp. 243-271). The terms are arranged by category: *Recht (ordo, testamentum, lex, iustitia, aequitas*, etc.), *Herrschaft und Gesetz* (*regnum, tyrannis, iubere, praeceptum,* etc.), and *Lohn und Strafe* (*merces, poena, satisfactio, retributio,* etc.).

Bible

391 Combridge, Rosemary. "*Aequitas* and *Iustitia* in Mediaeval German Psalters." *Mediaeval German Studies Presented to Frederick Norman.* London: University of London Press, 1965.

Comments on the failure of German translations of the Latin Psalter to distinguish between *aequitas* and *iustitia,* using instead a variety of terms for both (*reht, rehtecheit, ebene, ebenunge, ebenheit, rihtunge, geliche*). The surprising absence of *billicheit* is explained from both a semantic and grammatical point of view.

392 Pausch, K. F. "Die Rechtswörter in der gotischen Bibel und in den Skeireins." Diss. Heidelberg 1954.

Eike von Repgow (See *Sachsenspiegel*)

Fastnachtspiele

393 Holtorf, Arne. "Markttag—Gerichtstag—Zinstermin. Formen von Realität im frühen Nürnberger Fastnachtsspiel." *Befund und Deutung: Zum Verhältnis von Empirie und Interpretation in Sprach- und Literaturwissenschaft.* Ed. Klaus Grubmüller et al. Tübingen: Niemeyer, 1979, pp. 428-450.

Observes that the subject matter of the early Fastnachtspiele revolved around important social-legal events in the everyday life of the peasant: market day, court day, and tax day. The court cases treated in the plays tend to fall into two groups: marital disputes and complaints of insult and injury. Holtorf summarizes more than a dozen of these.

394 Michels, Victor. *Studien über die ältesten deutschen Fastnachtspiele.* Quellen und Forschungen zur Sprach- und Culturgeschichte der germanischen Volker, 77. Strassburg: Trübner, 1896.

Devotes several pages—much of it on textual matters—to the
Gerichtsszenen (pp. 194-202).

Friedrich von Hausen

395   Ludwig, Otto. "Die Rolle des Sprechers in MF 47,9." *ZDA* 93
       (1964), 123-132.

       A structural analysis of Friedrich von Hausen's *Kreuzlied* "Mîn
       herze und mîn lîp diu wellent scheiden." The dispute involves four
       parties: the heart, the body, the audience (i.e., the jury), and the
       speaker, who serves as advocate (*Fürsprecher*) for the body and
       accuser (*Ankläger*) of the heart. The pattern reflects medieval court
       procedure—only the judge is missing. Ludwig pays particular
       attention to the role changes of the speaker—in turn *Berichterstatter,
       Betroffener, Partei*, and *Mitleidender*—and suggests that these
       correspond to the stages of argument prescribed by the *genus
       iudiciale*, that is, *narratio, transitus, argumentatio*, and *peroratio*.

Gottfried von Strassburg

396   Combridge, Rosemary. *Das Recht im "Tristan" Gottfrieds von
       Strassburg*. Philologische Studien and Quellen, 15. Berlin: Schmidt,
       1964.

       An important study of the legal aspects of *Tristan*, with special
       attention to marriage and trial by ordeal. In Chapter 1, Combridge
       discusses: 1. the legal status of the characters (especially Rual), in
       terms of the *Heerschildordnung* put forward in the *Sachsenspiegel*;
       and 2. the marriage of Riwalin and Blanschflur, in order to establish
       Tristan's legitimacy under canon law. In Chapter 2 she discusses the
       legal questions raised by the "Ireland" material (lines
       5867-12674)—i.e., the combat over unpaid tribute (Morold episode),
       Isolde's betrothal to Mark *in absentiae*, and the dispute between
       Tristan and the *Truchsess*. Chapter 3 is concerned with Isolde's
       ordeal. Gottfried uses the incident, says Combridge, to criticize the
       practice of invoking God's help in matters of little importance.
       Chapter 4 stresses the weaknesses of Mark as a king. Combridge
       concludes that although Gottfried was very conversant in the law, he
       uses it in *Tristan* not for its own sake but as a vehicle for describing

human behavior; and where goodness conflicts with law, he is always on the side of the former. His main concern throughout is *Minne*.

397 Mersmann, Walter. *Der Besitzwechsel und seine Bedeutung in den Dichtungen Wolframs von Eschenbach und Gottfrieds von Strassburg*. München: Wilhelm Fink, 1971.

In Part I Mersmann provides an overview of the MHG vocabulary for *Besitzwechsel* (transfer of possession). He takes up in order such categories as inheritance, combat, service, loans, trade, tribute, etc. In Part II he examines the use of this vocabulary in *Parzival, Willehalm,* and *Tristan.* Mersmann concludes that Wolfram uses the terms with greater frequency and more artistic purpose than Gottfried. For example, Parzival's coming into possession represents an important stage in his quest. Of the three works, the historical reality of *Besitzwechsel* is most clearly reflected in *Willehalm.* The final third of the book consists of an exhaustive index (nearly a hundred pages), which cites every use of transfer of possession terms in the three poems.

398 Willson, H. B. "The Old and the New Law in Gottfried's *Tristan.*" *MLR*, 60 (1965), 212-224.

Sees an analogy between the biblical account of the woman taken in adultery and Gottfried's treatment of Isolde's ordeal: just as Christ forgave the woman, thereby showing the superiority of love (the New Law) over formalism (the Old Law), so He protects Isolde against her accusers. Thus, "there is absolutely no need to label as heretical Gottfried's description of Christ's behaviour in relation to Isolde's oath. As we have seen, the Gospel 'image' of the Saviour is of a controversial figure who was constantly at odds with those who represented the law...."

Grazer Marienleben

399 Streadbeck, Arval. "Juridical Redemption and the *Grazer Marienleben.*" *GR*, 31 (1956), 83-87.

A clear exposition of the idea of redemption as a legal transaction, as set forth in the mid-thirteenth-century *Grazer Marienleben* and other medieval works (e.g., its model, the *Vita beate virginis Mariae et salvatoris rhythmica*, and the *Annolied*).

Hartmann von Aue

400   Beyerle, Franz. "Der 'Arme Heinrich' Hartmanns von Au al
       Zeugnis mittelalterlichen Ständerechts." *Kunst und Recht. Festgabe
       für Hans Fehr*. Vol. I of *Arbeiten zur Rechtssoziologie und
       Rechtsgeschichte*. Karlsruhe: Müller, 1948, pp. 29-46.

       Evaluates the *Arme Heinrich* as a source of information not only
       on *Ständerecht* ("estates law") but also on the background of the
       author. For example, Hartmann's equation of *edelfrei* (noble and
       free) and *freibäuerlich* (peasant and free), as seen in his description
       of the marriage between a knight and a steward's daughter, "does
       not correspond to the social reality of the time, but is grounded
       instead in the basic religious assumption of the poem." In fact, the
       equation reflects the spirit of the reformed Church. Thus we are able
       to rule out the possibility of Hartmann's having been educated in the
       monastery school at Reichenau.

401   Cramer, Thomas. "'Saelde und êre' in Hartmanns 'Iwein."
       Euphorion, 60 (1966), 30-47; rpt. *Hartmann von Aue*. Ed. Hugo
       Kuhn and Christoph Cormeau. Darmstadt: Wissenschaftliche
       Buchgesellschaft, 1973, pp. 426-449.

       Argues that Iwein's guilt lies in his unlawful acquisition of land
       and wife ("Land und Frau") by killing the husband without proper
       warning, a violation of *Fehderecht*.

402   Fehr, Hans. "Das Recht im Iwein." *Festschrift Ernst Mayer zum
       70. Geburtstage*. Weimar: Böhlaus, 1932, pp. 93-110.

       Although both *Die Klage* and *Erec* contain legal elements, none
       of Hartmann's works is so steeped in legal terminology and motifs a
       Iwein. Fehr discusses four matters involving law: 1. the *Bahrprobe*
       2. an inheritance dispute, settled through trial by combat; 3
       Zweikampf as a "business transaction" (*Rechtsgeschäft*), in which
       the combat is described in commercial terms such as *Pfand, Leihe,
       Darlehen, Zins, Käufer, Verkäufer*, and *Wucher*; 4. the oath (*Eid*)
       of which several different kinds are presented (*Schwur, Gelöbnis,
       assertorisch* and *promissorisch* oaths, etc.). The final section of the
       essay consists of twenty-nine brief notices on individual lines in *Iwein*
       that have legal associations.

403   Gellinek, Christian J. "Iwein's Duel and Laudine's Marriage." *The Epic in Medieval Society: Aesthetic and Moral Values*. Ed. Harald Scholler. Tübingen: Niemeyer, 1977, pp. 226-239.

A critical look at the traditionally accepted opinion that "Laudine, the heroine, badly in need of a new defender of her magic Fountain, *marries the murderer* in undue haste because of the power of *minne*." In the first place, Gellinek denies that Iwein is a "murderer": of Iwein's two blows against Ascalôn, it is the first, struck in self-defense, that leads to his death, and "therefore the second blow cannot bear any legal or moral consequences one way or the other." As for Iwein's hasty marriage to the widow, Laudine, the necesssary legal ingredient of mutual consent is certainly present. Missing, however, is the quality of *"rehte güete,"* which "presupposes an affectionate volition of two persons"; the real basis of the marriage is not *caritas* but *ardor* or *Minne*, fueled by Laudine's beauty. This precludes atonement in any meaningful way (especially on the part of Iwein) and leads to an imbalance between "marriage law and marriage order."

404   Hagenguth, Edith. "Hartmanns Iwein. Rechtsargumentation und Bildsprache." Diss. Heidelberg 1969.

405   Jackson, William Henry. "Friedensgesetzgebung und höfischer Roman zu Hartmanns 'Erec' und 'Iwein.'" *Poesie und Gebrauchsliteratur im deutschen Mittelalter*. Ed. Volker Honemann, Kurt Ruh, Bernhard Schnell, and Werner Wegstein. Tübingen: Niemeyer, 1979, pp. 251-264.

Analyzes two "âventiure" episodes in the light of *Landfriedensgesetze* (laws concerning the public peace). The question is: under what circumstances can the wounding or killing of a man be justified? The answer turns on the legal distinction between a fight (*Gewaltverbrechen*) and a true feud (*echter Fehde*), which takes place only after a three-day notice (*Widersage*). King Guivreiz's insistence on immediate combat with Erec is thus a violation of law and *triuwe* and results, as justly it should, in his defeat. On the other hand, Iwein's failure to give a three-day notice before killing Ascalon is not a breach of law under the circumstances; Ascalon himself has violated the law by rejecting the peace-offer of Iwein's kinsman, Kalogrenant. Neither does the killing constitute "murder," since the act occurs in the open.

406   Jacobi, Bernhard von. "Rechts- und Hausaltertümer in Hartmanns Erec. Eine germanistische Studie." [Diss. Göttingen 1903. Göttingen: Haensch, 1903.

407   Markey, T. L. "The *Ex Lege* Rite of Passage in Hartmann's *Iwein*." *Colloquia Germanica*, 2 (1978), 97-110.

       Sees Iwein's progress from *ex lege* (outcast) to social re-integration as a kind of *rite de passage*.

408   Mertens, Volker. *Laudine. Soziale Problematik im Iwein Hartmanns von Aue*. Berlin: Schmidt, 1978.

       Touches upon the legal aspects of several topics in *Iwein* (e.g. combat, the legal status of noble wives, etc.).

409   Nobel, Hildegard. "Schuld und Sühne in Hartmanns 'Gregorius' und in der frühscholastischen Theologie." *ZDP*, 76 (1957), 42-79.

       Analyzes Gregorius's guilt in the light of church law and early Scholastic thought. Although Gregorius does not inherit his parents' guilt, he nevertheless participates in their *infamia*. His chief sin is pride (*superbia*). In this connection Hartmann's vocabulary shows the influence of penitential doctrine: *riuwe* (*contritio*), *bîhte* (*confessio oris*), and *buoze* (*satisfactio operis*).

410   Panzer, Friedrich. "Étude sur Hartmann d'Aue par F. Piquet." *ZDP*, 31 (1899), 520-549.

       Part of this review deals with the question of legal elements in Hartmann's *Klage*-Büchlein. "Meint Hartmann 'wehklage' oder 'anklage'?" Panzer is critical of those who, having answered "anklage," proceed unnecessarily to find legal meanings in the most ordinary words.

411   Pensel, Franzjosef. "Rechtsgeschichtliches und Rechtssprachliches im epischen Werk Hartmanns von Aue und im 'Tristan' Gottfrieds von Strassburg." Diss. Berlin (Humboldt-Universität) 1961.

412   Thum, Bernd. "Politische Probleme der Stauferzeit im Werk Hartmanns von Aue: Landesherrschaft im 'Iwein' und 'Erec'." *Stauferzeit*. Ed. Rüdiger Krohn, Bernd Thum, Peter Wapnewski. Stuttgart: Klett-Cotta, 1978, pp. 47-70.

Raises the question of whether the historical transition from feudalism to territorial states is reflected in Hartmann's writings. Of particularly legal interest is Thum's analysis of *Iwein*. He sees the hero's initial failure (rectified by a series of *âventiuren*) as consisting in his disregard for *landesherrliche Rechte*, his indifference to *Landfrieden*, and his neglect of his own territorial responsibilities for the sake of *Königsdienst*.

413   Tonamura, Naohiko. "Zur Schuldfrage im 'Gregorius' Hartmanns von Aue." *Wirkendes Wort*, 18 (1968), 1-17.

Finds the key to the question of Gregorius's guilt in the canonistic distinction between subjective and objective. Because Gregorius sinned without knowledge or intention, his guilt is "objective" and stands for the guilt of mankind as a whole (the guilt of *Erbsünde*, original sin). "The story of Gregorius is finally a lament for the world—precious, beautiful, yet bent on sin—and at the same time a creed-book filled with the hope and confidence that God, despite all, will lead us into the kingdom of heaven."

414   Willson, H. B. "*Triuwe* and *Untriuwe* in Hartmann's *Erec*." *GQ*, 43 (1970), 5-23.

Argues that Enite's *untriuwe* is actually *triuwe* of a higher order. Just as the New Law (*caritas*) transcends the Old, so Enite's love for Erec compels her repeatedly to break his commandments.

415   Wisniewski, Roswitha. "Hartmanns *Klage*-Büchlein." *Euphorion*, 57 (1963), 341-369.

Taking as a point of departure Anton Schönbach's thesis that the *Büchlein* is cast "in the form of a juristic debate," Wisniewski identifies more than seventy-five words and phrases with possible legal significance. She describes the poem as a mixed genre, both a "complaint" and "a meditation on the nature of *Minne*..., brought within the form of a debate and partially clothed as legal dispute."

Heinrich von dem Türlein

416   Jillings, Lewis. "Ordeal by Combat and the Rejection of Chivalry in
       Diu Crône." *Speculum*, 51 (1976), 262-276.

              Argues that *Diu Crône* (ca. 1230) is "the first literary rejection of
       the chivalric ordeal by combat in Germany." Jillings begins with a
       discussion of the aborted duel between Arthur and Gasozein
       ("Gasozein objects to the ordeal by combat strictly on the grounds
       that the resort to violence to solve a legal dispute is *infra dignitatem*
       for two princes") and then proceeds to show that the other duels and
       fights in *Diu Crône* are characterized by "a tone of constant
       trivialization." Heinrich's rejection of juridical combat is assessed in
       relation to contemporary attitudes toward the institution, specifically
       those of the Church, secular authorities, urban codes of law, and
       other literary works (*Vom Recht, Rolandslied*, Hartmann von Aue's
       Iwein, Konrad von Würzburg's *Der Schwanritter, Apollonius von
       Tyrland*, Gottfried's *Tristan*, Wittenwiler's *Der Ring*, and Dante's
       De Monarchia).

Heinrich von Veldeke

417   Hermesdorf, B. H. D. "Hendrik van Veldeke in het licht der
       Rechtsgeschiedenis." *Publications de la Société Historique et
       Archéologique dans le Limbourg*, 83 (1947), 175-206.

418   Schieb, Gabriele. "Rechtswörter und Rechtsvorstellungen bei
       Heinrich von Veldeke." *BGDSL*, 77 (1955), 159-197.

              Demonstrates that in his *St. Servatius* and *Eneid*, Veldeke
       skillfully incorporated into two passages, both having to do with
       territorial annexation, legal elements not to be found in his sources.
       His precise use of such words as *vesten, vrien, vedemen, wien*, and
       prime shows "an astonishing mastery of the relevant terminology."

419   Oonk, Gerrit J. "*Rechte Minne* in Veldekes *Eneide*."
       Neophilologus, 57 (1973), 258-273.

              An analysis of Veldeke's conception of *minne* on four levels:
       psychological, ethical, legal, and religious. Psychologically *rechte
       minne* comes about naturally and not as the result of a magic potion
       or kiss. Ethically it is based upon mutual *triuwe* (*fides*), *arbeit*

(*labor*), and *dinest* (*servitium amoris*). Legally, it is "the critical moment in the battle between right and wrong." Aeneas's victory over Turnus is the victory of trust in God's will over trust in human institutions, of divine *Recht* over "Recht als eine menschliche Satzung." Religiously speaking, *rechte minne* is unity with—that is, obedience and service to—God. It is "transcendental only when...it reaches out beyond the narrow, empirical boundaries of the man-woman relationship to the sphere of Law and of God."

Heliand

420 Langenpusch, E. "Das germanische Recht im Heliand." *Untersuchungen zur deutschen Staats- und Rechtsgeschichte*, 16 (1894).

421 Melicher, Theophil. "Die germanische Gefolgschaft im Heliand." *Mitteilungen des Instituts für österreiche Geschichtsforschung*, 51 (1937), 431 ff.

Attempts to show the pervasive influence of Germanic legal thought in both the poet's terminology and his portrayal of Christ as God's bravest and most faithful retainer.

422 Schmidt-Wiegand, Ruth. "Rechtswort und Rechtszeichen in der deutschen Dichtung der karolingischen Zeit." *Frühmittelalterliche Studien*, 5 (1971), 268-283.

This study is based primarily on two works, the *Heliand* and Otfrid von Weissenburg's *Evangelienbuch*. The *Heliand*'s use of *bôcan* ("sign") in reference to the star of Bethlehem leads Schmidt-Wiegand into a long discussion of the word's legal history and of the study of *Rechtssprachgeographie* in general. She emphasizes the value of such works as the *Heliand* in tracing the development of Germanic legal terminology, especially in view of the paucity of vernacular legal sources until the thirteenth century. Otfrid's work is put to similar use. In particular, Schmidt-Wiegand is interested in the light it sheds on three problems: 1. the *Rückgang* of words and symbols that have their roots in Germanic law (e.g., *âhten, Bann, Warg*; 2. the transfer of institutions and concepts from Frankish to German law (e.g., *ruagstab* "rod of reproof"), and 3. the formation of new legal ideas that are fully developed only at a

later period (e.g., the distinction between *reht* [= *ius*, "in gerader
Richtung...gehörig, richtig, wahr"] and *êwa* or *wizzôd* [= *lex*, "das
objektive Recht"]).

Hermann von Sachsenheim

423   Loersch, Hugo. "Der Prozess in der Mörin des Hermann von
Sachsenheim." *Drei Abhandlungen zur Geschichte des deutschen
Rechts. Festgruss an K. G. Homeyer.* Ed. F. Blume, R. Schröder,
H. Loersch. Bonn, 1871.

424   Martin, Ernst, ed. *Hermann von Sachsenheim.* Tübingen: Laupp
(Für den litterarischen Verein in Stuttgart), 1878.

Specifies in his introduction (pp. 19-21) the elements of juridical
procedure in *Moerin* and connects the author's extensive knowledge
of law to his position as assessor ("beisitzer") in a feudal court.

Hildebrandslied

425   Ehrismann, Gustav. "Zur Althochdeutschen Literatur. 3. Zum
Hildebrandsliede." *BGDSL* (Halle), 32 (1907), 260-292.

Considers the poem as an important source of information on
trial by combat as practiced in the author's own time. After an
extended discussion of the trial as a *Gottesurteil* in several other
works (e.g., *Beowulf, Strassburger Alexander, Tristan* and especially
Waltharius), Ehrismann turns to an analysis of the duel in the
Hildebrandslied as a form of trial process. He identifies five stages:
1. accusation (*Klage*); 2. denial; 3. counter plea of the accuser; 4.
pre-combat greeting (*Kampfgruss*), which consists of the
provocation (*Reizrede*) and words of self-praise (*Gelf*); and 5. the
combat itself, as *iudicium Dei.*

426   Kunstmann, John G. "*Hildebrandslied* 20-22a." *MLN,* 54 (1939),
501-506.

Addresses the legal questions raised by Hildebrand's desertion of
his family. "A man follows his lord into exile. What happens to his
wife, his issue, his property?" Part of the answer turns on the

interpretation of *furlaet* in line 20. Does it mean *dimisit* (in which case Hildebrand went into exile without consulting his wife) or *reliquit* (in which case he invited her along but received a negative reply)? The distinction is suggested by two *decreta* (the *decretum Compendiense* and the *decretum Vermeriense Pippini*) which belong to the period in which the *HL* was written down.

427   Northcott, Kenneth J. "'Das Hildebrandlied': A Legal Process?" *MLR*, 56 (1961), 342-348.

Focuses on the legal significance of the Zweikampf between Hadubrand and his father Hildebrand, and suggests that the tragic consequences of Hildebrand's desertion of his family must have struck the Anglo-Saxon missionaries of Fulda—where the poem was written down—as valuable propaganda for the Christian tenets of the sanctity of marriage and family life. Terms mentioned as having legal undertones are *dinc* (Lat. *causa*), *arbeo laosa, reccheo* (= *exsul*), *furlaet, wêttu, suasat chind*, and *reht*.

428   Puntschart, Paul. "Zur rechtsgeschichtlichen Auslegung des Hildebrandsliedes." *Festschrift zu ehren Emil von Ottenthals.* Innsbruck: Wagner, 1925, pp. 170-183.

Offers a legal interpretation of probably the most discussed word in the poem, *wettu*, which appears in Hildebrand's speech to his son ("wettu irmingot obana ab hevane, dat dû neo dana halt mit sus sippan man dinc ni gileitôs..."). Puntschart takes the word to be the instrumental form of the substantive *Wette* "pledge" and argues that Hildebrand, in conformity with ancient Germanic legal custom, is offering his own body as a pledge of the truth of his words.

Hugo von Trimburg

429   Genzmer, Erich. "Hugo von Trimburg und die Juristen." *L'Europa e il diritto romano. Studi in memoria di Paolo Koschaker.* 2 vols. Milan: Giuffrè, 1954, 1:291-336.

A very full treatment of Hugo's portrayal of jurists in *Der Renner* (ca. 1300). Adopting the European perspective of Paolo Koschaker (whom the volume honors), Genzmer cites parallels between Hugo's criticism of venal lawyers—"Judisten" (i.e., heirs of Judas) rather than "Juristen"—and similar complaints in Walter of Châtillon, Guiot de Provins, and the *Mariages des filles du Diable*. The attitudes reflected in these works are then tied to supranational events and movements, such as Pope Honorius III's *Constitutio super speculum* (prohibiting the study of civil law) and the Reception—and so-called "Renunciations"—of Roman law.

Johannes von Tepl (*Der Ackermann aus Böhmen*)

430 Bäuml, Franz H. *Rhetorical Devices and Structure in the Ackermann aus Böhmen*. University of California Publications in Modern Philology, 60. Berkeley and Los Angeles: University of California Press, 1960.

Denies the extensive influence of contemporary judicial usage on the poem, as argued by Burdach [432], and offers instead the model of medieval Latin rhetoric.

431 Borck, Karl Heinz. "Juristisches und Rhetorisches im 'ackerman.'" *Zeitschrift für Ostforschung*, 12 (1963), 401-420.

The abundance of legal terminology in *Der Ackermann* has led some scholars to see the work as a realistic rendition of the various stages in the trial process—from *Zeterruf* (outcry) to *Urteil* (verdict). Although the conclusion of the work—a philosophical dispute—is a departure from this scheme, Borck suggests that it too reveals legal influence, particularly in following closely the structure of the antique *genus iudiciale: exordium, narratio, confirmatio, confutatio,* and *conclusio*.

432 Burdach, Konrad (and Alois Bernt), ed. *Der Ackermann aus Böhmen*. Vol. 3, part 1, of Burdach's *Vom Mittelalter zur Reformation*. Berlin: Weidmann, 1917.

The seminal study on juridical elements in the *Ackermann*. See the editors' commentary, pp. 153-406. In his later study of the poem, *Der Dichter des Ackermann aus Böhmen und seine Zeit* (same volume, part 2 [Berlin: Weidmann, 1926-1932]), Burdach gives a great deal of attention to other works also showing the influence of law (for example, see pp. 460-511 on the "Satansprozess und der Prozess Belials gegen Christus").

433   Hahn, Gerhard. *Die Einheit des Ackermann aus Böhmen.* Münchener Texte und Untersuchungen zur deutschen Literatur des Mittelalters, 5. München: Beck, 1963.

In contrast to the *Satans-* or *Belialsprozess* [cf. 432], Hahn regards the juristic elements in *Ackermann* as governed more by literary concerns than by actual trial procedure. The study contains numerous legal observations, but the greatest concentration is in Chapter 3, where the quarrel between Death and the Plowman is analyzed specifically in terms of law and order. The disputants are said to represent two distinct orders: Death, the *ordnung* of natural law; and the Plowman, that of human existence ("die Ordnung eines sinnvollen, werthaltigen und beglückten *irdischen* Menschendaseins"). The death of the Plowman's wife creates a conflict between the two orders.

434   Hennig, Reinhard. "Die Rechtfertigung des Todes unter dem Status Qualitatis. Zur Interpretation der Todesfunktion im Ackermann aus Böhmen." *ZDP*, 91 (1972), 374-383.

Suggests that Death's entire argument rests upon his use in Chapters 6 and 8 of the *status qualitatis*, one of the four types of procedure described in the branch of rhetoric known as *genus iudiciale.* According to this line of argument, the defendant responds to the formal accusation "fecisti" with the words "feci, sed recte" ("I did it, but rightly or with good reason"). Thus, in Chapter 6 Death admits his deed but justifies it as part of his function as *lex naturalis.* In Chapter 8 Death argues that he serves as a representative of God himself for the purpose of destroying all superfluous life.

435   Hübner, Arthur. "Deutsches Mittelalter und italienische Renaissance im Ackermann aus Böhmen." *Kleine Schriften zur deutschen Philologie.* Ed. Hermann Kunisch and U. Pretzel. Berlin: Dr. E. Ebering, 1940.

436   Meissner, Rudolf. "Dein clage ist one reimen." *Vom Geiste neuer Literaturforschung. Festschrift für Oskar Walzel.* Ed. Julius Wahle and Victor Klemperer. Wildpark-Potsdam: Athenaion, 1924, pp. 21-38.

Raises objections to Burdach's emendation of "reimen" to "raunen" in Death's words to the Ackermann ("dein clage ist one reimen"). The emendation allowed Burdach to read the speech in an exclusively legal context: "Your suit is without the help of a *rauner*," i.e., one who gives secret advice in the course of a trial. Meissner points out that in Saaz and Prague, the *rauner* was called *stewer*, that the word had negative connotations in Bohemian law, and that no advocate or *rauner* is mentioned elsewhere in *Der Ackermann*. He takes the word to mean "rhyme" ("Your complaint is not in verse") and then points to the ancient association of rhyme with "furor." The remainder of the article is devoted to a discussion of the rational and irrational in art.

437   Natt, Rosemarie. *Der Ackermann aus Böhmen des Johannes von Tepl. Ein Beitrag zur Interpretation*. Göppinger Arbeiten zur Germanistik, 235. Göppingen: Kümmerle, 1978.

Denies the theory of Burdach, Hübner, et al. that the *Strafprozess* of the poem suggests the author's legal training and instead analyzes the debate in terms of the *genus iudiciale*, as outlined in H. Lausberg's *Elemente der literarischen Rhetorik* [51].

438   Roth, Jeremy Samuel. "The *Ackermann aus Böhmen* and the Medieval 'Streitgespräch.'" Diss. University of Chicago 1980.

Considers the *Ackermann* in the light of other *Streitgespräch* works in order to isolate its unique features—of which the Plowman's persistent assertiveness is the most outstanding.

439   Stutz, Ulrich. "Rechthistorisches in und zu dem 'Ackermann aus Böhmen.'" *ZRG*, Germ. Abt. 41 (1920), 388-390.

Points to the value of Burdach's commentary on *Der Ackermann* for legal historians.

Jüngerer Titurel

440   Meier, John. *Untersuchungen zur deutschen Volkskunde und Rechtsgeschichte. Erstes Heft. Ahnengrab und Brautstein*. Halle: Niemeyer, 1944.

Includes a short reference (pp. 38-39) to the *Jüngerer Titurel*, in which a marriage ceremony is described as taking place on a prehistoric grave, an important site for legal decisions (*briutestol*).

Konrad von Würzburg

441   Kesting, Peter. "Diu rehte Wârheit. Zu Konrads von Würzburg 'Engelhard.'" *ZDA*, 99 (1970), 246-259.

Konrad's seemingly shallow treatment of Engelhard's deceit (the use of a substitute in judicial combat) is actually part of a deeper moral purpose. The action is justified once our attention is shifted from the question of merely factual truth (*wârheit*) to that of perfect truth (*rehtiu wârheit*), exemplified in abundance by Engelhard's *wâre minne* and *hôhe triuwe*. The distinction between the two types or degrees of truth is supported by other writers as well—Hartmann von Aue, Wolfram von Eschenbach, and Gottfried von Strassburg.

Kudrun

442   Grimm, Gunter. "Die Eheschliessungen in der Kudrun. Zur Frage der Verlobten- oder Gattentreue Kudruns." *ZDP*, 90 (1971), 48-70.

Raises the question of whether Kudrun and Herwig were legally married at the time of her abduction (*Raub*). After a survey of the various forms of marriage in the Middle Ages (*laikale Muntehe, Entführungsehe, Friedelehe, Kebsehe*), Grimm concludes that Kudrun was Herwig's lawful wife as a result of their mutual consent and the exchange of rings—both acts considered legally binding.

443   Loerzer, Eckart. *Eheschliessung und Werbung in der 'Kudrun.'* München: Beck, 1971.

A comparative analysis of *Kudrun* and the *Nibelungenlied* in the light of the laws and customs governing courtship and marriage. Loerzer traces the abundance of *Rechtsformen* in *Kudrun* (especially the idea of "mutual consent") to the influence of the *Nibelungenlied*.

444   Schroeder, Richard. "Corpus Iuris Germanici Poeticum. 1. Kudrun." *ZDP*, 1 (1869), 257-272.

This is Schroeder's first (and last) contribution to the ambitious project described in his 1867 article [381], a *corpus iuris poeticum*, and deals exclusively with the legal aspects of *Kudrun*. He takes up in order the related issues of legal status (*Heerschildordnung*), succession to the throne, and marriage (focusing on the distinction between *Verlöbnis* and *Eheschliessung*).

See also 454, 460, 461.

Ludwigslied

445   Melicher, Theophil. "Die Rechtsaltertümer im Ludwigslied." *Anzeiger der phil.-historische Klasse der Österreichischen Akademie der Wissenschaften*, 1954 (No. 18). Wien: Rohrer, 1955, pp. 254-275.

Elaborates on the poet's use of *Gefolgschaft* as a metaphor for man's relation to God. God is seen as a *Gefolgsherr*, and Ludwig and all the Franks as "in der Gefolgschaft Gottes." The emphasis is on *triuwe*. "The ethical heart of the Germanic Weltanschauung is not Love but Fidelity." This legalistic attitude pervades the poem. Melicher discusses a number of passages in which law and notions of justice play a role—e.g., the importance of property rights, of "der Unterschied zwischen mein und dein" in Frankish ethical thought; "haranskara" (corporal punishment, loss of honor) and fasting as the penalties for crimes against property; the poet's view of battle as a *Gottesgericht*; and so on.

Memento Mori

446   Kuhn, Hugo. "Minne oder Recht." *Studien zur deutschen Philologie des Mittelalters*. [Festschrift for Friedrich Panzer.] Ed. Richard Kienast. Heidelberg: Winter, 1950, pp. 29-37; rpt. in Kuhn, *Dichtung und Welt im Mittelalter*. Stuttgart: Metzler, 1959, pp. 105-111.

Argues that the poet's use of *minne* in the eleventh-century *Memento Mori* was intended to evoke the legal formula "minne oder reht." The earliest evidence of the phrase was previously thought to be the *Sachsenspiegel* and (in a literary text) Stricker's *Pfaffe Amis* (V.833 ff.). Kuhn interprets the formula as distinguishing between amicable agreements (*minne*) and court-imposed settlements (*recht*); and he connects its rise with the Investiture Contest and the peace movement (*Friedensbewegung*), during which time the corresponding Latin phrases *consilio vel iudicio, iustitia et pax, lex et gratia,* etc. were much in fashion. Thus, the poem probably served as a document (1082-1085) for the party of Heinrich IV. [On the formula see also 377.]

Morant und Galie

447   Linke, Elisabeth. "Der Rechtgang in Morant und Galie." *BGDSL* (Halle), 75 (1953), 1-130.

Among *"Prozessepen"* (Konrad von Würzburg's *Schwanenritter*, Hermann von Sachsenheim's *Mörin*, the Reynard stories, etc.), *Morant und Galie* stands out as the only one based on Frankish legal procedure. Linke's very detailed analysis consists mainly of two parts: 1. an attempt to show the close correspondence between the structure of the poem and that of a trial process; 2. an exhaustive lexicon of legal terms and formulas that appear in the work (some 270 in all). A critical text of lines 2592-3030 (the deliberation and sentencing), edited by Linke and Theodore Frings, is appended.

Muspilli

448   Kolb, Herbert. "dia weroltrehtwîson." *Zeitschrift für deutsche Wortforschung,* 18 (1962), 88-95.

Defines the word *weroltrehtwîson,* as used by the author of *Muspilli* in his account of the battle between Elias and Antichrist, as "die Kundigen des weltlichen Rechts" (in contradistinction to divine *Recht*).

449   _____. "Himmlisches und irdisches Gericht in karolingischer Theologie und althochdeutscher Dichtung." *Frühmittelalterliche Studien,* 5 (1971), 284-303.

Shows the importance of legal analogies in four authors (Caesarius of Arles, Agobard of Lyon, *Muspilli,* and Otfrid von Weissenburg) as a means of explaining divine judgment to the newly-converted Germans. Even as these authors build up elaborate analogies, however, they are at pains to stress the *differences* [cf. 305] between secular and divine procedure (e.g., in God's court there will be no proof required, no argumentation, no advocates, no bribes).

Neidhart von Reuenthal

450 Bründl, Peter. "Minne und Recht bei Neidhart von Reuenthal." Diss. München 1972.

Nibelungenlied

451 Cometta, Marina. "La 'Bahrprobe' e la sua rappresentazione nel *Nibelungenlied* e in altri poemi epici medievali." *Acme*, 26 (1973), 331-357.

Studies the tradition in Germanic and Romance literature of the *iudicium feretri, Bahrprobe* or "judgment of the barrow," in which the corpse of a victim bleeds in the presence of its murderer. Cometta compares the treatment of the motif in Chrétien de Troyes' *Chevalier au Lion*, Hartmann von Aue's *Iwein*, the epic poem *Moriaen*, and the *Nibelungenlied*, noting that the *iudicium feretri* is regarded not so much as God's work but rather as something to be marveled at. He concludes that after Chrétien, the motif is more literary than popular, a fact which does not exclude, however, the authors' "precise consciousness of juridical-popular tradition."

452 Gengler, H. G. "Rechtsalterthümer im Nibelungenliede." *Zeitschrift für deutsche Kulturgeschichte*, 3 (1858), 191-215.

Following the methodology of Grimm's *Deutsche Rechtsalterthümer* [348], Gengler investigates the reflection of legal antiquities in the *Nibelungenlied*: kingship, vassalage, status, kinship, marriage, and criminal law.

453 Gentry, Francis G. *Triuwe and Vriunt in the Nibelungenlied.* Amsterdamer Publikationen zur Sprache und Literatur, 19. Amsterdam: Rodopi, 1975.

Focuses on the moral dilemma of those characters faced with conflicting obligations. In several major episodes—Hagen's decision to kill Siegfried, Kriemhild's revenge, Rüdiger's decision to fight against his friends, the Burgundians—"the protagonists act completely in accord with feudal and customary law. Yet in each case the characters do wrong according to the moral judgment of the poet." From his point of view, "the *triuwe* humanized by friendship is preferable to the cold legal bond in those instances when the two come into conflict" (pp. 87-88).

454 Hartung, Oskar. *Die deutschen Altertümer des Nibelungenliedes und der Kudrun*. Cöthen: Schulze, 1894.

A reference book on the life and thought of early Germanic people, as seen in *Kudrun* and the *Nibelungenlied*. Law has an important place in most of the entries, which are as follows: the family, the social structure, king, queen, the judicial system, vassalage, knighthood, tournaments, hunting, women, housing, clothing, food and drink, hospitality, messengers, warfare and weapons.

455 Mahlendorf, Ursula R. and Frank J. Tobin. "Legality and Formality in the *Nibelungenlied*." *Monatshefte*, 66 (1974), 225-238.

The purpose of this article is to reveal, by an examination of the question of legality and formality in the poem, "a unified code of ethics and its forms in the poem which underlies all actions." The tragedy of the *Nibelungenlied* arises from differing attitudes to legality and formality. On the one hand, there is Siegfried's disdain of law and formality, his reliance on personal qualities alone, which leads eventually to his downfall. On the other hand, there is Hagen's (and the Burgundians') violation of the spirit of the law, even as they scrupulously observe all the external forms. These two attitudes may be seen in the three *causae majores* from the first part of the poem: (1) Brünhild's libel suit and Siegfried's oath; (2) Siegfried's murder with Kriemhild's hue and cry and request for justice; (3) the rape of Kriemhild's treasure. From the legal point of view, the symbolic use made of Siegfried's sword gains added significance and, in fact, summarizes the point of the poem: "The wielder of this sword from the beginning of the poem on is one who disregards the law and takes matters into his own hands."

456   Mitteis,   Heinrich.   "Rechtsprobleme   im   Nibelungenlied."
      Juristische Blätter (Wien), 74 (1952), 240-242.

      Takes as his point of departure Zallinger's work on marriage law
      in the *Nibelungenlied* [460] and proposes that the poem may serve
      also "as a source for the *Verfassungsleben* of the period." Mitteis
      discusses Kriemhild's revenge ("a true medieval *Adelsfehde* rather
      than a merely Germanic *Sippenrache*"), the problem of *Landfrieden*
      in Bavaria, and the significance of the faithful Rüdiger as *Beamter*.

457   Neumann, Friedrich. *Das Nibelungenlied in seiner Zeit.* Göttingen:
      Vandenhoeck & Ruprecht, 1967.

      Numerous comments of a legal nature throughout (pp. 60-203).

458   Wapnewski, Peter. "Rüdigers Schild. Zur 37. Aventiure des
      Nibelungenliedes." *Euphorion*, 54 (1960), 380-410.

      Discusses in depth the points of law underlying the pattern of
      feudal obligations and the gift of Rüdiger's shield in *aventiure* 37.
      The behavior of Rüdiger, who subordinates friendship to his duty as
      a vassal (*Lehnsmannenpflicht*), is contrasted to that of Hagen, who,
      having received Rüdiger's shield, announces in defiance of the law
      that he will not fight his friend. The whole passage is rife with
      language that ought to be taken, Wapnewski insists, in a legal rather
      than in an ordinary sense (e.g., *ellende, bestân, widersagen*).

459   Wisniewski,   Roswitha.   "Das   Versagen   des   Königs.   Zur
      Interpretation   des   Nibelungenliedes."   *Festschrift für Ingeborg
      Schröbler zum 65. Geburtstag.* Ed. Dietrich Schmidtke and Helga
      Schüppert. Tübingen: Niemeyer, 1973, pp. 170-186.

      Traces the downfall of the Nibelungen to King Gunther's failure
      to exercise his legal obligations as husband, brother, head of the clan
      (*sippe*), and king. Because he does not stand by Kriemhild, for
      example, she is forced to take the law into her own hands.
      Eventually, his repeated violations of the laws and customs of the
      social "microstructure" (family and kin) leave him powerless to
      protect the social "macrostructure." He is the embodiment of the
      rex iniquus. Within the context of this argument, Wisniewski
      pursues a number of legal themes, e.g., Siegfried's oath
      (*Reinigungseid*), Kriemhild's revenge (*Blutrache*), *Bahrgericht* (the
      bleeding of a man's wounds in the presence of his murderer), the

theft of Kriemhild's *morgengabe*, the legal status of a woman (who stands in the *munt* or protection of her male relatives), and so on.

460   Zallinger, Otto. "Die Eheschliessung im Nibelungenlied und in der Gudrun." *SBAW*, 199 (Wien und Leipzig, 1923), 3-68.

461   _____. "Heirat ohne 'Trauung' im 'Nibelungenlied' und in der 'Gudrun.'" *Festschrift zu ehren Oswald Redlichs.* Veröffentlichungen des Museum Ferdinandeum in Innsbruck, 8. Innsbruck: Wagner, 1928, pp. 356 ff.

Notker of St. Gall

462   Köbler, Gerhard. *Stadtrecht und Bürgereinung bei Notker von St. Gallen.* Arbeiten zur Rechts- und Sprachwissenschaft, 4. Göttingen: G. Distler, 1974.

Argues that Notker's use of the translation words "burgreht" (*ius civile*) and "giwonaheit" (*consuetudo*) in his commentary on *De consolatio Philosophiae* was intended not to reflect contemporary German law but rather to convey in a scientific manner the *Rechtsstoff* of antique tradition. Underlying his use of the two terms is the crucial idea of a tension between positive and natural law.

Oswald von Wolkenstein

463   Lamberg, Gudrun. "Die Rechtsdichtung Oswalds von Wolkenstein." *ZDP*, 93 (1974), 75-87.

Sees Wolkenstein's song "Mich fragt ain ritter" as reflecting three main concerns: 1. the question of concordance between secular law (*irdisches Recht*), and divine justice (*göttliche Gerechtigkeit*); 2. the abuse of common law by the nobility and unscrupulous judges; 3. the advantages of written Roman law (*Corpus Iuris Civilis*). Lamberg compares the poet's concerns with those of Eike von Repgow and Ruprecht von Freising; and suggests that his work may be the earliest poetic attempt to popularize and clarify the content of Roman law.

Otfrid von Weissenburg

464   Siebert, Eberhard. *Zum Verhältnis von Erbgut und Lehngut im Wortschatz Otfrids von Weissenburg.* München: Wilhelm Fink, 1971.

Includes a brief discussion of the proportion of native and loan words pertaining to law and ethics in Otfrid's *Evangelienharmonie.* One purpose of the analysis is to refute the conclusion of other scholars that writers of the period were forced by a meager native vocabulary in these areas and others (e.g., feeling, thinking, art, literature, society, applied science) to draw heavily on Latin. Siebert shows that German words far outnumber Latin words in every case.

See also 422, 449.

Reinhart Fuchs (and Flemish *Van den Vos Reynaerde*)

465   Göttert, Karl-Heinz. *Tugenbegriff und epische Struktur in höfischen Dichtungen.* Köln: Böhlau, 1971.

Seeks to shed light on the title-subject by contrasting *untriuwe* in *Reinhart Fuchs* and *triuwe* in Konrad von Würzberg's *Engelhard.* Reinhart's trial serves to reveal the gap between Law and Authority (pp. 72 ff.).

466   Heeroma, K. "De *Reinaert* en het recht." *Tijdschrift voor Nederlandse Taal- en letterkunde,* 87 (1971), 260-274.

467   Jacoby, Frank Rainer. *Van den Vos Reinaerde: Legal Elements in a Netherlands Epic of the Thirteenth Century.* München: Wilhelm Fink, 1970.

"The study compares legal procedures and criminal law as presented in the thirteenth century Netherlands epic *Van den Vos Reinaerde* with actual legal customs in contemporary Flanders, as formulated in surviving Flemish documentation of the period." Chapter 1 describes the legal situation in Flanders at the time of the poem's composition. Chapter 2 then turns to the use of law in the poem and finds that "Reinaert's trial, his sentence and his reprieve conform, technically, to contemporary usage." Chapter 3 evaluates the literary significance of the poet's use of contemporary law. Deviations are explained as part of the author's satiric purpose, which was to expose the inadequacy of current laws and procedures.

468   . "The Conflict between Legal Concepts and Spiritual Values in the Middle High German *Reinhart Fuchs.*" *Revue des langues vivantes*, 29 (1973), 11-27.

Sees the contrast between the Old Law and the New, transposed to the secular realm, as the organizing principle of *Reinhart*. By sticking to the letter of the law and thereby perverting its spirit, the fox's accusers are unable to prevail. The author manipulates his source material—primarily through a crass presentation of Reinhart's moral and legal guilt—to show that *humilitas* is more effective in the conquest of evil than secular law and its procedures.

469 Meiners, Irmgard. *Schelm und Dümmling in Erzählungen des deutschen Mittelalters.* Münchener Texte und Untersuchungen zur deutschen Literatur des Mittelalters, 20. München: Beck, 1967.

Attempts to show in Chapter 3 ("Füchsische Reden") that the authors of *Reinaert I, Reinaert II,* and *Reinke de Vos* patterned the fox's defense in court after the Roman "oratio iudiciale" (*exordium, narratio, argumentatio, peroratio*). Meiners sees the speech as a literary parody rather than as a criticism of contemporary law and legal procedures. However, in an excursus on the topic of the combat before the court (Zweikampf vor Gericht) in *Reinaert II* and *Reinke de Vos*, she suggests that the authors here intended a parody of the *Gottesurteil* and thus a criticism of the misuse of God's help in insignificant quarrels.

470 Rombauts, E. "Grimbeert's Defense of Reinaert in *Van den Vos Reynaerde.* An Example of *Oratio Iudicialis*?" *Aspects of the Medieval Animal Epic.* Ed. E. Rombauts and A. Welkenhuysen. Louvain: Louvain University Press, and The Hague: Nijhoff, 1975, pp. 129-141.

Argues that Grimbeert's defense of Reinaert, even more than the fox's own "confession," represents an *oratio iudicialis*. The speech is analyzed in terms of the five main parts prescribed for the *genus iudiciale* by classical rhetoric: *exordium, narratio, probatio* or *argumentatio, refutatio,* and *peroratio* or *epilogus*.

471   Van den Brink, H., and J. Van Herwaarden. "Van den vos
       Reynaerde: Recht en macht." *Samenwinninge.* Zwolle: Willink,
       1977, pp. 75-91.

472   Wiezner. C. *Über einige deutsche Rechtsaltertümer in Willems*
       Gedicht van den vos Reynaerde. Breslau, 1891.

Reinfrid von Braunschweig

473   Koelliker, Beat. *Reinfrid von Braunschweig.* Bern: Francke, 1975.

       Touches upon the complaint that legal rhetoric has perverted the
       law (pp. 29-30) and upon the work's treatment of *Minne* and the law
       of nature (pp. 129-131).

Rolandslied

474   Gellinek, Christian. "À propos du système de pouvoir dans la
       Chanson de Roland." CCM, 19 (1976), 39-46.

       A contrastive analysis of the *Chanson de Roland* and the
       Rolandslied in terms of the authors' handling of the question of
       political authority. The didactic aims of the two poems are entirely
       different. The focus of the *Chanson* is ethical; of the *Rolandslied*,
       religious and theocratic. Consequently, "In the *Chanson*, the trial of
       Ganelon has the character of an epilogue to the episode of
       Roncevaux; while in the *Rolandslied*, by contrast, the stress is placed
       above all on the defense of a Christian-Carolingian 'légalité,'
       presented as necessary from the point of view of sacred history—a
       'légalité' which is identified with the cause of Christianity as a
       whole."

475   Wapnewski, Peter. "Der Epilog und die Datierung des deutschen
       Rolandsliedes." *Euphorion*, 49 (1955), 261-282.

       Assigns the poem to the time of Duke Heinrich der Löwe, partly
       on the basis of the line "ze gerichte er im nu stat" (9070), which
       Wapnewski thinks refers to Heinrich's trial (1178-80).

476   Wolff, Ludwig. "Ze Gerichte er im nu stat. Zur Datierung des
       Rolandsliedes." *BGDSL*, 78 (1956), 185-193.

       Rejects Wapnewski's interpretation [above] of verse 9069/70
       "swa er sich uirsumet hat, ze gerichte er im nu stat" as an allusion to
       the trial of Heinrich der Löwe and insists that the lines refer to the
       general judgment in which all sinners stand.

Sachsenspiegel (Eike von Repgow)

477   Jacobi, Johannes. "Die sittliche Forderung des christlichen 'Lebens
       im Recht' insbesondere nach dem Sachsenspiegel." *Deutsch-
       unterricht*, 8 (1956), 90-104.

       Calls attention to the verse prologue of the *Sachsenspiegel,* in
       which divine law is said to subsume secular law.

478   Kisch, Guido. "Biblical Spirit in Mediaeval German Law."
       Speculum, 14 (1939), 38-55.

       Stresses the pervasive influence of the Bible in the *Sachsenspiegel*
       and compares the author's concept of God as the source of law with
       two twelfth-century poems, *Vom Recht* and *Die Hochzeit.* To
       illustrate the "genetic" use made of Scripture in medieval law, Kisch
       describes at length Eike's attempt to prove that servitude has no legal
       justification in the Bible.

479   _____. "The Influence of the Bible on Medieval
       Legal Thought in England and Germany." *VIIIe Congrès
       International des Sciences Historiques, Zurich, 1938. Com-
       munications Présentées.* 2:317-319.

       Emphasizes the connection between the Bible and medieval law,
       as seen in two works: the introduction to King Alfred's code of laws,
       in which the Ten Commandments are translated, and the Prologue to
       Eike von Repgow's *Sachsenspiegel,* in which God and Holy Scripture
       are recognized explicitly as the source of all law.

480   _____. *Sachsenspiegel and Bible, Researches in the
       Source History of the Sachsenspiegel and the Influence of the Bible
       on Mediaeval German Law.* Notre Dame, Ind.: University of Notre
       Dame Press, 1941.

A contribution to "the history of the influence of the Bible on the secular law in the Middle Ages," especially on the *Sachsenspiegel*. Kisch attempts to show that the Bible influenced not only the content but also the author's technique of composition.

481   Kolb, Herbert. "Über den Ursprung der Unfreiheit. Eine Quaestio im *Sachsenspiegel*." *ZDA*, 103 (1974), 289-311.

Identifies the structure of Eike's treatment of servitude (Art. 3,42) with that of the *quaestio*. Kolb introduces the point with a long discussion on the mixed character of early lawbooks (in particular the *Spiegeln*)—part literary, part legal—as a result of which the genre has received little attention from scholars in either field.

Stricker

482   Brall, Helmut. "Strickers *Daniel vom dem blühenden Tal*. Zur politischen Funktion späthöfischer Artusepik im Territorialisierungsprozess." *Euphorion*, 70 (1976), 222-257.

Interprets the work from a socio-political point of view. The wealth of legal terminology in the text points to the historical conflict between feudalism (represented by Arthur and his court) and the rise of territorialism. Stricker is seen as a spokesman for the old order, and his work is considered an example for his contemporaries of how to react to the threat of the new. In this light the "aventiure" appears as an acceptable means of restoring feudalism and not as a danger to law and order. Some crucial terms: *Fehde, Dienst, Besitz, fri und eigen*.

483   Schwab, Ute. "Zum Thema des jüngsten Gerichts in der mittelhochdeutschen Literatur." *Annali Istituto Universitario Orientale*, Sezione Germanica (Napoli), 4 (1961), 11-73.

An edition and analysis of Stricker's *Die Beiden Königinnen*. The work, says Schwab, consists of two parts: 1. the *bispel* (*exemplum* and *expositio*); 2. a description of the Last Judgment. Stricker's didactic purpose in part 2 may be inferred from his inclusion of only certain traditional elements. These are: A. Adventus Christi ad iudicium (conflagratio aeris, timor iustorum, ira iudicis); B. Iudicium universale (quatuor ordines, discretio bonorum et malorum, accusatores [quatuor elementa], assistentes iudicis).

Making extensive use of possible sources and analogues, Schwab discusses each element in order. Although she refers occasionally to juristic concepts, her focus is primarily theological.

Vom Recht

484   Robl, H. "Reimwörter und Reimwortverzeichnisse zu den Gedichten 'Vom Recht' und 'Die Hochzeit.'" Diss. Wien 1948.

485   Schröbler, Ingeborg. "Das mittelhochdeutsche Gedicht vom 'Recht.'" *BGDSL*, 80 (1958), 219-252.

Useful for understanding both the poem and conventional legal thought. The analysis is in three parts: 1. The thought process of the poem; 2. The form; 3. Classical and New Testament influences. The basic assumption of the poem is the divine pre-eminence of law; to defy the law is to defy God. Three forms of law subsume all others, namely, truth or fidelity (*triuwe*), righteousness (*Gerechtigkeit*, as defined by the Golden Rule), and veracity (*Wahrhaftigkeit*). These are manifested in specific social relationships (lord-servant, husband-wife, priest-layman, etc.). As for the form of the poem, Schröbler argues for several influences: Rather of Verona's *Praeloquia*, Honorius of Autun's *Speculum Ecclesiae*, Alan of Lille's *Summa de arte praedicatoria*, and Bonizo of Sutri's *Decretum*. In part three Schröbler examines the relation between the poet's concept of order and the hierarchy of domestic order put forth in Paul's epistles and in certain classical writers (Aristotle, Xenophon, Seneca).

Walther von der Vogelweide

486   Hatto, Arthur T. "Walther von der Vogelweide's Ottonian Poems: A New Interpretation." *Speculum*, 24 (1949), 542-553.

Argues against the "hallowed assumption" that these six songs "were composed by Walther in the service of Otto and so expound his policy...."

487   Schmidt-Wiegand, Ruth. "Walthers *Kerze* (84, 33). Zur Bedeutung
      von Rechtssymbolen für die intentionalen Daten in mittelalterlicher
      Dichtung." *ZDP*, 87 (1969), 154-185.

      Explains Frederick II's gift to Walther (a candle) as a legal
      symbol of the emperor's protection; and then uses this interpretation
      to date Walther's *lied* of gratitude (spring 1224).

488   Wells, David A. "Imperial Sanctity and Political Reality: Bible,
      Liturgy, and the Ambivalence of Symbol in Walther von der
      Vogelweide's Songs Under Otto IV." *Speculum*, 53 (1978), 479-510.

      Shows how Walther's so-called *Ottenton* is "a plea for a return
      to the traditional values and condemnation of those who foster the
      state of disorder for their own short-sighted ends." Wells is
      particularly concerned with Walther's use of scriptural allusion as a
      vehicle for criticism of the emperor. The article, which touches upon
      several legal matters (e.g., the coronation ceremony, *pflegen* "to pay
      tax," *fronebote,* etc.), is especially valuable for its full review of
      previous scholarship on the political implications of the songs.

489   Willson, H. B. "The *ordo* of love in Walther's Minnesang." *DVLG*,
      39 (1965), 523-541.

      Sees Walther's addressing a *maget* as *frowe* not as "debasing the
      coinage of *Minnedienst*" but rather as part of a conscious effort to
      establish "a new order in MHG courtly love-poetry." Following the
      analogy of spiritual love (as described, for example, by Bernard of
      Clairvaux), Walther praises *herzeliebe* as a law and order unto itself.
      "Such is the paradox: inordinatio is the *ordo* of love, the measure of
      love is its lack of measure."

Wernher der Gärtner

490   Bonawitz, Achim. "Helmbrecht's Violation of 'Karles Reht.'"
      Monatshefte, 56 (1964), 177-182.

      "Helmbrecht's guilt consists not only in his criminal acts and in
      a revolt from the *ordo* established by civil and canon law (the
      desertion of his "God-given" social class), but also, quite simply, in
      the wearing of clothes that are not his by right...." That "Karles
      reht" prescribed the clothing of peasants is inferred from two

sources: Neidhart von Reuenthal's songs of winter and the *Kaiserchronik*. Bonawitz concludes: "The knightly clothing, forbidden a peasant by law, serves the author as an image of Helmbrecht's *unstaete*, his disloyalty to the farming class, and of his recourse to predatory knighthood, which goes awry and brings its burden of guilt."

491   Fischer, Hanns. "Gestaltungsschichten im 'Meier Helmbrecht.'" *BGDSL*, 79 (1957), 85-109.

Working from the assumption that the structure of *Meier Helmbrecht* is based on the biblical parable of the Prodigal Son, Fischer sees Helmbrecht's *inobedientia* (disregard for family) and generally lawless behavior as a threat to the earthly *Ordnungssystem*. As an extension of divine justice, however, earthly justice is able to re-establish equilibrium.

492   Göhler, Peter. "Konflikt und Figurengestaltung im 'Helmbrecht' von Wernher dem Gartenaere." *Weimarer Beiträge,* 20 (1974), 93-116.

Includes a brief discussion of the *Scherge* (pp. 105-106), whose commission seems to come not from any feudal authority but rather from God himself. The "supernatural power" of the *Scherge* betokens the supernatural status of the order which Helmbrecht has violated.

493   Lange, Günter. "Das Gerichtsverfahren gegen den jungen Helmbrecht. Versuch einer Deutung nach dem kodifizierten Recht und den Landfriedensordnungen des 13. Jahrhunderts." *ZDA,* 99 (1970), 222-234.

Analyzes *Meier Helmbrecht* under the aspects of codified law and *Landfriedensordnung*; and concludes that the author was well-versed in the law of his time. Topics discussed include the following: *Scherge, Richter, landschädliche Leute, Strafe des Hängens, Verstümmelungsstrafen, Munt, Friede,* and *Blutrache*.

494   Schindele, Gerhard. "'Helmbrecht.' Bäuerliche Aufstieg und landesherrliche Gewalt." *Literaturwissenschaft und Sozialwissenschaften, 5: Literatur im Feudalismus.* Ed. Dieter Richter. Stuttgart: Metzler, 1975, pp. 131-211.

An inquiry into the value of *Helmbrecht* as social history, with much attention to the legal implications of the younger Helmbrecht's actions. Several legal codes are quoted.

Wirnt von Grâvenberc

495   Steer, Georg. "Rechtstheologische Implikationen der Helmbrecht Dichtung Wernhers des Gartenaere." *Poesie und Gebrauchsliteratur im deutschen Mittelalter.* Ed. Volker Honemann, Kurt Ruh Bernhard Schnell, and Werner Wegstein. Tübingen: Niemeyer, 1979 pp. 239-250.

The details of law in *Helmbrecht* are less important to ar understanding of the work than the author's general conception of Right, which is theological rather than legal or moral. Subordinating all else—including the two modes of life exemplified in the work *rehte tun* and *unreht tun*—is the idea of Peace or *Gottesfrieden* Helmbrecht's pursuit of *unreht*, not only his outward acts of lawlessness but also his inward disposition (e.g., his avarice), is seen as a violation of this peace. The article concludes with a discussion of Wernher's distinction between *Richter* and *Scherge* as agents of divine retribution; the first is associated with the secular (*landesherrlich*) courts, the second with the ecclesiastical courts.

496   Kaiser, Gert. "Der *Wigalois* des Wirnt von Grâvenberc. Zur Bedeutung des Territorialisierungsprozesses für die 'höfisch ritterliche' Literatur des 13. Jahrhunderts." *Euphorion,* 69 (1975) 410-443.

In the Arthurian romance the town and its citizens appear on the horizon as a real social unit, an economic factor of government. The direct treatment of this development in the *Wigalois* not only affected the structure and central conflict of the work but also accounted, in part, for its appeal to a medieval audience.

Vittenwiler

97   Boesch, Bruno. "Fragen rechtl. Volkskunde in Wittenweilers
      Ring." *Schweizerisches Archiv für Volkskunde*, 71 (1975), 129-157.

98   Clifton-Everest, J. M. "Wittenwiler's Marriage Debate." *MLN*, 90
      (1975), 629-642.

      Devotes a paragraph (p. 641) to the medieval identification of
      prose as "the legal idiom" (cites Wittenwiler, *Der Ackermann aus
      Böhmen, Le Livre du chevalier de la Tour Landry,* and Chaucer).

99   Fehrenbach, Charles Gervase. *Marriage in Wittenwiler's Ring.* The
      Catholic University of America, Studies in German, 15. Washington,
      D. C.: The Catholic University of America, 1941.

      In Chapter 5 ("Legal Aspects of Marriage"), the author tries to
      determine how the marriage of Bertschi and Mätzli should be
      characterized ("civil," "clandestine," etc.). After a survey of
      marriage customs in law and in other literature *(Nibelungenlied,
      Kudrun, Iwein, Tristan*, etc.), Fehrenbach concludes that although
      the marriage was "gravely illicit" from a canonical point of view and
      hardly a civil marriage in the strict sense (for no civil official was
      present), it was nevertheless valid according to secular law and
      custom.

00   Mittler, Elmar. *Das Recht in Heinrich Wittenwilers 'Ring.'*
      Forschungen zur oberrheinischen Landesgeschichte, 20. Freiburg im
      Breisgau: Eberhard Albert, 1967.

      An extremely thorough and useful investigation of the legal
      character of the *Ring.* In contrast to Dante, who develops the
      metaphysical idea of God as the source of law, Wittenwiler is
      concerned almost entirely with law in the daily lives of his burgher
      audience. Part of his didactic purpose is to educate his readers in the
      practical matters of law, as is evident in his treatment not only of
      legal procedures themselves (suits, trials, etc.) but also of betrothal
      and marriage, the conduct of war, social class, and the sacraments of
      baptism and confession. He shows a substantial knowledge of
      Roman, canon, and common law—a good example of the medieval
      Dichterjuristen. From Wittenwiler's handling of many individual
      points of law and his attitude toward the Reception, Mittler infers

that the *Ring* was written "um die Wende zum 15. Jahrhundert."
An extensive bibliography on literature and law is appended.

Wolfram von Eschenbach

501   Becker, Ernst Wilhelm. "Das Recht im Parzival." Diss. Bonn 1956.

502   Schmid, Elisabeth. "Enterbung, Ritterethos, Unrecht: Zu
      Wolframs 'Willehalm.'" *ZDA*, 107 (1978), 259-275.

      Compares the disinheritance motif in *Willehalm* and various
      chansons de geste (e.g., *Le Narbonnais, Le Charroi de Nimes, La
      Prise d'Orange*). The father's unjust action, depriving Willehalm of
      land and position, leads the son to commit injustices of his own (e.g.,
      Landraub). He is not another Parzival.

503   Schmidt-Wiegand, Ruth. "Der 'Wisch' als Bann- und
      Verbotszeichen." *Zeitschrift für Volkskunde*, 64 (1968), 203-222.

      Touches upon (p. 213) the different legal implications of *wisc*
      and *schoup* in Wolfram. The objects function as symbols for taking
      possession, respectively, of land and of office (kingship).

504   Schumacher, Marlis. *Die Auffassung der Ehe in den Dichtungen
      Wolframs von Eschenbach*. Heidelberg: Winter, 1967.

      Stresses the "modern" characteristics of Wolfram's conception
      of marriage. There are several discussions of marriage as a legal
      institution. For example, in opposition to some critics, Schumacher
      declares that Sigune's "marriage" has no validity under human law
      and therefore permits no inferences about the legal foundation of
      marriage in Wolfram's work (pp. 49-60). Elsewhere the author notes
      that although Wolfram basically affirms the legal jurisdiction of
      husband over wife, "Recht und Sitte" are often in conflict (pp.
      92-94).

505   Weiss, Paula Barran. "Personal Clothing in Wolfram's *Parzival*
      and *Willehalm*: Symbolism and Significance." Diss. University of
      British Columbia 1976.

06   Wiegand, Herbert Ernst. *Studien zur Minne und Ehe in Wolframs Parzival und Hartmanns Artusepik*. Berlin: de Gruyter, 1972.

Grounds his discussion of *Minne* and *Ehe* in the legal and political history of marriage among the feudal aristocracy of France and Germany.

ee also 397.

ICELANDIC

507   Andersson, Theodore M. *The Icelandic Family Saga: An Analytic Reading*. Cambridge, Mass.: Harvard University Press, 1967.

Comments intermittently on the extent and purpose of the law in the sagas. For example, Andersson notes that revenge—a theme in all the sagas—could be effected by blood vengeance, by legal prosecution of the slayer, or by a combination of both. "The least common mode of revenge is the purely legal, perhaps because this mode offered the poorest dramatic possibilities, perhaps because it was felt by the Icelandic audience to be the least honorable alternative, and perhaps because in fact legal recourse *was* the least frequent solution" (p. 19).

508   Ashdown, M. "The Single Combat in Certain Cycles of English and Scandinavian Tradition and Romance." *MLR*, 17 (1922), 113-130.

A rambling discussion of the literary treatments of single combat as a solution to national or international difficulties. The article focuses on romances "linked by the presence of the Scandinavian adventurer, Anlaf Cuaran." Appended is a list of instances of single combat, drawn from early Germanic tradition and medieval romance.

509   Baetke, Walter. "Geschichte, Überlieferung und Dichtung in den Isländersagas." *Kleine Schriften*. Ed. Kurt Rudolph and Ernst Walter. Weimar: Böhlau, 1973, pp. 256-279.

Provides a few examples of the way in which historical material, much of it legal, was transformed by the saga-writer's artistic purpose.

510   Barlau, Stephen B. "An Outline of Germanic Kingship." *Journal of Indo-European Studies*, 4 (1967), 97-130.

Provides an overview of Germanic kingship as a system of a given type (one based upon kindreds), and in the process of examining its vital features (language, inheritance, and wergild) draws primarily upon the evidence of language, law, and literature (e.g., *Egil's saga, Saga af Tristram ok Isönd, Saga of Harald Fairhair, Reykdale saga, Gripisspa, Gylfaginning*).

511   Berger, Alan J. "Old Law, New Law, and *Hoensa-Þóris saga.*" *Scripta Islandica*, 27 (1976), 3-12.

Suggests that the author of the saga reworked parts of Ari Þorgilsson's account of the reform of the Old Icelandic judicial system in *Íslendingabók* (Chapter 5). The discussion centers on two episodes involving the conflict of the old law of the republic and the new law announced by the adoption of *Jónsbók* in 1281. Although neither issue was alive in his day, "The author was content to indicate to his audience that the original conflict between individuals grew into a national issue, and the paragraph from Ari served principally to give his story the very ring of truth."

512   —————————. "Lawyers in the Old Icelandic Family Sagas: Heroes, Villains, and Authors." *Saga-Book*, 20 (1978-79), 70-79.

Seeks to explain why the sagas are so full of law and lawyers. Typical examples of legal episodes are cited from *Víga-Glúms saga, Vápnfirðinga saga, Hoensa-Þóris saga* and *Valla-Ljóts saga*. Berger suggests that the authors found in the law "a catalogue of conflicts useful to a conflict-hungry literature" and that, moreover, "narrative contrivances could be made convincing with the addition of daubs of legal detail." Because so many episodes turn on points of law, he notes, both heroes and villains must be made lawyers, e.g., Helgi Droplaugarson (*Droplaugarsona saga*), Guðmundr the Powerful (*Ljósvetninga saga*), Áskell goði (*Reykdoela saga*). In many cases there is a recurring pattern: the conflict "between the letter of a primitive old law and the spirit of a new, as yet unadopted law."

513   Bergsgård, Arne. "Skaldane um land og lands styring." *Festskrift til Halvdan Koht*. Oslo: Aschehoug, 1933, 112-120.

514   Bø, Olav. "*Hólmganga* and *einvígi*: Scandinavian Forms of the Duel." *MScan*, 2 (1969), 132-148.

Attempts to distinguish between the two words for duel in the sagas. *Einvígi* seems to be the older and more general form;

hólmganga refers to a later development that was clearly "a much more ordered affair." In any case, the custom died out about the year 1000; and it is understandable that the sagas, written nearly 300 years later, should have confused the two terms. Though inconclusive (and not well organized), the article is helpful as a guide to scholarship on the subject.

515   Brown, Ursula, ed. *Þorgils saga ok Hafliða*. London: Oxford University Press, 1952.

Legal matter is especially prominent in the narrative. See the notes to this edition, pp. 46-95.

516   Ciklamini, Marlene. "The Old Icelandic Duel." *SS*, 35 (1963), 175-194.

Discusses various aspects of the duel in law and literature and notes several features unique to the north. The common man was allowed to challenge the rich, making the duel an attractive road to wealth and glory; the contest was mainly secular and not a judgment of God, as it was in Western Europe and Norman England; and finally the combatants themselves, and not a court, decided beforehand the consequences of victory and defeat.

517   Dahl, Willy. "Kjøpmannsbolken i konungs skuggsjá—en parafrase over Hávamál, str. 57-65." *Maal og Minne*, 1960, pp. 48-55.

518   Duncan, Annelise Marie. "A Study of Ethics and Concepts of Justice in Two Sagas of Icelandic Outlaws." Diss. Rice University 1969.

Examines reflections of the ethical "spirit" of *Hávamál* (a collection of gnomic verse) and the legal "spirit" of *Grágás* (the Old Icelandic lawbook) in two family sagas, *Gísla Saga Súrssonar* and *Grettis Saga Ásmundarsonar*.

519   Einarsson, Bjarni. "On the Status of Free Men in Society and Saga." *MScan*, 7 (1974), 45-55.

Although feudal ideals were imported by way of the Church and literature (cf. use of the word *kurteisi* after 1200), these ideals were in basic conflict with the equality of free men under Icelandic law. The sagas provide a record of this conflict. For example, the shipwreck

episode in *Eiríks saga rauða* may be seen as a protest against the
increasing inequality of the age. The author's view is expressed by
Bjarni Grímólfsson who says that place in the lifeboat is not to
depend on rank. This view is in deliberate contrast to the apparent
source of the episode, *Maríu saga*, in which the places go first to the
most prominent.

520   Engfield, Roy. "Der Selbstmord in der germanischen Zeit."
       Seminar, 8 (1972), 1-14.

       The author summarizes his article as follows: "The Germanic
       peoples, before contact with Christianity, did not, as a rule,
       condemn suicide, and this attitude, reflected in laws and narratives,
       changed only slowly under the influence of the Church. The earliest
       known cases of suicide occurred among both sexes after the battle of
       Vercellae and Aqua Sextiae. They are explainable by reference to
       religious beliefs and the position of women in the Germanic tribe.
       These explanations also hold for suicides among the early
       Norwegians and Icelanders; hanging particularly is found to be
       meant as a sacrifice. In suicides of women, however, there may be
       seen traces of *suttee* (Witwentötung). *Suttee* probably existed among
       Germanic peoples at a very early time and was given up as they
       turned from a migratory to an agricultural way of life."

521   Evans, Virginia. "The Ethics of Survival: A Critical Approach to
       the Icelandic Family Saga." Diss. Queen's University at Kingston
       (Canada) 1979.

       "By examining concerns common to the group—the role of the
       law, the place of the warrior, the ambiguities of chance—as well as
       the overall structure of individual works, this thesis arrives at a view
       of the saga as thematically coherent and artistically discreet."

522   Fleck, Jere. "Konr—Óttarr—Geirroðr: A Knowledge Criterion for
       Succession to the Germanic Sacred Kingship." *SS*, 42 (1970), 39-49.

       Argues that numinous knowledge, not primogeniture or
       ultimogeniture, is the crucial factor in succession to the sacred
       kingship in at least three Eddic poems—*Rigsþula* (runic knowledge),
       Hyndlolióð (royal genealogy), and *Grímnismál* (magic spell)—and
       that once the knowledge criterion is accepted in these mythological
       cases, "its practice in the world of Germanic reality becomes a
       logical conclusion."

523   Foote, Peter. "On Legal Terms in *Faereyinga saga.*" *Fróðskaparrit*, 18 (1970), 159-175.

As part of the larger question of "how much the Icelandic author of *Faereyinga saga* actually knew about Faroese conditions," Foote isolates numerous legal terms that seem more appropriate to the Faroes (or to Norway) than to Iceland. Among the terms: *orvarþing* (an assembly summoned immediately after an offense); *svá sem log yður liggja til* (a reference to compurgation, hardly existent in Iceland); *óbótamaðr* (irredeemable outlaw); *logsogumaðr* (title of legal office); *landbúi* (tenant); *áverki* (effect, result of action); *útlagi, útlagr, útlaegr* (outlaw); *útlegð* (outlawry); *þingmaðr* (man who attends the *thing*).

524   Frank, Roberta. "Marriage in Twelfth- and Thirteenth-Century Iceland." *Viator*, 4 (1973), 473-484.

An entertaining description of marriage customs, drawn from both *Grágás* (the national law of the twelfth and thirteenth centuries) and the sagas.

525   Gløersen, Ingeborg. *Kongespeilet og Las Siete Partidas.* Oslo: Universitetsforlaget, 1972.

Suggests that the author of *The King's Mirror* was influenced by the Spanish lawbook *Las siete partidas*, especially on the topics of the king's authority and his role as judge. The study also includes a discussion of the historical relation between Norway and Spain in the 1250's, the decade in which the *Kongespeilet* presumably was written.

526   Gurevich, Aron Ya. "Edda and Law. Commentary upon *Hyndlolióð.*" *Arkiv för Nordisk Filologi*, 88 (1973), 72-84.

Sees behind the puzzling genealogy in *Hyndolioð* a trial involving the ancestral property. "There is a complete congruence between Ottarr's genealogy of five generations in *Hdl* and the necessity according to the injunction of the *Gulathings-lov* to enumerate five generations of the *óðal-menn* in order to prove the right of the sixth to the land in dispute." Gurevich insists repeatedly on the close association between early law and poetry: "There are in the earliest codes of law the 'microsagas,' small juridical narratives....On the other hand, it is not difficult to find in the

Eddaic lays some legal terminology and situations....If one wants to understand their poetry and law, it is necessary to take into consideration this singularity of the mentality of those days.''

527   Heusler, Andreas. *Die altgermanische Dichtung*. Berlin: Athenaion, 1924; rpt. Darmstadt: Gentner, 1957.

Includes several brief discussions of "Poesie im Recht" [cf. 9], e.g., pp. 50 ff., 82 ff., 212 f. et passim.

528   _____. *Das Strafrecht der Isländersagas*. Leipzig: Duncker & Humblot, 1911.

The classic treatment of crime and punishment in the sagas, focusing on the concepts of outlawry and wergild. The discussion of legal terminology is unusually full. Chapter 1 takes up the question of the sagas' reliability as sources of law.

529   _____. *Zum isländischen Fehdewesen in der Sturlungenzeit*. Berlin: Verlag der königlichen Akademie der Wissenschaften, 1912.

530   Holm-Olsen, Ludvig. "Konungs skuggsjá og norrøn poesi." *Einarsbók. Afmoeliskveðja til Einars Ól. Sveinssonar*. Reykjavik: Útgefendur Nokkir Vinir, 1969 [1970], pp. 114-120.

531   Jones, Gwyn. "Landnámabók: Its Contribution to the Study of Icelandic Feud." *MLR*, 28 (1933), 217-225.

Attempts to clear up the most doubtful passages concerning feud procedure, primarily by comparison with the sagas. *Landnámabók* describes 49 cases, 33 of which are settled by private vengeance, 5 by arbitration, and 11 by legal procedure. The sagas describe 520 cases, and the same proportion holds more or less: 297, 104, 119. Based on the evidence of *Landnámabók,* the treatment of the three types in the sagas seems to be relatively faithful to historical fact. Exceptions are noted. Of particular interest to Jones are the concepts of outlawry and of "balance" (a principle used by arbitrators to reach their award).

532 _____. "Some Characteristics of the Icelandic *Hólmganga.*" *JEGP*, 32 (1933), 203-224.

Collates the evidence from seventeen sagas for the existence of *hólmganga* or wager-of-battle and attempts to shed new light on the custom itself. Although it surrendered law to the blood-thirsty principle of private vengeance, *holmgang* at least confined the strife to two men; moreover, it was strictly governed by an etiquette of the duel (*hólmgöngulög*), in contrast to the unregulated fight known as *einvígi* [cf. 514]. There is no convincing evidence to support the theory of battle by proxy; to refuse a challenge was to bring the greatest shame upon oneself, a fate worse than death. Jones concludes with a discussion of the legal attempts to ameliorate and then to suppress the custom.

533 _____."Fjörbaugsgarðr." *Medium Aevum*, 9 (1940), 155-163.

Proposes to explain the difference between the use of the term *fjörbaugsgarðr* ("life-ring-garth") in the sagas and in the thirteenth-century lawbook *Grágás.* Jones concludes that there is nothing to show that the *fjörbaugsgarðr* of *Gragas* (calling for a banishment of three years) was part of feud procedure in the period 870-1030 "and next to nothing to show that it was practical law to the end of the twelfth century." Like Heusler [528] Jones is sceptical of the authority of the lawbooks for the study of feud in the sagas.

534 _____. "History and Fiction in the Sagas of the Icelanders." *Saga-Book*, 13 (1964), 285-306.

Comments briefly on the legal evidence in *Víga-Glúms saga*, which "while always interesting is sometimes dubious and once or twice incorrect." As errors, Jones cites the saga's account of the outlawry of *Vigfúss* and the "*Hrísteigr*-mowing."

535 Koht, Halvdan. *The Old Norse Sagas.* New York: The American-Scandinavian Foundation, 1931.

In the chapter titled "Historical Value of the Sagas," Koht talks briefly about the sagas' interest in law and lawsuits. He describes the narratives as "balancing between fiction and history." In general these thirteenth-century works "are stamped by the law practice of the first Christian century, the eleventh century...."

536   Larson, Laurence M., trans. *The King's Mirror*. New York: The
       American-Scandinavian Foundation, 1917; rpt. New York: Twayne
       Publishers and the American-Scandinavian Foundation, n. d.

           In his Introduction (pp. 1-71) Larson calls attention to the
       literary qualities of the *Mirror*, which is in dialogue form, and to its
       relation to other literary works. Specific influences cited are the
       Vulgate Bible, the *Disciplina Clericalis* (a collection of tales by Petrus
       Alphonsus), the *Elucidarium* of Honorius of Autun, the
       Topographia Hibernia of Giraldus Cambrensis, and the letter of
       Prester John to the Byzantine emperor.

537   Lehmann, Karl and Hans Schnorr von Carolsfeld. *Die Njálssage,
       insbesondere in ihren juristischen Bestandtheilen*. Berlin: Prager,
       1883.

           After a close examination of legal elements in the work—the
       legal expressions, the *Rechtsgeschäfte* (marriage, divorce), and the
       six law-suits—the authors reject the widely-held view that the saga
       can be used to plug the gaps in our knowledge of early Icelandic law
       (i.e., *Freistaatsrecht*). On the contrary, most of the legal elements
       are traceable to the lawbooks, and those that are not can be
       explained as misinterpretations, more recent post-republican law,
       Norwegian rather than Icelandic law, or finally plain nonsense. On
       the basis of the representations of law in the work, the authors assign
       it to the last third of the thirteenth century.

538   Lehmann, Winfred P. "On Reflections of Germanic Legal
       Terminology and Situations in the *Edda*." *Old Norse Literature and
       Mythology: A Symposium*. Ed. Edgar C. Polomé. Austin:
       University of Texas Press, 1969, pp. 227-243.

           Focuses on the roles of individuals in and out of society.
       Lehmann is particularly interested in the changing concept of the
       outlaw—a change influenced by the coming of a wider society and a
       Christian outlook. At first merely a temporary outcast from a small
       social group (a "wanderer"), the outlaw becomes (especially in the
       Eddic poems with a southern background) a figure of universal
       scorn, the member of a criminal race, "like the monsters in
       Beowulf." (The English poem, in fact, is used extensively as a basis
       of comparison.) Among the legal terms treated are *vargr* (wolf,
       outlaw), *sekr* (free to be hunted), *bót* (recompense), *iafnendr*
       (arbiter), *saetta* (settle a suit), *baug* (payment of wergild).

539   Liestøl, Knut. *The Origin of the Icelandic Family Sagas.* Instituttet
       for Sammenlignende Kulturforskning, Serie A: Forelesninger, 10.
       Oslo: Aschehoug, 1930.

       Repeats Heusler's point [528] that criminal law in the sagas was
       unaffected by the legal conceptions of the twelfth and thirteenth
       centuries but represented instead the ancient legal system which was
       in force in the *söguöld* (pp. 222 f.).

540   Maurer, Konrad von. *Vorlesungen über altnordische
       Rechtsgeschichte.* 5 vols. Leipzig: Deichert, 1907-1939; rpt.
       Osnabrück: Zeller, 1966.

       Judicious use of the sagas for illustrative purposes. (For
       Maurer's comments on the value of saga literature to the legal
       historian, see 5:291.)

541   McGrew, Julia Helen. "Character and Tragedy in Eight Family
       Sagas." Diss. Bryn Mawr College 1954.

       Makes extensive use of the laws in order to establish "the
       concept of personality" in thirteenth-century Iceland. "The
       Icelandic laws indirectly reflect the concept of personality. They
       express no idea of legal personality, no philosophy of abstract
       Justice; but they give concrete empirical statements of the
       individual's responsibilities and the law's penalties in acts of revenge
       and feud."

542   Mezger, F. "Did the Institution of Marriage by Purchase Exist in
       Old Germanic Law?" *Speculum*, 18 (1943), 369-371.

       Rejects the existence of marriage by purchase ("Kaufehe"),
       which some historians infer from the language of Germanic law.
       Mezger's argument is based on two kinds of evidence: 1. the Family
       Sagas, which show that the gift of the bridegroom belongs to the
       bride alone and not to the person who gives her away, and 2. the
       history of the crucial term for "purchase" (Gmc. *kaupon*, Icelandic
       kaupa, bruðkaup), which originally referred to the broader concept
       of "exchange" or "agreement."

543   _____. "The Publication of Slaying in the Saga
       and in the Nibelungenlied." *Arkiv för Nordisk Filologi*, 61 (1946)
       208-224.

       Using the story of Sigfrid's death in the *Nibelungenlied* and in
       Þidreks saga as his primary example, Mezger discusses problems
       related to "the publication of the slaying" (i.e., the delivery of the
       body to Kriemhild). Several analogues are cited from other sagas
       (*Droplaugarsona saga, Gísla, Njála, Bjorn Hitdoelakappa, Grettis
       saga, Fóstbroedra saga*). The publication is crucial to the definition
       of the act and thus to the punishment: a concealed slaying is,
       technically speaking, a "murder." Mezger also treats the idea of a
       dead man's rights.

544   Nordal, Sigurdur. *The Historical Element in the Icelandic Family
       Sagas.* The Fifteenth W. P. Ker Memorial Lecture. Glasgow
       Jackson, 1957.

       Includes a brief discussion of the account of the proceedings at
       the Althing after the burning of Njál, an account copied out of a
       lawbook (pp. 28-29).

545   Phillpotts, Bertha S. *Kindred and Clan in the Middle Ages and
       After.* Cambridge: Cambridge University Press, 1913.

       Relies heavily on the sagas for information about wergild laws in
       Iceland (the whole of Chapter 1).

546   Rehfeldt, Bernhard. "Recht, Religion und Moral bei den früher
       Germanen." *ZRG*, Germ. Abt. 71 (1954), 1-22.

       Investigates the close connection between law and religion,
       especially in early Scandinavia, with Snorri Sturluson's *Ynglinga
       saga* as a major source of information. A great deal of the discussion
       centers on the distinction between religion and magic.

547   Rulfs, Jane L. "Narrative Techniques in *Njáls Saga*." Diss. Rice
       University 1974.

       Among other devices, "parallel quasi-histories of Republican
       law, from *hólmganga* to the law's disintegration, and of the
       Christianizing of Iceland further aid the overall continuity of the
       saga."

548   Schach, Paul. "An Anglo-Saxon Custom in *Tristrams saga*?" *SS*,
       42 (1970), 430-437.

       Accepts York's conclusion [567] that the *salle aux images*
       episode in *Tristrams saga* was influenced by Anglo-Saxon law but
       questions certain aspects of his reading of the text.

549   Schwartz, Stephen P. *Poetry and Law in Germanic Myth*. University
       of California Publications, Folklore Studies, 27. Berkeley:
       University of California Press, 1973.

       Seeks to verify and elaborate upon Jacob Grimm's theory [9]
       concerning the interrelationship of law and poetry. The Introduction
       provides a summary and critique of the main points in Grimm's
       theory. In Chapter 1 Schwartz argues for the importance of the
       Frisian legend "Van da tweer Koningen Kaerl ende Radbod" as "the
       only self-contained account in a Germanic language of the divine
       origin of law." Chapter 2 deals with the transformation of the
       Frisian god Foseti (the law-giver) into the Old Norse god Forseti, and
       hypothesizes that his integration into the Norse pantheon
       contributed to the rise in importance of the juridical function of
       Oðinn. How the chief of the gods acquired this function is the
       subject of Chapter 3: by displacing Tyr (the god of law), Oðinn (the
       god of battle and poetry!) came to embody both law and poetry at
       once, important testimony of their connection at the mythological
       level. Chapter 4 illustrates other versions of the story, in which the
       pagan gods have been replaced by the heroes of traditional literature
       (the most outstanding example being the Latin account of the
       adventures of Waltharius, i.e., Walter of Aquitane).

550   Scovazzi, Marco. "L'origine dei negozi giuridici individuali
       nell'antico diritto nordico." *Rivista di storia del diritto italiano*,
       40-41 (1967-68), 13-33.

       Scovazzi examines Nordic law in the context of the sagas to give
       "a clear indication of how the human conscience strives to liberate
       itself from the subjection of a public law, strongly dominated by
       religion, and to attain the satisfaction and expression of individual
       petition that private juridical channels allow."

551   See, Klaus von. *Altnordische Rechtswörter. Philologische Studien zur Rechtsauffassung und Rechtsgesinnung der Germanen.* Hermaea. Germanistische Forschungen, N. F. 16. Tübingen: Niemeyer, 1964.

Important discussion of legal terms in Old Norse. The study is divided into nine categories: law and privilege (*réttr*), law and custom, law and religion, peace, power and violence, faithfulness, truth, justice, and the meaning of *lög* ("law"). The author treats in several places the relation between *Rechtsprache* and *Dichtersprache*, observing that what is legal in one context (law book) may not be in another (poem) [cf. 556]. Literary art and legal science are obviously two different things, he says, and "the predilection of the Icelandic sagas for legal proceedings is no testimony for the popularity of law."

552   _____. *Germanische Heldensage. Stoffe, Probleme, Methoden.* Frankfurt: Athenäum, 1971.

Touches upon (pp. 70-72) the use of legal formulas (e.g., "saxi oc með sverði," showing Hloðr's legal status) and the influence of legal rhetoric in the "Hunnenschlachtlied."

553   _____. "Strafe im Altnordischen." *Anzeiger für deutsches Altertum und deutsche Literatur*, 90 (1979), 283-298.

Traces the development of the abstract idea of punishment (Strafe) through the more concrete terms *hefna, refsa, hegna, pína, víti,* etc. (several examples taken from Scaldic verse). The author stresses the influence of the Bible and Church doctrine, in which "the king executes punishment not out of personal vengeance but out of service to and by mandate of his superior, that is, as a deputy of God."

554   Simpson, Jacqueline. "A Note on the Word *Friðstóll.*" *Saga-Book*, 14 (1955-56), 200-210.

Suggests that the use of the word *friðstóll* ("chair of peace") in *Guðmundar saga*, the single appearance in Old Icelandic, "provides a clear example of the influence of English ecclesiastical vocabulary on Icelandic." The discussion centers on the notion of sanctuary in English canon law.

555   Spoelstra, Jan. "De Vogelvrijen in de Ijslandsche Letterkunde."
       [Diss. University of Utrecht 1938.] Haarlem: Tjeenk, 1938.

       Concerns the outlaw tradition in Icelandic folklore, both old and
       new.

556   Ström, Folke. *On the Sacral Origin of the Germanic Death
       Penalties*. Trans. Donald Burton. Stockholm: Wahlström &
       Widstrand, 1942.

       Points out among other things that *nið, níðingr,* etc. had a moral
       rather than juristic meaning when used in literary texts.

557   _____. *Nið, Ergi, and Old Norse Moral Attitudes*.
       The Dorothea Coke Memorial Lecture in Northern Studies. London:
       Viking Society for Northern Research, 1973.

558   Turville-Petre, G., ed. *Víga-Glúms Saga*. 2d ed. Oxford: Clarendon,
       1960.

       The legal statements of the saga "seem generally to be based on
       sound tradition, even though they conflict in a few instances with
       other records" (p. xvi), for which see notes to pp. 24, 43, 48 et
       passim.

559   Tveitane,   Mattias.   *Studier   over   Konungs   Skuggsiá*.
       Bergen-Oslo-Tromsø: Universitetsforlaget, 1971.

       Anthology of studies by various authors, in which the *King's
       Mirror* is treated as a literary work and as a source of legal history.
       There is a full bibliography at the end.

560   _____. "The 'Four Daughters of God' in the Old
       Norse *King's Mirror*." *NM*, 73 (1972), 795-804.

       Calls attention to the allegory of the Four Daughters of God in
       The King's Mirror, a *Fürstenspiegel* (ca. 1260) usually overlooked in
       scholarly treatments of the theme, and suggests as possible sources:
       1. the *Château d'Amour* attributed to Robert Grosseteste, 2. Hugh
       of St. Victor, or 3. "some unknown or hitherto unnoticed
       intermediate version."

561   Vigfússon, Gudbrand [Guðbrandur], ed. *Sturlunga Saga*. Oxford: Clarendon, 1878.

The editor's Prolegomena includes a survey of legal sources in Icelandic and Norwegian (pp. cxcvii-ccviii) and a brief commentary on *Njals Saga* (pp. xlii-xlv), about which the editor says: "The Saga of Law, *par excellence*, it is based on that most important element of early society [the althing], and the lesson it teaches is of a Divine retribution, and that evil brings its own reward in spite of all that human wisdom and courage, even innocence, can do to oppose it....This story is, from internal evidence, the work of a lawyer, well acquainted with Icelandic history and genealogies...."

562   _____, and F. York Powell, eds. *Corpus Poeticum Boreale*. 2 vols. Oxford: Clarendon, 1883.

Copious notes on the legal aspects of Icelandic poetry, indexed separately in Vol. 2 as "Law, Family and Constitutional" (pp. 699 ff.).

563   Voigt, Helmut. "Zur Rechtssymbolik der Schuhprobe in Þiðriks saga (viltina þáttr)." *BGDSL*, 87 (1965), 93-149.

Uses the *Kniesetzung*, a sign of engagement in Scandinavian law, as a basis for speculating on the source, date, and textual history of the saga.

564   Wagner, F. "L'Organisation du combat singulier au moyen âge dans les états scandinaves et dans l'ancienne république islandaise." *Revue de Synthèse*, 11 (1936), 41-60.

Surveys the practice of single combat as described in seventeen sagas. The discussion treats in separate sections the following topics: the causes, the prize, types of provocation (especially *niðing*), the *holmganga* as distinguished from *einvigi*, the place of combat (*holmgongustaðr*), the size of the ring, the prescribed weapons, assistants, compensation, religious overtones (the sacrifice of animals afterwards), instances of magnanimity, and the legal suppression of duels in 1004. Several of Wagner's assumptions (e.g., that the duel represented a *iudicium Dei*, or that the coming of Christianity hastened its demise) are questioned by later scholars.

565 Widding, Ole. "Alcuin and the Icelandic Law-Books." *Saga-Book*, 14 (1953-55), 291-295.

Shows borrowings from Alcuin's *De virtutibus et vitiis* in the *Jónsbók* and other legal material.

566 Williams, Carl O. *Thraldom in Ancient Iceland.* Chicago: University of Chicago Press, 1937.

A broad study of the historical development of thraldom in Iceland, based on the Eddic poems, the genealogical sagas (*Islendingasögur*), and the laws (*Grágás*, etc.). The work is marred, however, by the author's uncritical acceptance of the sagas as "a realistic picture of the material, social, and political conditions in ancient Iceland" and by his stance as the champion of an oppressed class.

567 York, Ernest C. "An Anglo-Saxon Custom in the *Tristrams saga*." *SS*, 41 (1969), 259-262.

Sees in the description of the giant Moldagog's boundaries and in the way Tristram defiantly announces his trespass (by hornblowing) the influence of Anglo-Saxon law. [For a reply see 548.]

FRENCH AND PROVENÇAL

General and Miscellaneous

568   Andrus, Toni Wulff. "The Devil on the Medieval Stage in France."
       Diss. Syracuse University 1979.

       A study of the Devil's role in French medieval drama (*Sponsus*,
       Jeu d'Adam, *Miracle de Théophile*, *Miracles de Nostre Dame*, and
       numerous Passion and mystery plays). Chapter Five investigates
       "the Devil's role in the dramatization of two social concerns of the
       late Middle Ages: juridical affairs and anti-Semitic prejudice."

569   Baldinger, Kurt. "Die Coutumes und ihre Bedeutung für die
       Geschichte des französischen Wortschatzes." *ZRP*, 67 (1951), 3-48.

       A lexicon of nearly 150 French words drawn from vernacular
       legal sources (mainly fifteenth and sixteenth centuries).

570   Barrow, Sarah Field. "The Medieval Society Romances." Diss.
       Columbia University 1920.

       Studies French chivalresque and courtly society as depicted in the
       works of Beaumanoir, compiler of the *Coutumes de Beauvaisis*, and
       Jean Renart.

571   Bender, Karl-Heinz. *König und Vasall. Untersuchungen zur*
       "chanson de geste" des XII. Jahrhunderts. Studia Romanica, 13.
       Heidelberg: Winter, 1967.

       An important study of the political and legal elements in fifteen
       chansons de geste.

572   Benkov, Edith Joyce. "Les Fabliaux: jugements risibles." Diss.
       University of California at Los Angeles 1979.

       This dissertation deals with two aspects of the Old French
       fabliaux: (1) "the reduction of the 'divine answer' as manifested in
       the *chansons de geste* to the human question as it appears in those

fabliaux in which a judgment is an integral element of the plot" and
(2) "the emergence of the collaborating reader in a number of
fabliaux in which the reader is called upon by the narrator to supply a
judgment. It is through this direct address to the audience that the
human question is able to discover its voice." A comparison of the
fabliaux to the legal tracts of the period reveals the authors'
"thorough and complete knowledge of the judicial system...."

573   Bertoni, Giulio. "Riflessi di costumanze giuridiche nell'antica poesia
       di Provenza." *Archivum Romanicum*, 1 (1917), 4-20.

       Identifies a number of legal motifs and customs where one might
       least expect to find them—"among the flowers of the lyric and in the
       field of the imagination."

574   Birkett, G. C. "The Words for 'Deceit,' 'Treachery' and
       'Promise-Breaking' in Middle French." M.A. Thesis Manchester
       University 1965.

575   Bloch, R. Howard. *Medieval French Literature and Law*. Berkeley:
       University of California Press, 1977.

       The most elaborate study of the connection between literature
       and law in medieval France. Argues, among other things, "that all
       the major aristocratic forms—epic, courtly novel, and lyric—are
       deeply rooted in the evolving legal ethos of their time, and that many
       of the essential distinctions between them may be interpreted as
       divergent responses to a common legal crisis." Several of the
       chapters were published previously as separate essays [666-668].

576   Coulin, Alexander. *Der gerechtliche Zweikampf im altfranzösischen
       Prozess*. Berlin: Guttentag, 1906.

577   Daucé, Fernand. *L'Avocat vu par les littérateurs français*. [Thesis
       University of Rennes 1947.] Rennes: Imprimeries Oberthur, 1947.
       [Repeated 673.]

578   Delachenal, Roland. *Histoire des Avocats au Parlement de Paris,
       1300-1600*. Paris: E. Plon, Nourrit et cie, 1885.

       Chapter Sixteen (pp. 299-329) looks at the representations of
       lawyers in medieval French literature including the following authors
       and works: Jacques de Vitry, *Le Dit des avocats*, Eustache

Deschamps, Coquillart, the farce of *Pathelin*, Villon, the theatre of the Basoche, and various sermons and anecdotes.

579   Dessau, Adalbert. "L'Idée de la trahison au moyen âge et son rôle dans la motivation de quelques chansons de geste." *CCM*, 3, (1960), 23-26.

Traces the evolving idea of treason as a motivating factor in several *chansons de geste*. In the majority of cases, Dessau observes, the guilty party is not the vassal but rather the lord. What recourse did the wronged vassal have? According to a capitulary of Charlemagne—military reprisal. This right is rejected, however, by the revised ending (mid-twelfth century) of the *Raoul de Cambrai*, in which "a juridical solution hostile to the felon lord is replaced by a moral solution condemning the right of the vassal to vengeance against his seigneur." This shift in attitude, visible as well in the *Roman de Thèbes*, reflects certain changes taking place in the feudal structure itself of twelfth-century France.

580   Foerster, Wendelin. "Der Feuertod als Strafe in der altfrz. erzählenden Dichtung." *SzEP*, 50 (1913), 180-189.

A brief study of Celtic practice as the source of the burning at the stake motif in *Tristan* and other Old French narratives.

581   Fundenburg, George Baer. *Feudal France in the French Epic*. Princeton: Princeton University Press, 1918.

Divides the history of French epic poetry into three periods: pre-feudal (ninth century), feudal (tenth and eleventh centuries), and later feudal (twelfth century). Only the poetry of the feudal period—*Auberi le Bourgoing, Raoul de Cambrai*, the cycle of *Garin le Loherain*, including the *Garin, Mort Garin, Gerbert de Metz*, and *Anseis de Metz*—"is a direct outgrowth of the epoch in which it originated." Only in this poetry will we find an accurate and unselfconscious representation of contemporary life and manners, geography and politics, customs and institutions.

582   Gersbach, Markus. "Eine altfranzösische Formel zu einem Gottesurteil." *Vox Romanica*, 24 (1965), 64-75.

Edits, with commentary, one of the oldest prose texts in

French—the ritual formula spoken before a trial by "the judgment of God."

583   Griffin, Parker Currier. "Chivalric Institutions at the Court of Burgundy as Reflected in the Life of Jacques de Lalaing: A Study of the Epoch of Philippe le Bon." Diss. University of Virginia 1955.

Under the Valois duke Philippe le Bon (1419-1467), observance of the chivalric code assumed the character of a national policy: the romances and epics of earlier centuries were used—just as a codification of law would be—as source-books for examples of social conduct. The life of Jacques de Lalaing, "one of the last and one of the greatest medieval *preux*," reflects the spirit of this period.

584   Halley, Anne M. "Arts, Law and Other Studies in Orleans in the Twelfth, Thirteenth and Fourteenth Centuries." Diss. City University of New York 1979.

Challenges the conclusion of Rashdall's *Universities of Europe in the Middle Ages*, Vol. 2 [63], that studies at Orleans were basically restricted to law after 1200, and emphasizes instead the continuity of literary studies there as documented in university statutes, contemporary literature, "and the even more compelling evidence found in student letters."

585   Helfer, Elisabeth. "Das Prozessmotiv in der Literatur des mittelalterlichen Frankreich." Diss. Erlangen 1923.

586   Junge, Adolf. "Über Gerichtsbeamte und Gerichtsverhältnisse in der Literatur des alten Frankreichs." Diss. Göttingen 1906.

587   Kendrick, Laura Jean. "Criticism of the Ruler, 1100-1400, in Provençal, Old French, and Middle English Verse." Diss. Columbia University 1978.

Analyzes the poetry of Marcabru, Bertran de Born, Rutebeuf, Eustache Deschamps, and Anglo-Norman authors with respect to literary tradition, ideals of kingship, and the contemporary social and political situation.

588 Knobloch, Heinrich. *Die Streitgedichte im Provenzalischen und Altfranzösischen*. Breslau: Korn, 1886.

589 Lacaze, Yvon. "Le Rôle des traditions dans la genèse d'un sentiment national au XVe siècle: La Bourgogne de Philippe le Bon." *Bibliothèque de l'Ecole de Chartes*, 129 (1972 [for 1971]), 303-385.

Emphasizes the important role played by poets and chroniclers as propagandists for the policies of Philippe le Bon, duke of Burgundy.

590 Langlois, Charles-Victor. *La Vie en France au moyen âge*. 4 vols. Paris: Hachette, 1924.

Volume One notes incidentally that French literature of the Middle Ages reflects the status of law at the time.

591 Leibecke, Otto. *Der verabredete Zweikampf in der altfranzösischen Litteratur*. Göttingen: Dieterich, 1905.

592 Lian, Andrew-Peter. "Les Procédés comiques des fabliaux." Diss. University of Paris-IV 1971.

593 Marquiset, Jean. *Les Gens de justice dans la littérature*. Paris: Librairie Générale de Droit et de Jurisprudence, 1967.

Chapter Two illustrates the satirical treatment of law in medieval French literature, with excerpts from Bozon, Villon, *La Farce de Maistre Pierre Pathelin*, and the sermons of Michel Menot and Olivier Maillard.

594 Meneghetti, Maria Luisa. "*Conseil des Barons:* L'Oratoria deliberativa dall'epopea al romanzo." *Retorica e Politica. Atti del II Convegno Italo-Tedesco* (Bressanone, 1974). Ed. D. Goldin. Padua: Liviana Editrice, 1977, pp. 43-54.

Examines the "informal" rhetoric of deliberative discourse in narrative French verse from the *Chanson de Roland* to Wace's *Brut*. Meneghetti is sensitive throughout to the legal significance of words used in the council scenes. For example, the discussion in *Roland* (laisses XIV, XV, and XVI) resembles "un *plait* giudiziario, immagine del resto corroborata dall'uso di verbi 'tecnici' (*otroier, cuntredire*)." Notes in investigating the rigid, formal structure of the *jugement* in *Wace* that the assembly in the work "è invero ur autentico *conseil*...."

595   Oulmont, Charles. *Les Débats du clerc et du chevalier dans la littérature poétique du moyen âge*. Paris: Champion, 1911; rpt Geneva: Slatkine, 1974.

This work consists of two parts: (1) an analysis of the genre from several aspects—historical context, literary genealogy, conventiona elements, and so forth; (2) an anthology of examples from primary texts. Although the genre lends itself to the development of lega themes [cf. 602], Oulmont does not explore its evolution from thi point of view.

596   Ourliac, Paul. "Troubadours et juristes." *CCM,* 8 (1965), 159-177.

Distinguishes among the troubadours three successive attitude toward the law: (1) a feeling of solidarity with the social and juridica order; (2) then criticism and even hatred toward a society that nc longer included them; and (3) grave misgivings about the restoratior of Roman law in southern France in the thirteenth century, a movement to which they opposed more rigid concepts taken from the moral law. Ourliac highlights a number of legal themes and terms ir the poetry of Guillaume de Poitiers, Peire Ramon, Marcabru, anc especially Peire Cardenal.

597   Pfeffer, M. "Die Formalitäten des gottesgerichtlichen Zweikampf: in der altfranzösischen Epik." *ZRP*, 9 (1885), 1-74.

An influential attempt to establish the detailed procedure of the Old French trials by combat through an examination of legal text and various epic poems. Notes that eleven steps were legally sanctioned and generally followed: 1. Accusation before the counci of barons; 2. Challenge and acceptance of the challenge; 3. Taking o hostages; 4. Night vigil in a church; 5. Mass; 6. Confession; 7 Swearing of an oath; 8. Proclamation of the bans; 9. Combat; 10 Punishment of the loser; 11. Judgment on (or freedom for) the hostages.

598   Riedel, F. Carl. *Crime and Punishment in the Old French Romances* New York: Columbia University Press, 1938.

Seeks to explain the crucial function of crime as a theme ir nearly two dozen Old French romances. Using Beaumanoir's *Coutumes de Beauvaisis* (1280-83) as his main authority, Riedel concludes that the romances reflect "with a fair degree of accuracy the actual procedure used in the twelfth and thirteenth centuries." Particularly interesting is the author's discussion of treason and the problem of intent. The book is organized under the following chapter titles: Criminal Law in the Thirteenth Century, Criminal Law in the Old French Romances, Moral Law in the Old French Romances, and Literary Significance of Crime and Criminals in the Romances.

599 Rossman, Vladimir R. *Perspectives of Irony in Medieval French Literature*. The Hague: Mouton, 1975.

The author's purpose is to distinguish the various types of irony at work in Old French literature, with particular emphasis on that type now thought of as "modern." The discussion occasionally touches upon legal process as a context for irony, e.g., Ganelon's trial in the *Chanson de Roland* (pp. 78-85) and Iseut's ordeal in Béroul's *Tristan* (pp. 85-93).

600 Rousset, Paul. "La Croyance en la justice immanente à l'époque féodale." *MA*, 54 (1948), 225-248.

A general treatment of the concept of immanent justice as seen in twelfth and thirteenth-century chronicles (e.g., Raoul Glaber, Orderic Vital, *Miracles de Saint-Benoît*). The recurring phrase *peccatis exigentibus* sums up a nearly universal concept of history during the period: all catastrophes are the result of sin. The same concept, however, underlies the practice of judicial combat, essentially an effort "to force God to indicate on which side justice lies." (Literary examples include the *Chanson de Roland* and *Fierabras*.) Rousset explains the prevalence of the concept by reference to "primitive" thinking and the influence of the Old Testament.

601 Scott, Nora Kay Burmester. "The Thematic Structure of the Twelfth Century Provençal *Canso*." Diss. University of Michigan 1972.

On the basis of the poetry of Guillaume IX (the first known troubadour), Marcabru, Bernart de Ventadorn, Raimbaut d'Aurenga, and Arnaut Daniel, Scott proposes that the underlying composition of the twelfth century *canso* "is that of a persuasive argument." Models described in Chap. 4 show "the contractual relationship of vassalage which forms the grounds for many legal cases of the Middle Ages; the feudal court system on the baronial level; "courts of love"; the *tenso*; and the *partimen*. Chapter 5 treats as a model the structure of argumentative discourse as contained in the *Rhetorica ad Herennium*.

602   Scully, Terence Peter. "The Love Debate in Mediaeval French Literature with Special Reference to Guillaume de Machaut." Diss. University of Toronto 1966.

Follows the shift of interest in the love debate from courtly love to casuistry. The first love debates proper are found in the *clerc-chevalier* cycle of poems (twelfth to thirteenth centuries). A change of emphasis in the mid-fourteenth century can be attributed to one poet: Guillaume de Machaut. He discovered the genre's potential for parody, and in his *Jugement dou roy le Behaingne* and *Jugement dou roy de Navarre* he "follows the main lines of formal scholastic and juridical debates." By the second quarter of the fifteenth century, the interest was centered entirely on the debate, "the procedure of which is authentically and in detail that of a legal trial."

603   _____, ed. *Le Court d'Amours de Mahieu le Poirier et la Suite anonyme de la "Court d'Amours."* Waterloo, Ont.: Wilfrid Laurier University Press, 1976.

An edition of two poems based on the "Court of Love" motif. In that of Mahieu le Poirier, some thirty-two figures bring their complaints and problems into Love's court "and in turn receive official decisions pronounced by the bailiff or by his assessors." In the anonymous sequel, all the lovers are expelled by Envy, who sets up his own court. Scully's notes contain several references to contemporary legal practice.

604   Thompson, James Westfall. "Catharist Social Ideas in Medieval French Romance." *RR*, 27 (1936), 99-104.

Ascribes the favorable portrayal of bastards in French romance (e.g., Bel Inconnu, Gawain's son Guigins, the son of Bohort, Galahad) to Catharist social and moral ideas. "Feudal tradition and practice favored interfamily marriages for the purpose of preventing the splitting up and diffusion of the lands of the house. But in 1066 the Church condemned the age-long principles of the Roman law with regard to consanguinity and established a new series of prohibited degrees....Were these changes made in the interest of social morality? Or was the Church, a great landholder, interested in breaking up the great fiefs?'' At any rate the Catharists, not acknowledging the authority of the Church, continued to ''live Roman law''; and their more liberal attitude toward marriage, Thompson argues, permeates the romance tradition.

Ami et Amile

605 Calin, William. *The Epic Quest: Studies in Four Old French "Chansons de Geste."* Baltimore: Johns Hopkins University Press, 1966.

As in numerous other *chansons de geste*, a dominant trait in *Ami et Amile* is "the point of feudal law." Calin identifies three legal issues raised by the poem: whether Amile is guilty of the charge that he dishonored Belissant; whether Ami's leprosy can be justified according to the theory of immanent justice; and whether Amile deserves condemnation for sacrificing his sons in order to cure Ami. In each case the hero is condemned by the letter but acquitted by the spirit of the law. "The discussion of juridical problems, crucial to so many *chansons de geste*, is seen to be hollow. The poet cuts through them to propose a totally different attitude toward life."

606 Dembowski, Peter. "Ami's Crime and Punishment. A Problem in Interpretation." *Essays in Romance Philology from the University of Chicago in Honor of the XII International Congress of Romance Linguistics and Philology.* Chicago: Univ. of Chicago Departments of Romance Languages and Literatures and of Linguistics, 1968, pp. 24-40.

Dembowski's purpose is "fundamentally method-ological"—that is, to show the interpretative value of materials external to the text (i.e., Rodulfus Tortarius's *Epistula II ad Bernardum* and the *Vita Amici et Ameli carissimorum*). A comparison of *Ami et Amile* with these works shows that the author injected the theme of the tricked oath and connected it with the problem of disobedience to God's will. "The legal casuistry is thus a necessary element in our version."

607   Modersohn, Hermann. *Die Realien in den altfranzösischen Chansons de geste "Amis et Amiles" und "Jourdains de Blaivies."* [Diss. Münster 1886.] Leipzig: Koehler, 1886.

Comments on legal aspects of family and feudal relationships in the two works. Following Pfeffer's eleven steps [597], he also provides a detailed examination of trial by combat.

Béroul (See *Tristan*)

Bible de Guiot de Provins

608   Meynial, Eduard. "Remarques sur la réaction populaire contre l'invasion du droit romain en France aux XIIe et XIIIe siècles." *RF*, 23 (1907), 557-584.

Illustrates popular and ecclesiastical reactions to the Reception of Roman law as reflected in a number of literary works—"Le dit des mais," poems by Gautier de Coinci, d'Andeli's *Bataille des Sept Arts*, and above all the *Bible de Guiot de Provins*, a rich satire on the legal establishment.

Brisebarre, Jean

609   Taylor, Steven Millen. "A Critical Study and Edition of the Unpublished *Le Dit de l'Evesque et de Droit* by Jean Brisebarre." Diss. Wayne State University 1976.

Brisebarre, a fourteenth-century *trouvère*, "made a major contribution to the genre of the *dit*, an allegorical poem in octosyllabic verse sharing a moral insight with the reader or listener." This *dit*, which presents the personified Virtues and Vices in the roles of attorneys and legal advisors, "is a unique vernacular transcription of ecclesiastical and secular court procedure in the early fourteenth century." Taylor includes a discussion of its influence on subsequent legal satire in France.

Chanson de Guillaume

610 Györy, Jean. "Le Refrain de la *Chanson de Guillaume*." *CCM*, 3 (1960), 32-41.

Finds in the puzzling refrain of the *Chanson de Guillaume* a reflection of the peace movement or popular attempt to enforce a "truce of God." In fact, the poem's origin is "more intimately tied to the *trêve de Dieu*...than any other *chanson de geste*." A number of its motifs are seen to point to interdicts concerning combat that were issued by various synods and councils of France between the tenth and twelfth centuries; and these interdicts provide a basis for interpreting the principal difficulty of the text, the expression *bataille Dé*, which Györy takes to refer simply to the judicial duel. The unique appearance of the phrase in the *Chanson de Guillaume* "proves the poet's preoccupation with distinguishing collective and public battle from the individual and private duel."

Chanson de Roland

611 Baist, Gottfried. "Der gerichtliche Zweikampf, nach seinem Ursprung und im Rolandslied." *RF*, 5 (1890), 436-448.

Looks for possible origins of the judicial duels of the *Chanson de Roland* in Germanic law. Finds three details that do not correspond to later French law, as described by Beaumanoir and others: the trial is fought by champions and not by the actual parties involved (a precedent seen to have derived from Burgundian laws); there is no oath before combat; and Ganelon is required to find thirty hostages or *pleges*.

612 Bercovi-Huard, Carole. "L'Exclusion du sarrasin dans la chanson de Roland: Vocabulaire et idéologie. 'Co est une gent ki unches ben ne volt' (v. 3231)." *Exclus et systèmes d'exclusion dans la littérature et la civilisation médiévales*. Collection "Senefiance," 5. Aix-en-Provence: Cuer Ma, and Paris: Champion, 1978, pp. 345-361.

The *Chanson de Roland* depicts two parallel worlds, Christian and Saracen. Although bound by the same feudal ideals as their Christian enemies, the Saracens are excluded from society as "felons" and "traitors." In order to become true members of

society they must renounce "la false lei" and accept "la lei de
Chrestiens."

613   Bresslau, H. "Rechtsalterthümer aus dem Rolandsliede." *Archiv
       für das Studium der neueren Sprachen und Literaturen*, 48 (1871)
       291-306.

       Like other early studies of *Rechtsaltertümer* [139], Bresslau's
       article is concerned less with literature as such than with its function
       as a mirror of social and legal institutions: kingship, vassalage
       family, and criminal law.

614   Brook, Leslie C. "Le 'Forfait' de Roland dans le procès de Ganelon
       encore sur un vers obscur de la *Chanson de Roland*." *Société
       Rencesvals IVe Congrés*. Heidelberg: Winter, 1969, pp. 120-128.

       An attempt to justify the reading "Rollant me *forfist* en or e er
       aveir" in Ganelon's self-defense, and to elucidate the meaning—
       partly legal—of the word *forfist* [cf. 623].

615   Burger, André. "Le Rire de Roland." *CCM*, 3 (1960), 2-11.

       Roland's laugh in derision of Ganelon "sets in motion
       irremediably, the drama of Roncevaux." Humiliated, Ganelon issues
       his "desfi." "It is clear that in this quarrel Roland is the offender
       and that Ganelon, the offended, has a right to vengeance."
       Tragically, he is unable to avenge himself on Roland and at the same
       time remain faithful to his emperor.

616   Burrell, Margaret A. "Ganelon's Act of Treason." *Olifant*, 4 (1976),
       84-86.

       Qualifies Stranges' definition of Ganelon's guilt [633]. In
       attacking Roland, one of the Twelve Peers protected by
       Charlemagne's personal *maimbour*, Ganelon was guilty of an
       offense against the king himself. His crime "should ultimately be
       judged not by formal feudal law, which proves inadequate, but by a
       custom which is prefeudal, yet still powerfully alive."

617   Forsyth, Elliott. *La Tragédie française de Jodelle à Corneille
       (1553-1640): Le Thème de la vengeance*. Paris: Nizet, 1962.

       Chapter 1 includes a brief history of attitudes toward revenge, as
       seen in the legal and literary sources of medieval France.

518   Gérard, Alb[ert]. "L'Axe Roland-Ganelon: valeurs en conflit dans la *Chanson de Roland.*" *MA*, 75, (1969), 445-465.

"The tragic error of Roland was to have subordinated the good of the nation (that is, the victory of France) to his personal glory and to that of his family; similarly, the juridical crime of Ganelon is to have placed his right to private vengeance above his duty to the person of his sovereign." Gérard quotes from Beaumanoir's *Les coutumes de Beauvaisis* in order to clarify the precise nature of Ganelon's treason.

519   Gibellini, Pietro. "Droit et philologie: L'Ordre des laisses dans l'épisode de la colère de Ganelon dans la *Chanson de Roland.*" *Revue Romane*, 7 (1972), 233-247.

Drawing upon the evidence of the council scenes, Gibellini attempts to present an integrated view of the juridical system in the *Roland* in order to confirm the Oxford version's sequence of *laisses* in the episode known as the anger of Ganelon. The "anti-Oxfordian" manuscripts "have a tendency to change all the passages that deal with the role of the assembly and to attribute to the king an absolute power, because they no longer understand the primitive juridical structure of the *chanson.*"

520   Goldin, Frederick. "Die Rolle Ganelons und das Motiv der Worte." *Beiträge zum Romanischen Mittelalter* [*ZRP* Anniversary Volume]. Tübingen: Niemeyer, 1977, pp. 128-155.

Analyzing Ganelon's speech at the first council, Goldin suggests that he intended from the beginning to betray Roland. The trial by combat settled the boundary between revenge and betrayal, and Ganelon died a traitor's death.

521   Halverson, John. "Ganelon's Trial." *Speculum*, 42 (1967), 661-669.

The poem raises one of the most essential questions of the earlier Middle Ages: Where is loyalty due? For the usual answer—to one's honor and then to the tribe—Thierry substitutes a new one—to one's king, to right, to God's justice. "The issue of political loyalties is at least momentarily resolved in the supremacy of the monarchial prerogative." The clash is ultimately between Germanic tradition and a new pattern of social organization that "asserts the precedence of a loyalty higher than the traditional bonds, which in turn implies a denial of the vendetta ethic for the sake of the common good."

622   Herman, Gerald. "V. 578 and the Question of Ganelon's Guilt in *la Chanson de Roland*." *Romance Notes*, 14 (1973), 624-630.

Despite Ganelon's trial defense, in which he claims merely to have taken revenge on Roland and not to have committed treason against the emperor, his words in verse 578 ("Carles verrat sun gran orguill cadeir") suggest otherwise. "Implicit in the words 'sun gran orguill' is a deep and smoldering feeling of resentment against Charlemagne."

623   Jenkins, T. Atkinson. "Why Did Ganelon Hate Roland?" *PMLA* 36 (1921), 119-133.

Argues on the basis of a new reading of Ganelon's words in line 3758 ("Roll' me forfist en or & en aveir") that Ganelon's "primary motive, the real spring of the action" was his envy of Roland' greater wealth. In support of this thesis, Jenkins would eliminate the pronoun *me* on metrical grounds and emend *forfist* to *sorfist*, "in overweening in, arrogant, intolerably boastful about" [cf. 614] Jenkins also considers the laws governing council procedure in order to explain the suddenness of Ganelon's anger at his nomination by Roland for the mission to Spain.

624   _____, ed. *La Chanson de Roland*. Boston: Heath 1924.

Notes that the phrase used by Ganelon, "Jo ne vos aim nïent" (l. 306), is a legal one, "still in use with diplomats who speak of 'friendship' and 'unfriendly' acts" (p. 31).

625   Jones, George Fenwick. *The Ethos of the Song of Roland* Baltimore: Johns Hopkins University Press, 1963.

Among other semantic and ethical influences on the *Chanson de Roland*, Jones considers the strong influence of law. "While fully at home in the language of literature," he says, "many terms in the *SR* clearly derive from the language of law, and some of these retain their precise legal meanings." In order to infer something about the ethical values of the poet and his audience, Jones examines such legally significant terms as *amer*, *dreit*, *tort*, *honte*, *orgoill*, etc.

626 _____. "Friendship in the *Chanson de Roland*." *MLQ*, 24 (1963), 88-98.

"The purpose of this paper is to show that the *Chanson* often uses *amer* in a non-emotive sense, namely, that of making or keeping peace or forming alliances, and that its cognates can also have diplomatic or political rather than intimate or personal connotations." Like a modern sovereign state, Jones suggests, the medieval individual protected himself with all sorts of personal and political alliances. "Although these alliances were conventionally expressed by the words *amer, amis, amur*, and *amistiet*, they were often a matter of practicality rather than affection." The word *amer* is used when Ganelon gives his "desfi" to Roland [cf. 624], when he forms an alliance with Marsile, and when Roland confirms his bond with Oliver.

627 Keller, Hans-Erich. "The *Song of Roland*: a Mid-Twelfth Century Song of Propaganda for the Capetian Kingdom." *Olifant*, 3 (1976), 242-258.

Assigns a date of about 1150 to the composition of the Oxford version of the poem—partly on the basis of legal attitudes expressed therein. Following Halverson [621], Keller interprets the trial of Ganelon as "a denial of the vendetta ethic for the sake of the common good." The poet's emphasis throughout on royal sovereignty and judicial power is explained as propaganda for the policies of Louis VII.

628 _____. "The *Song of Roland* and Its Audience." *Olifant*, 6 (1979), 259-274.

Just as the original version of the *Roland* was composed "in order to further Capetian interests," so its redaction in England was meant to support the policies of Henry II. Indeed, the prototype of the Oxford *Roland* "achieved its popularity due to the political ambitions of Henry II, since they aimed precisely at the thaumaturgical function of kingship advocated by the poem—especially in its last part, the trial of Ganelon."

629 Köhler, Erich. *"Conseil des barons" und "jugement des barons": Epische Fatalität und Feudalrecht im altfranzösischen Rolandslied.* Sitzungsberichte der Heidelberger Akademie der Wissenschaften. Phil.-historische Klasse. 1968 (4 Abh.). Heidelberg: Winter, 1968.

An elaborate study of feudal law in the *Roland*, organized around the distinction between the institutions of *conseil des barons* (the vassal's duty to give *consilium* or advice) and *jugement des barons* (*judicium parium* or judgment by peers). Köhler argues that the poet was less concerned to give a true representation of Carolingian practice than to comment on his own period.

630   Mickel, Emanuel J., Jr. "The Thirty *Pleges* for Ganelon." *Olifant*, 6 (1979), 293-304.

Attempts to answer the following questions: "Why did Ganelon need thirty *pleges* and Thierry none? What do the thirty *pleges* represent in legal terms? What precedence and significance is there in the hanging of the thirty?" The solution lies in Germanic law. The *pleges* are not merely bondsmen but compurgators or oath-helpers. In effect they "have pledged their support to an open and shut case of treason."

631   Payen, Jean Charles. "Une Poétique du génocide joyeux: devoir de violence et plaisir de tuer dans la *Chanson de Roland*." *Olifant*, 6 (1979), 226-236.

Sees the problem of Ganelon's guilt in terms of a conflict between the legal right to vendetta and a higher obligation to the safety and preservation of Christendom.

632   Ruggieri, Ruggero M. *Il processo di Gano nella Chanson de Roland*. Florence: Sansoni, 1936.

Seeks to demonstrate the archaism of the procedure of Ganelon's trial, arguing that his role in the *Chanson* is the nucleus around which the poem was constructed. In the judicial duel, the legal process is seen to be indistinguishable from the divine process, "human will from godly will, positive law from divine law."

633   Stranges, John A. "The Character and the Trial of Ganelon, a New Appraisal." *Romania*, 96 (1975), 333-367.

"The purpose of this study is to penetrate the intricacy of Ganelon's character, to put to light the psychology which has motivated him in his behavior, and to devote particular attention to the trial and to its technicalities." Stranges holds that Ganelon had every right to avenge his humiliation by Roland at the first council—he was not a traitor. As the trial makes clear, however, his right to private revenge conflicted with his higher duty of service to the emperor. [Reply in 616.]

634 Thomas, Jacques. "La traîtrise de Ganelon." *Romanica Gandensia*, 16 (1976), 91-117.

Modern attempts to rehabilitate Ganelon's character, beginning as early as Ruggieri's monograph [632], will not stand up to a careful reading of the text. Ganelon is "essentially evil." It is his nature, and not the situation, that explains his treachery.

635 Wais, Kurt. "Rolands Tränen um Ganelon." *Australian Journal of French Studies*, 6 (1969), 465-483.

Deals in passing with the legal ramifications of Ganelon's threat of revenge before the first Council of Barons.

Chrétien de Troyes

636 Cohen, Gustave. "Le Duel judiciaire chez Chrétien de Troyes." *Annales de l'Université de Paris*, 8 (1933), 510-527.

Cohen compares certain details of the duels in *Charrette* and *Yvain* (e.g., the role of the judges, the *quarantaine le roi*, the formal initiation of combat, the swearing of an oath on relics, etc.) with the juridical information available from the *Assises de Jérusalem*, *Assises de Romanie*, *Coutumes de Beauvaisis*, *Coutume d'Amiens*, and certain royal *Ordonnances*. One is struck, he concludes, by the exactitude with which Chrétien has transposed into the chimerical realm of fiction "la réalité juridique des seigneuries contemporaines."

637 Euler, Heinrich. *Recht und Staat in den Romanen des Crestien von Troyes*. [Diss. Marburg 1906.] Marburg: Heinrich Bauer, 1906.

Essentially an annotated anthology of excerpts that illustrate legal or political themes in Chrétien's Arthurian works. The examples are organized in the following groups: feudal obligations, social structure, brotherhood in arms, rules of combat, family, criminal law, trial procedures, perjury, and courtly love.

638   Grimbert, Joan Tasker. "Treachery and Conflict of Loyalties in Chrétien de Troyes." [Resumé of paper given at the Eleventh Triennial Conference, Exeter, 1975.] *BBSIA*, 27 (1975), 226-227.

    "The purpose of the study is to analyze the concept and role of treachery in the romances of Chrétien de Troyes, paying particular attention to the resolution of potential conflicts of loyalties. Three basic types of treachery are discussed: 1) breach of allegiance with respect to one's liege lord or kin, 2) failure to honor a self-imposed pledge, 3) betrayal of trust in love situations."

639   Jonin, Pierre. "Le Vasselage de Lancelot dans le *Conte de la Charrette*." *MA*, 58 (1952), 281-298.

    Taking Chrétien's *Conte de la Charrette* as his chief example, Jonin questions the presumed analogy between feudal vassalage and the lover's service to his lady. Despite certain shared phrases (e.g., one is the "man" of another), feudal homage and amorous homage are based on totally different hierarchies of social, moral and religious values. "The two systems cannot coexist and the application of the second supposes the ruin of the first."

640   _____. "Aspects de la vie sociale au XIIe siècle dans *Yvain*." *IL*, 16 (1964), 47-54.

    Includes a detailed explanation of the technical aspects of the "Pucelle déshéritée" episode in *Yvain* (inheritance laws, appeal for novel disseisin, trial by battle, etc.). Chrétien appears to have been meticulously faithful to the law of his day.

641   Köhler, Erich. "Le Rôle de la 'coutume' dans les romans de Chrétien de Troyes." *Romania*, 81 (1960), 386-397.

    The various "coutumes" of the court of Arthur and of other monarchs in the works of Chrétien provide a basis for juridical order and allow the exposition of realistic medieval themes. Included among these customary laws are hunting ordinances in *Erec*; the law of the "don" (whereby vassals were legally given freedom of action); and the statutes which governed lord-vassal relationships.

642   Mandel, Jerome. "Proper Behavior in Chrétien's *Charrette*: The Host-Guest Relationship." *FR*, 48 (1975), 683-689.

Mandel characterizes the *Charrette* as a "poem about order, about the relation between people in society, and about behavior proper in those relationships which lie at the very heart of medieval society." All of the characters were meant to be judged by the standard of order. "Bademagu is a truth-character....He speaks for order, for courtesy, for proper behavior at all times." Meleagant is "the Grand Perverter...antithetical to order and, hence, to organized society." By subordinating all else to the courtly love relationship, Lancelot "reveals his lack of concern for order" and thus deserves the humiliation of the cart.

643   Matthias, Anna-Susanna. "Yvains Rechtsbrüche." *Beiträge zum romanischen Mittelalter*. [*ZRP* anniversary volume.] Tübingen: Niemeyer, 1977, pp. 156-192.

Finds Yvain guilty of six major crimes: 1. he leaves Arthur's court without permission; 2. he duels in violation of the "treuga Dei"; 3. he duels without giving a formal "desfi"; 4. he violates the general rule against killing one's opponent in a feud; 5. he pursues the quarrel even after his opponent, mortally wounded, has conceded him the victory; and 6. he doesn't admit to his actions. Matthias supports each point by reference to the laws and legal treatises of the period (Beaumanoir's *Coutumes de Beauvaisis*, *Le Grand Coutumier de Normandie*, *Le Livre de jostice et de plet*, etc.). She believes, however, that Yvain's marriage and voluntary exile atone for his crime.

644   Riquer, Martín de. "Un aspecto jurídico en *Li Contes del Graal*." *Romania*, 82 (1961), 403-405.

Sees influence of Spanish legal codes in vss. 7371-7392 and 8411-8413 of the *Contes*. After the defeat of the nephew of Greoreas in single combat, Gauvain is reminded by the *notonier* that it is he, and not Gawain, who has the right to the horse of the conquered man: "je doi avoir le destrier" (v. 7390). Later, after Gauvain's conquest of another knight, Chrétien writes simply, "mes sire Gauvains an prant/ la fiance et puis si le rant/ au notonier qui l'atandoit" (vss. 8411-8413). Such details are consistent with the *Fuero real de España*, promulgated in 1255, which states that the horse and arms of him who is conquered *por alevoso* "as treacherous" should become the property of the king's *mayordomo*.

645   Rohr, R. "Zur 'Schuld' Percevals." *Mélanges de philologie romane offerts à Charles Camproux.* Montpellier: Centre d'Estudis Occitans, 1978, 1:459-468.

       Discusses Perceval's "fault" in the context of natural law, especially in terms of the commandment "honor thy father and mother."

646   Shirt, David J. "Chrétien de Troyes et une coutume anglaise." *Romania,* 94 (1973), 178-195.

       The primary concern of this article is the function of the cart in *Le Chevalier de la charrette.* In recounting the episode of the cart, Shirt argues, Chrétien had in mind an English form of punishment for petty offenses: the wrongdoer was bound to a *tumbril,* a kind of stool on wheels, and pulled through the streets past a mocking public. But Chrétien also had in mind the French "charrete patibulaire," a wagon used to transport felons to the gallows. His *charrete* is thus a fusion of two instruments of punishment—one associated with *causae minores,* the other with *causae majores*—and the invention allows him to stress the dual and contradictory obligations of Lancelot as devoted lover of Guinevere and faithful vassal of Arthur. "Seen in this manner, the episode of the *charrete* plays a very significant role in the action of the poem—a role that justifies the title which Chrétien gives to his poem...."

Couronnement de Louis

647   Frappier, Jean. "Réflexions sur les rapports des chansons de geste et de l'histoire." *ZRP,* 73 (1957), 1-19.

       A stimulating look at the way in which historical fact is incorporated—and often transformed—in the *chansons de geste.* For example, the coronation scene in the beginning of the *Couronnement de Louis* is clearly based on a ninth-century chronicle (Thegan's *Vita Hludowici imperatoris*), which describes the coronation of Louis the Pious by his father Charlemagne (813); yet the twelfth-century poet has altered the account to conform more nearly to the coronation of Louis VII in his own time (1131). "Thus, the ceremony of Rheims is superimposed on that of Aix-la-Chapelle in the poet's imagination; he has fused in his epic picture two ages, the Carolingian and the Capetian." His purpose was undoubtedly political: to support the Capetian claim to hereditary kingship.

648   Van Waard, Roelof. "*Le Couronnement de Louis* et le principe de l'hérédité de la couronne." *Neophilologus*, 30 (1946), 52-58.

Sees the *Couronnement* as a chapter in the history of the struggle between two political principles: heredity and election. Probably written during the troubled era of 1131-1137, when the Capetian dynasty's whole fortune rested on the slender shoulders of a boy, the future King Louis VII, the poem recalls the exemplary role taken by William as protector of Charlemagne's son, Louis the Pious, during his minority. May we not suppose, then, that a desire to maintain the Capetian line of succession led the poet "to write a *roman* that would celebrate fidelity to the legitimate and hereditary king, even if that king was young, weak, timid?"

Cuvelier

649   Faucon, Jean-Claude. "Un Curieux duel judiciaire rapporté par Cuvelier." *Romania*, 100 (1979), 382-397.

Cuvelier's history of the life and exploits of Bertrand Du Guesclin raises a curious question: "How can the judgment of God manifest itself in a judicial duel, when the combatants are both Jews and scoundrels?" Cuvelier reports that during the battle, a dark cloud suddenly arose; lightning struck both men, consuming them to the bone; and at this "sign" from God 1,600 Jews had themselves baptized the same day. The story has no basis in fact. It seems to serve two purposes: as a burlesque of the judicial combat and as an expression of anti-Semitic feeling.

Daurel et Beton

650   Caluwé, Jacques de. "Les Liens 'féodaux' dans *Daurel et Beton*."
       Études de philologie romane et d'histoire littéraire offertes à Jules
       Horrent à l'occasion de son soixantième anniversaire. Liège: n. p.,
       1980, pp. 105-114.

       Instead of a clearly defined hierarchy of feudal relations, an
       analysis of this *chanson de geste* reveals a social framework of
       "egalitarian relations (*convenientiae*) and of spontaneous feudal
       service." The study is confined to the relations between Beuve and
       Gui, Beuve and Charlemagne, and Gui and Charlemagne.

Drama (See also individual plays)

651   Bryant, Lucie M. "La Satire du droit et de la justice dans le théâtre
       comique de la fin du moyen-âge et du XVIe siècle." Diss. University
       of Kansas 1973.

       The author distinguishes two different comic theaters. The
       comedies of the Pléiade, elite and erudite, contain very little satire
       against the administration of justice. However, the popular comic
       theater, born among the lower classes in the fourteenth century,
       "attacks with verve the social injustices which are corrupting the
       country." The satire (at least before 1550) is directed mainly against
       litigants and lawyers; judges and institutions are generally respected.

652   Cohen, Gustave. *Le Théâtre en France au moyen âge*. 2 vols. Paris:
       Rieder, [1928]-1931.

       One of the early standard histories of medieval French drama.
       Cohen touches upon the legal theme in Rutebeuf's *Le Miracle de*
       Théophile; Eustache Deschamps' portrait of the advocate Maître
       Trubert; a fifteenth-century farce by Verconus, in which a single
       actor plays all the roles (gentleman, fool, melancholic, doctor,
       orator, advocate, pleader, and judge); the *Farce de Maistre Pierre*
       Pathelin—inspired (says Cohen) by the *Advocacie de Notre-Dame*
       and *Chapellerie de Notre-Dame de Bayeux*—and its imitations, *Le*
       Testament Pathelin and the *Nouveau Pathelin*.

653   Fabre, Adolphe. *Les Clercs du palais. Recherches historiques sur les Bazoches des Parlements & les Sociétés dramatiques des Bazochiens & des Enfants-sans-souci.* 2nd ed. Lyon: Scheuering, 1875.

A history of the society of Paris law clerks known as the Basoche and its contributions to French comedy of the fifteenth and sixteenth centuries. Among the works discussed are *La Farce de Maistre Pathelin, Le Testament de Pathelin, Le Cry de Gringoire,* and those of Martial d'Auvergne, André de la Vigne, Jean d'Abundance, Jean Bouchet, and Villon.

654   _____, ed. *Les Clercs du palais, la Farce du cry de la bazoche: Les légistes poètes, les complaintes et épitaphes du Roy de la Basoche.* Vienna: Savigné, 1882.

655   Harvey, Howard Graham. *The Theatre of the Basoche: The Contribution of the Law Societies to French Mediaeval Comedy.* Harvard Studies in Romance Languages, 17. Cambridge, Mass.: Harvard University Press, 1941.

Harvey states his purpose as follows: "The object of this book is to study, in the light of this professional attitude [i.e., of the Paris law clerks or "Basochiens"], the role played by the law and the lawyers in the medieval comic theatre." The scope is roughly 1450-1550, "the heyday of the theatre of the Basoche." Influence of the Basoche may be seen not only in the prevalence of legal terms in the comedy of the period—"the point of view from which a play is written is at least as good a clue." There is an almost universal respect for law and for the legal profession; "it is the shameless, quarrelsome, ridiculous litigants, and their stupid or malicious witnesses who bear the brunt of the satire." Harvey's admirable study illuminates a wide variety of related problems: the history and organization of the Basoche, its role in the writing and production of comedy, the authors' use of legal terms and concepts, and so forth [Harvey's chapter on *Pathelin* was published previously as a separate essay; see 675].

Ferget, Pierre

656   Robson, Walter Wilson, III. "*Le Procès belial a l'encontre de Jhesus*: A Critical Edition." Diss. University of Kansas 1972.

Pierre Ferget's *Le Procès Belial a l'encontre de Jhesus*, a French translation of Jacobus de Theramo's *Consolatio pauperum peccatorum*, "consists of a suit brought against Jesus by Belial who is acting in the name of all the devils of Hell." The suit seeks to recover possession of the souls lost by the devils at the Harrowing of Hell. Robson's introduction includes a discussion of the place of juridical debates and trials in medieval French literature, and the function of the trial in *Belial* specifically as a metaphor of the human condition. Ferget's translation was the source for several Provençal plays, notably *Lo Jutgamen general*.

Gerbert de Mez

657   Rossi, Marguerite. "La Réprobation sociale est-elle un critère d'exclusion? Les traitres dans *Gerbert de Mez*." *Exclus et systèmes d'exclusion dans la littérature et la civilisation médiévales*. Collection "Senefiance," 5. Aix-en-Provence: Cuer Ma, and Paris: Champion, 1978, pp. 27-40.

Because of their high social status, the traitors in *Gerbert de Mez* (Fromont and his son Fromondin) "are extraordinarily protected against all chastisement....Exclusion in the form of a judicial sentence against them seems inconceivable."

Lancelot en prose

658   Kennedy, Elspeth. "Social and Political Ideas in the French Prose *Lancelot*." *Medium Aevum*, 26 (1957), 90-106.

Comparing passages in *Lancelot* with passages in Beaumanoir's *Les Coutumes de Beauvaisis* and in the *Assises de Jérusalem*, Kennedy tries to authenticate the realism of the writer's treatment of kingship, chivalry, and the relation between lord and vassal.

659 York, Ernest C. "The Concept of Treason in the Prose *Lancelot*." *Kentucky Foreign Language Quarterly*, 12 (1965), 117-123.

> The study of twenty-five cases of "treason" (limited here to murder and crimes against women) in the prose *Lancelot* leads York to three major conclusions: (1) the work "depicts French law to a much greater extent than it does English law"; (2) "the French law prior to the twelfth century and of the earlier thirteenth century, as represented by the *Etablissements de Saint Louis*, is depicted more often than the later law of Beaumanoir"; and (3) "the reflections of these laws in the prose *Lancelot* support Frappier's theory of multiple authorship...."

Le Fèvre, Jean

660 Hasenohr-Esnos, Geneviève, ed. *Le Respit de la mort*. Paris: Picard, 1969.

> *Le Respit de la Mort* shows everywhere the legal background of its author, a "procureur en Parlement du roy nostre sire" and licentiate in both Roman and canon law ("in utroque jure"). The plot of the poem is "a judicial fiction taken from the theory of obligations." Death is seen as a debt that every man must pay on a day fixed by God. The title of the poem arises out of the efforts of the speaker (called upon to pay his debt) to obtain a "letter of respite"—a legal instrument in fourteenth-century France to block coercive action by one's creditors.

Marcadé, Eustache

661 Desobry, Jean. "Moine, juriste et compositeur de théâtre: Eustache Marcadé." *Bulletin trimestriel de la Société des Antiquaires de Picardie*, 4 (1967), 145-161.

> Pieces together a biographical account of this paradoxical figure: "le contemplatif qui se cantonne dans le droit ne perd jamais le sens des valeurs pécuniaires; le religieux qui devient rimeur se retrouve au milieu d'une 'court amoureuse'; le juriste qui se bat pour faire valoir ses titres les abandonne quand il a gagné son procès." The study ends with a review of the circumstantial evidence for Marcadé's authorship of the *Passion d'Arras*.

Marie de France

662   Francis, E. A. "The Trial in *Lanval*." *Studies in French Language and Mediaeval Literature Presented to Professor Mildred K. Pope by Pupils, Colleagues and Friends*. Manchester: University of Manchester Press, 1939, pp. 115-124.

A comparison of the trial scene in *Lanval* with that in the *Roman de Thèbes*. Although Marie may have been copying the trial of Daire in her *lai*, as Hoepffner argued [663], "it appears probable that she was affected also by models of legal procedure of a different kind." An analysis of the trial shows "how little her legal vocabulary corresponds to that of the *Thèbes* model and how closely to that used by Maitland [*History of English Law*] in description of actual trials."

663   Hoepffner, Ernst. "Pour la chronologie des *lais* de Marie de France." *Romania*, 59 (1933), 351-370, and 60 (1934), 36-66.

As part of a larger attempt to establish the chronology of Marie's works, Hoepffner argues that the trial in *Lanval* was inspired by the trial of Daire in the *Roman de Thèbes*. Several similarities are noted.

664   Rothschild, Judith Rice. "A *Rapprochement* between *Bisclavret* and *Lanval*." *Speculum*, 48 (1973), 78-88.

Discusses Marie's use of law as one of several analogues between *Bisclavret* and *Lanval*. Rothschild's primary concern is with the ramifications of the word *felunie* as used in *Bisclavret*.

665   Rychner, Jean, ed. *Le Lai de Lanval*. Geneva: Droz, and Paris: Minard, 1958.

This edition of the *Lanval* includes a detailed point-by-point discussion of the trial scene (pp. 78-84). More than fifty words and phrases are explained.

La Mort Artu

666   Bloch, R. Howard. "The Death of King Arthur and the Waning of the Feudal Age." *Orbis Litterarum*, 29 (1974), 291-305.

Examines *La Mort Artu* against the background of rapidly changing legal and social institutions of thirteenth-century France. Although politically a model of the feudal world, the "values and institutions—the judicial duel, entrapment *in flagrante delicto*, the system of vendetta and private war—no longer function to insure the unity of [Arthur's] realm."

667   _____. "From Grail Quest to Inquest: The Death of King Arthur and the Birth of France." *MLR*, 69 (1974), 40-55.

"The decline of Arthur's world reflects a crisis of values and institutions—in particular judicial procedures—that is traceable to the decline of feudalism in France in the century and a half that preceded the poem's composition." Bloch considers the two trial scenes in *La Mort*, concluding that they "only serve to undermine credence in the fundamental tenets of feudal justice." This reflects the historical transition from trial-by-combat, the *judicium Dei*, to the trial of the courtroom based on established procedure.

668   _____. "The Text as Inquest: Form and Function in the Pseudo-Map Cycle." *Mosaic*, 8 (1975), 107-119.

In *La Mort Artu* "we detect the basic formula of judicial inquest.... [The work] is a contemporary crisis of values and institutions, especially feudal judicial procedure...." Bloch notes the strong affinity between inquest and literary creation during the period, and says that the creative process "serves exactly the same purpose, which is the substitution of a verbalized non-confrontive means of resolving conflict for a directly confrontive one."

669   entry deleted

670   Vale, Juliet. "Law and Diplomacy in the Alliterative *Morte Arthure.*" *NMS*, 23 (1979), 31-46.

    Includes a comparison of Maillart's approach in the *Roman du Comte d'Anjou* to that used in the alliterative *Morte Arthure*. Like the English poet, Maillart (a notary in the French royal chancery) inherited his subject matter and transformed it "with a remarkably similar emphasis on contemporary legal issues." (The article notes that Gervais de Bus, author of the *Roman de Fauval*, was also a notary in the French royal chancery.) [Item repeated 317.]

Pathelin, Farce de Maistre

671   Brévonnes, Roland, and Francine Rachmühl. *Une Oeuvre, la "Farce de Maistre Pierre Pathelin." Un thème, la satire de la justice.* Paris: Hatier, 1978.

672   Cons, Louis. *L'Auteur de la Farce de Pathelin.* Princeton: Princeton University Press, and Paris: Les Presses Universitaires de France, 1926.

    Denies that the legal vocabulary of the farce points toward any association with the Basoche. Indeed, "when Charles d'Orléans speaks of love he uses more legal expressions than when the author of *Pathelin* portrays a trial." Cons attributes the play instead to Guillaume Alecis, a monk of Lyre.

673   Daucé, Fernand. *L'Avocat vu par les littérateurs français.* [Thesis University of Rennes 1947]. Rennes: Imprimeries Oberthur, 1947.

    Suggests that the farce of Pathelin gives us a picture of the professional life of medieval advocates (see pp. 66-68, 78, 90, 95). [Repeats 577.]

674   Fischler, Alexander. "The Theme of Justice and the Structure of *La Farce de Maître Pierre Pathelin.*" *Neophilologus*, 53 (1969), 261-273.

    Argues that the theme of the work is the fallibility of human justice, which fails and yields "to a justice that is infallible"—that of God. Believes that the work was written by "an ecclesiastical author rather than a member of the *basoche*."

675   Harvey, Howard Graham. "The Judge and the Lawyer in the
       Pathelin." *RR*, 31 (1940), 313-333; rpt. *The Theatre of the Basoche:
       The Contribution of the Law Societies to French Mediaeval Comedy.*
       Harvard Studies in Romance Languages, 17. Cambridge, Mass.:
       Harvard University Press, 1941 [655], pp. 144-173.

       "A searching study of contemporary customs in respect to
       litigation...is a necessary prelude to a critical analysis of some of the
       social aspects of the play." Accordingly, Harvey sets about to show
       that the court scene involves "an ecclesiastical tribunal of the lowest
       order," that Pathelin "represents a cleric of the lowest class, a
       lecteur who ekes out a meager stipend by offering his services as an
       'advocate' to litigants attracted to the local sittings of the *official*,"
       and that the judge represents law and order: "his artistic function in
       the play is to set off the gibberish of the draper, the idiocy of the
       shepherd and the abnormality of Pathelin."

676   Lejeune, Rita. "Le Vocabulaire juridique de *Pathelin* et la
       personnalité de l'auteur." *Fin du Moyen Âge et Renaissance:
       Mélanges de philologie française offerts à Robert Guiette.* Anvers:
       Nederlandsche Boekhandel, 1961, pp. 185-194.

       Building upon the works of Harvey [675] and Lemercier [678],
       Lejeune comments on forty legal terms used in the trial scene of
       Pathelin (vss. 1215-1501). Her conclusion coincides with theirs—that
       the farce owes a great deal to the milieu of Paris law clerks and
       advocates. "From one end of the piece to the other, from one
       personage to another, one finds repeatedly the same precision in
       juridical details, the same evident delight in the case, the same
       superabundance of technical terms that betray the experience of a
       professional."

677   _____. "Pour quel public *La Farce de Maistre
       Pierre Pathelin* a-t-elle été rédigée?" *Romania*, 82 (1961), 482-521.

       Like the legal terms in the farce [see above], the names and
       place-names point to a Parisian origin. Details of the trial scene point
       even more precisely to St.-Germain-des-Prés.

678   Lemercier, P. "Les Éléments juridiques de *Pathelin* et la localisation
       de l'oeuvre." *Romania*, 73 (1952), 200-226.

       Proposes "to review as a whole the juridical elements of the celebrated farce in order to penetrate its meaning, to isolate its interest for the historian of institutions, and above all to inquire into what these elements can teach us about its provenance." The legal elements in the work can be grouped under three headings: the judicial organization itself, procedure, and the formalities involved in closing a sale of personal property. Lemercier follows Harvey [675] in arguing that Pathelin is not an advocate, properly speaking, but rather a clerk in minor orders who assumes some of the duties of that profession. Both the nature of the court proceedings, presided over by "un juge seigneurial," and the use of certain legal terms—in particular, *retrait des rentes*—point strongly toward a Parisian audience.

Peire Cardenal

679   Goldin, Frederick. "The Law's Homage to Grace: Peire Cardenal's
       Vera Vergena, Maria." *RPh*, 20 (1967), 466-477.

          The *Vera* "repeatedly uses terms that have a legalistic or
       quasi-legalistic connotation" (e.g., *de dreitura ples*, *restauriest*,
       clarifia, *sobrepres*, Christ as Mary's "heir," salvation as Christ's
       "inheriting a soul," and so forth). "The poem begins and ends its
       praise of the Virgin in terms of activities that are defined, or
       prescribed, or preserved by law—by the explicit and formal
       codification of justice, or by the articles of contractual obligation."
       A brief history of the Virgin as advocate in legend and patristic
       writings is included.

680   Ourliac, Paul. "Glose juridique sur le troubadour Peire Cardenal."
       Anuario de Derecho Aragonés (Mélanges Sancho Izquierdo), 10
       (1959-1960), 57-72.

          Discusses the "notions juridiques" that recur in Peire Cardenal's
       poetry, particularly in *Clergia non Vale*, vss. 23-24, which suggest
       that he studied the *legalis scientia*—probably at the canonical school
       of Puy. Observes that the troubadour can be identified with the
       "Petrus Cardinalis" employed at the chancellery of Raymond VI.

Le Preudome qui rescolt son compere de noier.

681   Pearcy, Roy J. "A Classical Analogue to *Le Preudome qui rescolt son compere de noier.*" *RomN*, 12 (1971), 422-427.

Finds an analogue to the ungrateful serpent of *Le Preudome* in Quintilian's example of the ungrateful gladiator, whose sister brought about his safe retirement by cutting off his thumb (*Institutio oratoria* III, 288-289). "If the core of the Old French fabliau is the legal crux resulting when someone injured in the course of an action intended to aid him sues for damages, then *Le Preudome* and this story from Quintilian are very similar."

Quinze joies de mariage.

682   Coville, Alfred. *Recherches sur quelques écrivains du XIVᵉ et du XVᵉ siècle.* Paris: Droz, 1935.

Argues that the canonist Gilles Bellemère (1337-1407) wrote the *Quinze joies de mariage.*

Raoul de Cambrai

683   Settegast, F. "Erde und Gras als Rechtssymbol im *Raoul de Cambrai.*" *ZRP*, 31 (1907), 588-593.

Traces the source of the phrase "terre ne erbe" in *Raoul de Cambrai* to old Germanic law, specifically the *Lex Salica* and *Lex Alamannorum*. The phrase is associated with the passing on of possessions by warriors in a trial by combat, or with the oath invoking God's judgment before the battle begins.

Roman de Guillaume de Dole

684   Lejeune, Rita. "L'Esprit 'clérical' et les curiosités intellectuelles de Jean Renart dans le *Roman de Guillaume de Dole.*" *Travaux de linguistique et de littérature*, 11 (1973), 589-601.

Identifies but does not discuss twenty-seven terms with legal significance drawn from the trial conducted by Liénor. "The treatment itself of the episode reveals an author singularly imbued with that knowledge of the law which he attributes to his heroine."

Roman de Renart

685   Graven, Jean. *Le Procès criminel du "Roman de Renart": Étude du droit criminel féodal au XIIe siècle.* Geneva: Georg, 1950.

An important study of criminal procedure in the *Roman de Renart.* Part One provides a historical sketch of criminal law in the medieval period; Part Two, an analysis of this law in the *Renart* itself. Graven's work loses some of its value, however, in drawing upon a modern translation of the *Renart* rather than upon the original text.

686   Nieboer, Etty. "Le Combat judiciaire dans la Branche VI du *Roman de Renart.*" *MRom*, 28 (1978), 59-67.

The theme of judicial combat is elaborated in great detail by the author of the sixth branch of the *Roman de Renart.* Why? Did the author wish "to parody judicial combats such as those that figure in the *chansons de geste* and chivalric romances?" Nieboer calls for further study of this and other questions.

687   Peel, C. D. "Feudal Institutions and Vocabulary in the *Roman de Renart.*" Diss. University of Leeds 1968-1969.

688   Subrenat, Jean. "Trois versions du jugement de Renart (*Roman de Renart*, branches VIIb, I, VIII du Manuscrit de Cangé)." *Mélanges ...offerts à Pierre Jonin.* Paris: Champion, 1979, pp. 623-643.

Subrenat's purpose is to compare the treatments of Renart's trial in three different branches "without lingering particularly on the technical aspects of the procedures."

689   Van Dievoet, G. "Le *Roman de Renart* et *Van den Vos Reynaerde*: Témoins fidèles de la procédure pénale au XIIe et XIIIe siècles?" *Aspects of the Medieval Animal Epic.* Ed. E. Rombauts and A. Welkenhuysen. Leuven: The University Press, and The Hague: Nijhoff, 1975, pp. 43-52.

"The legal historian will find no juridical heresies or striking anachronisms in the *Roman de Renart*, nor in the Flemish poem. The course of the trial, the system of proofs, the functioning of the feudal court, all correspond to the data furnished by the historical documents of the twelfth and thirteenth centuries.''

Roman de Thèbes

690   Grout, P. B. "The Trial of Daire and the Dating of the *Roman de Thèbes*." *FS*, 19 (1965), 392-395.

Maintains that Harris [691] was misled by the use of the number forty in the reconstructed text of L. Constans. "In fact this is not an instance of the *quarantaine le roy*, but of the *diffidatio*, or formal defiance of an overlord by his vassal." Thus, the trial of Daire cannot be used to date the text after 1150.

691   Harris, R. "A *Terminus a Quo* for the *Roman de Thebes*." *FS*, 11 (1957), 201-213.

Argues on the basis of the trial of Daire that the date of the *Roman* should be moved from 1150 to about 1180. The key evidence is an allusion to the *quarantaine le roy*, instituted by Philip Augustus in 1179-80. The *quarantaine* required a forty-day truce between offense and revenge, and any breach was considered an act of treason against the king himself. In fact, this breach of the *quarantaine* is the very crime (*trahison*) charged against Daire by Creon, spokesman for the "prosecution."

Rutebeuf

692   DuBruck, Edelgard. "The Theme of Self-Accusation in Early French Literature: *Adam* and *Théophile*." *Romania*, 94 (1973), 410-418.

Primarily a stylistic comparison of the lament of Adam in the *Jeu d'Adam* and of Théophile in Rutebeuf's *Miracle de Théophile*, both among the earliest lyrical self-accusations in French literature. Like Adam, Théophile does not dare to ask God for mercy, "as he has become a vassal of the devil (image in feudal terminology: 'que j'ai fet hommage au deable mains jointes,' stanza 11)...."

Sermon de la Choppinerie

693 Aubailly, J. C., ed. *"Le Sermon de la Choppinerie." RLR*, 80 (1972), 73-88.

The editor of this late fifteenth-century *sermon joyeux* calls attention to the legal overtones of the word *vaisseaulx* (line 12), which appears in the midst of a satire on the pedantry of scholastic disputation.

Songe du Vergier (See also Latin *Somnium viridarii*)

694 Shahar, Shulamith. "Une Source encore inconnue du *Songe du Vergier:* l'Ordonnance de 1372." *MA*, 76 (1970), 285-291.

Shows in parallel columns those portions of the *Songe* copied from the Ordonnance of 1372 (on the inalienability of sovereignty).

Thomas (See *Tristan*)

Tristan

695 Bédier, Joseph, ed. *Le Roman de Tristan par Thomas*. 2 vols. Paris: Société des Anciens Textes Français, 1902-1905.

Bédier's commentary (vol. 2) compares the treatments of Isolt's judgment in Thomas and Béroul, and touches upon other legal aspects of the tale.

696 Blakey, Brian. "Truth and Falsehood in the *Tristan* of Béroul." *History and Structure of French: Essays in the Honour of Professor T. B. W. Reid*. Ed. F. J. Barnett, et al. Oxford: Blackwell, 1972, pp. 19-29.

An analysis of the equivocal oaths and unequivocal lies in Béroul's *Tristan*. Drawing on the evidence of the chronicles (Froissart, Joinville, *Estoire d'Eracles*) in order to define "the underlying machinery of the oath" in medieval times, Blakey concludes that Béroul "is adhering to a system of truth, or rather truthfulness, patently different from our own, a system in which one was not bound to be truthful, unless one had sworn to be so."

697   Frappier, Jean. "Structure et sens du *Tristan*: version commune, version courtoise." *CCM*, 6 (1963), 255-280 and 441-454.

Calls for a more precise rationale for the traditional distinction between a "version commune" (Eilhart, Béroul) and a "version courtoise" (Thomas of England). Part One of the study (pp. 255-280) is devoted to the two versions' handling of the love-potion theme. Béroul presents the philtre as "the material cause of the lovers' attraction, the symbol of their fatal passion and the absolution of their sin...The entire destiny of Tristan and Iseut can be explained at bottom by this conception." By contrast Thomas sees no reason for a moral alibi: "Obedience to Love has become their sole law." Part Two (pp. 441-454) attempts to show that the moral contexts established by the love-potion theme are carried over into the differing treatments of the "judgement of God" scene, particularly in its legalistic aspects.

698   Jonin, Pierre. *Les Personnages féminins dans les romans français de "Tristan" au XIIe siècle: étude des influences contemporaines.* Publication des Annales de la Faculté des Lettres, N. S. 22. Aix-en-Provence: Ophrys, 1958.

The chapter "Le Procès d'Iseut" provides extensive information on the judicial duel during the twelfth century.

699   Newstead, Helaine. "The Equivocal Oath in the Tristan Legend." *Mélanges offerts à Rita Lejeune.* Gembloux: Duculot, 1969, 2:1077-1085.

Calls attention to the differences in treatment of Isolt's ambiguous oath in Béroul and Thomas. Béroul's version is far more elaborately developed and, with its robust enjoyment of the clever ruse, "closer than Thomas's version to the spirit of the source from which both were derived, a widely disseminated popular tale of Oriental origin about a similar equivocal oath." Legal aspects of the trial are commented on briefly.

200 LITERATURE AND LAW

700 Nichols, Stephen G., Jr. "Ethical Criticism and Medieval Literature: *Le roman de Tristan.*" *Medieval Secular Literature: Four Essays.* Ed. William Matthews. Berkeley and Los Angeles: University of California Press, 1965, pp. 68-89.

Béroul manages to retain our sympathy for Tristan and Iseut mainly "by shifting the moral focus from the fact of the affair to its social setting." For example, much of the reader's potential criticism of the adulterous pair is drawn off by the reprehensible behavior of King Mark. He has no proof of their guilt. Yet he proceeds "as though he had caught the lovers *en flagrant délit.*" Nichols' discussion of law serves two purposes: to show the full and shocking extent of Mark's violation of due process, and to find further evidence of twelfth-century attitudes toward adultery.

701 Ranke, Friedrich. "Isoldes Gottesurteil." *Medieval Studies in Memory of Gertrude Schoepperle Loomis.* Paris: Champion, and New York: Columbia University Press, 1927, pp. 87-94; rpt. Geneva: Slatkine, 1974.

Surveys the motif of the falsified *Gottesurteil*, especially in the Tristan narrative as treated by Thomas and Béroul.

702 Schoepperle, Gertrude. *Tristan and Isolt: A Study of the Sources of the Romance.* New York University Ottendorfer Memorial Series of Germanic Monographs, 6-7. 2 vols. Frankfurt: Baer, and London: Nutt, 1913.

Denies (*pace* Bédier) that the peculiar ideas of justice in the *estoire* furnish any basis for dating the poem: "There were probably men who doubted the validity of the judicial duel in the time of Charlemagne; there are probably men in our own time who would trust it still." Analyzes the Tristan-Morholt duel in terms of the eleven steps of conventional judicial combat offered by Pfeffer [597]. In all, some twenty-two other versions of island combat are discussed.

703 Vàrvaro, Alberto. *Il Roman de Tristan de Béroul.* Turin: Bottega d'Erasmo, 1963. Trans. John C. Barnes. *Beroul's Romance of Tristan.* Manchester: Manchester University Press, and New York: Barnes and Noble, 1972.

Like many writers of the period, Vàrvaro observes, Béroul

showed "a lively interest in legal forms." The sin of the lovers does not compromise their relationship with God, which is "obviously understood in the strictly feudal juridical sense." In Tristan's demand for a trial and in Isolt's oath, we see that "the claims of the conscience seem to be replaced by those of the law, which are again fully respected as a whole and meticulously observed in their detail, with a true lawyer's scrupulousness." Among the terms discussed are *loial, garanti, revoir le cri, se fier, escondit, deraisne, lever blasme, desloier* and *felon*.

704 Whitehead, Frederick. "The Early Tristan Poems." *Arthurian Literature in the Middle Ages: A Collaborative History*. Ed. Roger Sherman Loomis. Oxford: Clarendon, 1959, pp. 134-144.

In contrast to Eilhart's treatment of the lovers' guilt, Béroul "tries to vindicate the lovers' conduct in terms of feudal law. What matters is not whether Tristan and Isolt are guilty, but whether they can be proved to be so by the standards of feudal justice. Tristan behaves correctly in submitting to the king...and he has therefore the right to trial by battle. In refusing this right, Mark becomes in a sense the offender...."

705 York, Ernest C. "Isolt's Trial in Béroul and 'La Folie Tristan d'Oxford." *M&H*, N. S. 6 (1975), 157-161.

Based on its treatment of Isolt's trial, York concludes that the Oxford *La Folie Tristan* drew on the work of Béroul rather than of Thomas. "Thomas chose the ordeal; Béroul the trial by oath." Both authors, however, were depicting "historical legal procedure of their own periods."

Villon

706 Brockett, Mervyn Neil. "Dramatic Aspects of Villon's *Testament.*" Diss. Cornell University 1978.

Villon's *Testament*, "a pastiche of a last will and testament," may be best viewed as a dictation from a deathbed—which would "explain why on a number of occasions the testator turns and addresses his notary clerk, Fremin. A comparison with earlier examples from the genre of the literary testament confirms that Villon's poem is unique in its presentation of the whole ceremony as a continuous stream of direct speech....[I]t seems probable that, like Deschamps before him, Villon was influenced by the two traditions, courtly and popular."

707   Burger, André. *Lexique de la langue de Villon*. Geneva: Droz, and Paris: Minard, 1957.

Key-word-in-context lexicon of the collected works of Villon, including the *Testament*. Indispensable for documentation of legal terminology in Villon's corpus.

708   Guiraud, Pierre. *Le "Testament" de Villon, ou le gai savoir de la Basoche*. Paris: Gallimard, 1970.

Theorizes that the *Testament* was written not as an autobiography but rather as a satire on contemporary society. Guiraud's method consists largely of "decoding" the legatees' names, many of which contain hidden legal significance. The work had its origin, Guiraud believes, "in the folklore of the Basoche" (the society for Paris law clerks).

ITALIAN

General and Miscellaneous

709 Grassi, Carmelo. *Il folklore giuridico dell'Italia*. Catania: Sorace & Siracusa, 1932.

710 Kantorowicz, Ernst H. "The Sovereignty of the Artist. A Note on Legal Maxims and Renaissance Theories of Art." *De Artibus Opuscula XL. Essays in Honor of Erwin Panofsky*. Ed. Millard Meiss. New York: New York University Press, 1961, 1:267-279.

Because "poets and humanists...not infrequently started their careers by studying law," it follows that the writings of medieval jurists (glossators and commentators of Roman and canon law) might have been relevant to the development of Renaissance theories of art. Kantorowicz discusses several analogies between the two. For example, jurisprudence, commonly defined as an art (*ius est ars boni et aequi*) "imitated nature" just as every other art was supposed to do. By nature the legislator had in mind "the law of nature." His art was supposed to direct "the particular application of the general law of nature to a limited space and a limited time, yet in such a fashion that the *particulare* still reflected the *generale* of the law of nature." But further still, legislators shared with poets—and even with God himself—the prerogative of creation. "For by fiction the jurist could create (so to say, from nothing) a legal person, a *persona ficta*—a corporation, for example—and endow it with a truth and a life of its own." Concerning these two analogies, Kantorowicz quotes ample commentary from jurists themselves such as Cino da Pistoia, Baldus, Hostiensis, Durandus, Tancred, and others.

Boccaccio

711   Branca, Vittore. "L'incontro napoletano con Cino da Pistoia."
       ("Notizie e documenti per la biografia del Boccaccio.") *SBoc*, 5
       (1969), 1-12.

       While a student of canon law at the Studio Napoletano (1330-31
       and 1336-37), Boccaccio would have met the distinguished poet and
       professor of civil law Cino da Pistoia. The relationship between the
       two is obscure; however, Branca indicates that a manuscript of
       Cino's *Lectura supra codicem* now in the Czartoryski Library of
       Cracow (MS. 2566) may contain annotations by Boccaccio himself.

712   _____. *Boccaccio: The Man and His Works*. Trans.
       Richard Monges and Dennis McAuliffe. New York: New York
       University Press, 1976.

       Touches upon Boccaccio's training in canon law (alluded to in
       De Casibus III,10) and his debt to Cino da Pistoia, professor,
       lawyer, and "standard-bearer of the new poetry" (pp. 31-32 et
       passim).

713   Kirkham, Victoria E. "The *Filocolo* of G. Boccaccio with an English
       Translation of the Thirteen *Questioni D'Amore*." Diss. The Johns
       Hopkins University 1971.

       The last chapter discusses "the origin of the scholarly legend that
       accepted courts of love as legal bodies with binding jurisdictional
       authority" as well as the "literary sources, precedents, and
       analogues for each single question."

714   Ricci, Pier Giorgio. "La pretesa immatricolazione del Boccaccio
       nell'Arte dei giudici e notai." ("Notizie e documenti per la biografia
       del Boccaccio.") *SBoc*, 3 (1965), 18-24.

       Maintains that Boccaccio was not a member of the Florentine
       Arte dei giudici e notai ("Justices' and Notaries' Guild").

715   _____.   "Dominus   Johannes   Boccaccius."
       ("Notizie e documenti per la biografia del Boccaccio.") *SBoc*, 6
       (1971), 1-10.

       Discussion of the title *dominus* that was accorded Boccaccio by
       the city of Florence in the year 1350, a designation that was reserved

exclusively for "noblemen and justices." Ricci notes that although Boccaccio studied canon law for six years at Naples, he never became a doctor or joined the *Arte dei giudici e dei notai.* What, then, was the justification for this honor? Ricci provides evidence in the form of a letter that Boccaccio wrote to Zanobi da Strada in 1347 or 1348, in which it is documented that the author of the *Decameron* served as *arbiter* in the private army of Francesco Ordelaffi during its progression towards Naples. This, coupled with other honors received in Florence, provides the justification for Boccaccio's title.

Cino da Pistoia

716   Boggs, Edward L., III. "Cino da Pistoia: a Study of His Poetry." Diss. The Johns Hopkins University 1977.

Cino da Pistoia was at the same time a jurist (see his *Lectura in Codicem*) and a poet (he wrote a lyrical collection, the *Canzoniere*).

717   Chiappelli, Luigi. *Vita e opere giuridiche di Cino da Pistoia, con molti documenti inediti, ricerche.* Pistoia: n. p., 1881.

718   Marti, Mario. "Cino da Pistoia." *Enciclopedia dantesca.* Rome: Istituto della Enciclopedia Italiana, 1970, 2:6-9.

Examines the literary relationship between Cino and Dante, which probably began around 1290; the former was already oriented to the modes and principles of the *poetica stilnovistica* by that time. Points out Cino's interest in the literary *quaestio*—which has its analogue in the law—as manifested in his poem "Novellamente Amore me giura e dice." Extensive bibliography.

719   Monti, Gennaro Mario. *Cino da Pistoia giurista, con bibliografia e tre appendici di documenti inediti.* Città di Castello: "Il Solco," 1924.

720   Zaccagnini, Guido. "Cino da Pistoia: l'uomo, il giurista, il poeta." *Cino da Pistoia: nel VI centenario della morte.* Ed. Comitato Pistoiese per le onoranze. Pistoia: Pacinotti, 1937.

Dante

721   Abegg, Hans. "Die Idee der Gerechtigkeit und die strafrechtlichen Grundsätze in Dante's Göttlicher Comödie." *Jahrbuch der deutschen Dante-Gesellschaft*, 1 (1867), 177-257.

Sees in the *Commedia* the first completely developed system of justice and order in European literature. Especially noteworthy is the poet's knowledge of criminal law. Abegg studies the details of his penal system at some length.

722   Angelini, Antonio. "Fondamenti del diritto penale di Dante: Giustizia e giurisprudenza nell'*Inferno* dantesco." *Due studi danteschi*. Ed. Antonio Angelini. Aquila: Romano, 1960, pp. 23-39.

Without relying on traditional architectonic structures, Dante, through an acute sense of juridical equilibrium, systematically distributes punishments in the *Inferno*. His system of ethics accommodates the sphere of law by means of an authentic line of demarcation between good and evil, without admitting the subtle distinction between morality and legality espoused by Roman jurisconsults. In the *Inferno*, moral and social justice are differentiated in their nature and in their applications, but in the end are united for the attainment of spiritual well-being. The concept of obligation as a juridical phenomenon is seen to be a significant element of Dante's penal system, particularly in the cases of Pier delle Vigne, and Paolo and Francesca.

723   Arias, Gino. *Le Istituzioni giuridiche medievali nella Divina Commedia*. Florence: Lumachi, 1901.

Describes the relationship between Dante and the juridical institutions of his time, noting that he "non fu nè cultore, nè giudice benevolo, o semplicemente equo della scienza del diritto."

724   Barbi, Michele. "L'ideale politico-religioso di Dante." *Problemi fondementali per un nuovo commento della "Divina Commedia."* Florence: Sansoni, 1955 [1956], pp. 53-60.

Maintains that Dante was certainly conscious of the fundamental parts of the *Corpus Iuris Civilis*, and probably the juridical literature of his day, without being a jurist in the strict sense of the word or having a juridical "forma mentis."

725 Belardi, Walter. "Dante e la dottrina stoica dell'onomatopea." *Studi Sapegno*, 1 (1974), 179-195.

Touches on the meaning of legal terminology in the *Vita Nuova*.

726 Biagi, Guido. *Giunte e correzioni inedite alla "Bibliografia del De Batines."* Florence: n. p., 1888.

Documents at p. 198 the literature on Dante and his penal system.

727 Bozzi, Carlo. *Dante e il diritto*. Turin: Società Editrice Internazionale, 1965.

Bozzi traces Dante's concept of *libertà* throughout his works in addition to examining particular aspects of law in the *Commedia*.

728 Bozzoli, Adriano. "Postilla dantesca: su Pier delle Vigne." *Aevum*, 38 (1964), 388-390.

Bozzoli finds that the dominant note in the character of Pier delle Vigne, the principal figure of *Inferno* XIII, is his strong sense of justice. Pier had been *censor juris* during the reign of Frederick II (d. 1250); was known as "Pietro Giudice"; and was immortalized in stone by Frederick at his fortress in Capua. Vss. 70-72 contain the *mea culpa* of the condemned man, who had once enjoyed glory but became the victim of "devastating envy" and unjust fortune, dying a suicide, "credendo col morir fuggir disdegno/ ingiusto fece me contra me giusto."

729 Brandileone, F. "Perchè Dante colloca in paradiso il fondatore della scienza del diritto canonico?" *Rendiconti della R[eale] Accademia Nazionale dei Lincei: Classe di scienze morali, storiche e filologiche*. Ser. VII, 2 (1926), 65-149.

Seeks to explain the comment by St. Thomas Aquinas in *Paradiso* X, 104, that Gratian aided "the one forum and the other for peace in Paradise." Is the author of the *Decretum* here credited with contributions to both civil and canon law? Brandileone concludes that both forums refer to ecclesiastical matters: the *foro esterno* to judicial affairs, and the *foro interno* to penitential or sacramental ones. Provides numerous citations from the *Decretum* and other texts that reflect the distinctions between the *ius poli* (i.e., canon law) and the *ius fori* (i.e., civil law).

730   Cancelli, Filippo. "Diritto romano in Dante." *Enciclopedia dantesca*. Rome: Istituto della Enciclopedia Italiana, 1970, 2:472-479.

A very useful article. In the midst of the debate as to whether Dante was trained as a jurist, Cancelli takes the moderate position of Barbi [724], that is, that Dante knew the appropriate parts of the *Corpus Iuris Civilis* and other texts without necessarily having the "forma mentis" of a lawyer. Cancelli reviews specific references and allusions to Roman law in Dante's writings. Extensive bibliography.

731   Carmignani, Giovanni. *La Monarchia di Dante, considerazioni. Opere Minori di Dante*. Ed. A. Torri. Livorno: Vannini, 1844; rpt. Pisa: Nistri, 1865.

Describes Dante as a jurisconsult, examining from a philosophical perspective his ideas on law, liberty, and justice.

732   Chiappelli, Luigi. "Dante in rapporto alle fonti del diritto ed alla letteratura giuridica del suo tempo." *ASI*, Ser. V, 41 (1908), 3-44.

Chiappelli proposes that the roots of Dante's political thought may be found in a strong, autodidactic *cultura giuridica*, given the allusions to the works of Justinian and to Gratian's *Decretum* that appear in *Purg*. VI, 88-90; *Parad*. VI, 10-13; *Parad*. X, 103-106; and elsewhere. Despite this juridical *cultura* and direct knowledge of Justinian sources, however, Chiappelli recognizes that proof of Dante's legal studies at Bologna is lacking.

733   _____. "Ancora su Dante e il diritto romano." *GD*, 20 (1912), 202-206.

Chiappelli here responds to Chiaudano's rebuff [see below] to his assertion [732] that the roots of Dante's political thought stemmed from a juridical background. Citing Dante's familiarity with the definition of *ius* as *ars boni et aequi* found at the beginning of the *Digestum Vetus*, Chiappelli attempts to demonstrate that if his knowledge *qua* jurist of Justinian texts does not appear to have been profound, it was at least direct.

734   Chiaudano, Mario. "Dante e il diritto romano." *GD*, 20 (1912), 37-56 and 94-119.

In opposition to Chiappelli [732] and Rosadi [781], Chiaudano argues that Dante's political and legal thought was not necessarily conditioned by an autodidactic *cultura giuridica*, and that he did not have a profound and direct knowledge of Justinian sources. Rather, the poet had a simple, non-organic knowledge of the law based on daily life experience that resulted in an essentially organic, rational vision of juridical relationships—a vision which at the same time reflects his familiarity with Aristotelian philosophical-juridical thought.

735   Cospito, Antonio. "La giustizia di Dante." *Dante giudice, ovvero, trattato giuridico su la "Divina Commedia."* Taranto: Filippi, 1949, pp. 18-20; rpt. *Dante giudice: Problemi di critica dantesca* ("Il pensiero critico": Collana di studi letterari, Ser. I, 3). Padua: CEDAM, 1952, pp. 18-20.

Rejects Zingarelli's view (*Nuova Antologia*, 16 August 1927, 411-421) that Dante did not follow "un concetto assoluto di virtù." The punishments meted out in the *Inferno* reflect the *legge de contrapasso*, an important concept in contemporary juridical thought. Were it not for the intervention of Grace, there would necessarily be a profound difference between Dante's positive law and his divine law.

736   _____. "Originalità del giure dantesco ovvero dell' ampliamento della legge del taglione." *Dante giudice: Problemi di critica dantesca.* ("Il pensiero critico": Collana di studi letterari, Ser. 1, 3). Padua: CEDAM, 1952, pp. 7-9.

Using as a point of departure the episode of Cacciaguida (*Paradiso* XV-XVI), Cospito notes that it is Dante's emphasis on divine law rather than public law that gives the *Commedia* its peculiar character. The poet's novel contribution lies in his depiction of the relation between crime and punishment, a depiction accomplished through the presentation of non-traditional antitheses rather than through commonplace analogies. As a jurist Dante's greatness lies in his ability to resolve, by means of the application of divine law, issues that are punishable by laws with a solely materialist orientation (e.g., the traditional *legge del taglione*).

737   De Antonellis, Ciriaco. *De' principi di dritto penale che si contengono nella Divina commedia*. Naples: Iride, 1860; rpt. Città di Castello: Lapi, 1894.

As a source of penal law legislation, the *Divina Commedia* heralds Dante as the "first penal legislator not only of Italy, but of all Europe...." Unlike modern penal justice, which views crime as a debt to be paid objectively, Dante's system of punishment is subjective—to be paid eternally. The study provides an interesting context of juridical-philosophical thought for the *Commedia*, ranging from Epicurus to Bentham and Blackstone, in outlining the relationship between the crimes of the individual and society. Also notes the distinction between the use of the term *diritto* "right" in Dante and the connotation of "command" that it held for the Roman jurisconsults. Classifies the crimes of the *Inferno* and their respective punishments (which are viewed from a utilitarian perspective) according to type, motivation, and degree of complicity.

738   De Florio, Anthony. "Il concetto dantesco della giustizia divina." Dante Prize Winner, 1928. Harvard Library [unpublished; cited in *DSARDS*, 15 (1930), 47-48].

739   Delhaye, Philippe. "Giustizia." *Enciclopedia dantesca*. Rome: Istituto della Enciclopedia Italiana, 1971, 3:233-235.

The topic is treated under the following categories: "The Triumph of Justice," "The Just Monarch as Restorer of Justice," "The Just God," "Justice and Men," and "Justice in the Philosophical-Theological Tradition." Delhaye takes a psychological tack in viewing Dante as having a "persecution complex" in his intense and constant yearnings for justice.

740   De Mattei, Rodolfo. "'Misericordia e giustizia' nella patristica e in Dante." "Varietà." *GSLI*, 109 (1937), 239-252.

De Mattei examines the meaning of the phrase "misericordia e giustizia gli sdegna" as applied to the slothful (*Inferno* III, 50), finding that Dante's view of God's mercy and justice as a unified concept corresponds to the opinions of the Church Fathers: St. Paul in the *Epistola ad Ephesios*, Chap. 5; Saints Hilary and Augustine on the Psalms; and others. In the *Commedia* as well as in *De Monarchia* (L.i.11[13]), Dante emphasizes the importance of equity through justice and mercy, two forces that are the same manifestation of the Supreme Tribunal.

741 Donadoni, Eugenio. "Dante poeta della giustizia." *Studi danteschi e manzoniani.* Florence: La Nuova Italia, [1963]; rpt. *Dante nella critica: Antologia di passi su Dante e il suo tempo.* Ed. Tommaso Di Salvo. Florence: La Nuova Italia, 1965, pp. 210-211.

The driving force of the *Commedia* is the ethical system that has been instilled by the poet. Indeed, all of Dante's spiritual orientation is toward the triumph of justice among men. In distributing justice in the poem, however, Dante is neither overly charitable nor does he (as some critics have maintained) exhibit traits of Franciscanism.

742 Dyroff, Adolf. "Dante als Rechtsphilosoph." *Archiv für Rechts- und Wirtschaftsphilosophie*, 14 (1920-21), 251-276.

A study of the legal and political ideas in the *Commedia, De Monarchia,* and *Convivio* reveals a unified system of thought; however, it is more metaphysical than empirical, more indebted to Aristotle and Aquinas than to civil law and contemporary juridical science.

743 Ercole, Francesco. Review of Mario Chiaudano's *Dante e il diritto romano* [734]. *BSDI,* N. S. 20 (1913), 161-178; rpt. as "La cultura giuridica di Dante" in Ercole's *Il pensiero politico di Dante.* Milan: Alpes, 1928, 2:7-37.

Disagrees with Chiaudano's negation of Dante's *cultura giuridica,* noting that an essential and fundamental element of the Italian culture of the thirteenth and fourteenth centuries was law and juridical tradition, and that almost all the first poets and writers of Italian "nascente letteratura" were notaries, judges, or men of law. Dante, as "uomo del suo tempo," appears to have had direct knowledge of his juridical sources. Ercole also examines the juridical element in the *Convivio* and in *De Monarchia,* as well as the legal character of Dante's theories on ecclesiastical patrimony and the relationship between Church and State.

744 _____. "Per la genesi del pensiero politico di Dante: I. La base aristotelico-tomistica e l'idea dell'umana civiltà." *GSLI,* 71 (1918), 1-46 and 72 (1918), 245-291; rpt. in Ercole's *Il pensiero politico di Dante.* Milan: Alpes, 1928, 2:39-131.

Comments on law and justice as the only equalizing *proportio* in an otherwise unequal world of men. In Dante's works, the concept of *proportio* corresponds to the functional definition of *ius*. Parts 4 and 5 of Ercole's study emphasize the restraining nature of *giustizia* in the *Commedia*, *De Monarchia*, and elsewhere, as typified by Marcus Lombard's discourse in *Purgatorio* XVI, 94, "convenne legge per fren porre." Just as in the Aristotelian system of ethics, so in Dante's works can two concepts of human justice can be discerned: one that is generic, and another that is specific.

745   Falco, Giorgio. "Dante giudice dei suoi tempi nella *Divina Commedia*." *RSI*, 77 (1965), 500-511.

Treats Dante's severe judgment on universal corruption in the Roman Church and his condemnation of three simoniacal popes: Niccolo III, Bonifacio VIII, and Clemente V. As noted several times throughout the poem, the origin of this greed for temporal wealth was the Donation of Constantine—the authenticity of which Dante never appears to have doubted.

746   Fedele, Pius. "Dante e il diritto canonico." *Ephemerides Iuris Canonici*, 21 (1965), 213-396.

Detailed study in ten sections of Dante's concept of canon law as developed in *De Monarchia*, the *Commedia*, and other works. Central to Fedele's thesis is the importance of the concept of *proportio* ("Ius est realis et personalis hominis ad hominem proportio" [*Monarchia*, II, v]), which is upset in the individual and society by *cupiditas* (the "cieca cupidigia" of *Inferno*, XII, 49-51). As for the judicial duel (*giudizi di Dio*), Dante was neither totally opposed to contemporary jurists on the matter nor the last to uphold it.

747   _____. "Dante e il concetto di diritto." *Scritti in memoria di Antonino Giuffrè. Vol. I: Rievocazioni, filosofia e storia del diritto, diritto romano, storia delle idee*. Ed. F. Antolisei, E. Betti, B. Biondi, et al. Milan: Giuffrè, 1967, pp. 421-489.

On Dante's considerations of juridical science and jurists; his attitude toward juridical phenomena; his conceptions of positive law, natural law, and divine law; and his use of judicial reasoning. Finds evidence in the *Paradiso*, cantos V, XII, XXII, XXXI; the

Inferno, III, V, XI; and elsewhere for Dante's concern with the "validità trascendente del diritto."

748 Filosa, Carlo. "La 'Virtù' dei romani nel giudizio di S. Agostino e di Dante." *Dante e Roma. Atti del Convegno di Studi a cura della "Casa di Dante."* Florence: Le Monnier, 1965, pp. 195-210.

St. Augustine is at once "sottile e severo" in his rationalization (*De Civitate Dei*, XIV, 24) of the earthly virtues of the Romans and their empire as being providentially linked to the founding of the Church of Christ. A similar rationalization also appears in several verses of canto II of the *Inferno*. In contrast to Augustine, however, Dante treats the "sacred" character of Roman virtue—heroic justice—as a *political* concession.

749 Ferrante, Joan M. "The Relation of Speech to Sin in the *Inferno*." *DSARDS*, 87 (1969), 33-46.

Discusses sins of the tongue in the *Inferno*. Gregory the Great in the *Moralia* had noted that he who talks too much cannot stay on the right side of justice (VII, 58), a relevant point of departure for a study of the liars, blasphemers, and other verbal miscreants of Dante's Hell. Pier's speech in XIII, 67-72, the lament of a suicide, is seen to be particularly ironic in light of its allusion to justice: "ingiusto fece me contra me giusto." On the contrary, it is Pier's own act against the highest justice that has made him finally and irreparably "ingiusto."

750 Friedrich, Hugo. *Die Rechtsmetaphysik der Göttlichen Komödie.* Frankfurt-am-Main: Klostermann, 1942.

A general study of Dante's legal philosophy directed toward an explication of the Francesca da Rimini material in the *Commedia*.

751 Frosini, Vittorio. "Misericordia e giustizia in Dante." *Rivista internazionale di filosofia del diritto*, Ser. III, 42 (1965), 310-320.

Holds that mercy and justice are by-words for the understanding of all moral judgments that Dante exercises over the characters in the *Divina Commedia*. If Dante's justice is Roman, his mercy is Christian—i.e., Marian—as evidenced in canto II of the *Inferno*: "Donna è gentil nel ciel, che si compiange.../ si chè duro giudicio là sù frange" (stzs. 94, 96). The harsh justice of the *Inferno* is

covered, however, "di un roseo lume di misericordia o pietà" in the
Purgatorio, and even more so in the *Paradiso*, "in quella Roma onde
Cristo è romano." By keeping in mind the close association of
misericordia and *giustizia* in Dante's poem, one avoids confusion
when dealing with other juridical and ethical terms (e.g., *carità*).
Human and divine law—the law of justice and of mercy—do not
diverge for Dante, but represent two moments of an *unicum* that
describes the relationship between the Old and New Testaments, in
which the law of love overcomes the law of vendetta.

752   Gilbert, Allan H. *Dante's Conception of Justice*. Durham, N.C.:
        Duke University Press, 1925.

        According to Gilbert, "the commentary of St. Thomas Aquinas
        on the fifth book of the *Ethics* of Aristotle, which is wholly
        concerned with justice, [forms] the chief systematic work on justice
        familiar to Dante....Justice lies at the heart of the *Commedia*. The
        poem cannot be morally or even aesthetically acceptable unless the
        punishments and rewards of which it treats are accepted as justly
        assigned." Treats the *Commedia* in general as a poem of justice
        (Chap. 3); the *Inferno* as justice in the life of the wicked (Chap. 4);
        the *Purgatorio* as justice in human suffering (Chap. 5); and the
        Paradiso as justice of variation in human talents (Chap. 6).

753   Grassi, Carmelo. "Il giudice nel concetto di Dante." *RASLA*, 17
        (1902), 1 ff. and 238 ff.

754   _____. "Il diritto nel concetto di Dante." *RUGD*,
        16 (1902), 25 ff.

755   _____. "La giustizia nel concetto di Dante."
        RUGD, 16 (1902), 118 ff.

756   _____. "La legge nel concetto di Dante." *RUGD*,
        16 (1902), 37 ff.

757   _____. "Una pagina biografica su Dante
        giureconsulto." *RASLA*, (1903), 489.

        Affirms that although Dante lacked formal training in the
        subject, he nevertheless had a solid knowledge of the law.

758   Hatzfeld, Helmut. "The Art of Dante's *Purgatorio*." *American Critical Essays on "The Divine Comedy."* Ed. Robert J. Clements. New York: New York University Press, and London: University of London Press, 1967, pp. 64-88.

Section 2 of this study, "The Foundation of the Poetical Myth," notes that in cantos VIII, IX and XXI the souls who died in excommunication, uttering only a last sigh of contrition, reflect the fact that "Dante poeticizes everything, even canon law. He knew that the threat of excommunication gave the person warned thirty days for a possible resipiscence before the excommunication itself took place."

759   Heggelbacher, Othmar. "Das frühchristliche Kirchenrecht in Dantes *Divina Commedia*." *ZRG*, Kan. Abt. 84 (1967), 1-14.

Finds precedents in canon law for the details of penance in the *Purgatorio* and places Dante in the mainstream of canonistic thought.

760   Jaeger, Nicola. "Il diritto al tempo di Dante." *CeS*, 4 (1965), 167-179.

Sees the terms in Dante's *poesia/diritto* dichotomy as more akin to spiritual and moral exigencies than to the sphere of material interests of men. Although Dante was not a jurist in the strict sense of the word, the influence that he exerted on the world of jurists cannot be ignored. Dante recognized the insufficiency of the law of his time and dreamed of a better, unified world of peace and justice in *De Monarchia* and the *Commedia*. "Diligite iustitiam qui iudicatis terram" are the words that he sees composed by the blessed in canto XVIII of the *Paradiso*; indeed, his arguments for a universal empire sprang solely from a desire for justice.

761   Kaske, Carol V. "Mount Sinai and Dante's Mount Purgatory." *DSARDS*, 89 (1971), 1-18.

Moses in Dante's Limbo was "Moïsè legista" (*Inferno*, IV, 57); moreover, the Exodus motifs in the opening cantos of the *Purgatorio* "are distinct and cry out for some representation of the giving of law on Mount Sinai." Mount Purgatory, identified with Mount Sinai, is consistently a mountain of law. The kind of law it embodies develops through three phases: Natural Law in the Prologue [*Inf.* I-II], Old

Law in the cavern of Hell, and New Law in Mount Purgatory itself. Law is given such a central place in the poem because Dante wished to represent human effort or will-power fulfilling its potential in achieving a state of justice.

762   Kaulbach, Ernest N. "*Inferno* XIX, 45: The 'Zanca' of Temporal Power." *DSARDS*, 86 (1968), 127-135.

Elucidates the use of the term *zanca* as applied to Pope Nicholas, who usurped temporal power. While Machiavelli believed the word to refer to the pope's legs, it also was "roughly equivalent to 'caliga' [slipper]..." and in antiquity had political and ecclesiastical significance, "its use...restricted by Theodosian law."

763   Kay, Richard. "Dante's Unnatural Lawyer: Francesco d'Accorso in *Inferno* XV." *Studia Gratiana*, 15 (1972), 147-200; rpt. as "Francesco d'Accorso the Unnatural Lawyer" in Kay's *Dante's Swift and Strong. Essays on "Inferno" XV*. Lawrence: The Regents Press of Kansas, 1978, pp. 39-66.

Francesco d'Accorso was an avaricious professor of law who exploited his students and either ignored the letter or misrepresented the sense of the law; his sin against nature was this continued violation of professional ethics and a distorted desire for fame. Son of Master Accursius, the author of the *Glossa Ordinaria* to the *Corpus Iuris Civilis*, Francesco had "a reputation for putting his legal knowledge to serve his avarice." Like the usurers condemned in *Inferno* XI, 97-111, he did violence to nature by gaining reputation through his father's prestige and labor as if his own. [Cf. 776.]

764   Koenen, Ferdinand. "Anklänge an das Busswesen der alten Kirche in Dantes Purgatorio." *DDJ*, 7 (1923), 91-105.

Seeks to demonstrate that the punishments in *Purgatorio* closely adhere to contemporary canon law.

765   Koffler, Judith Schenck. "Capital in Hell: Dante's Lesson on Usury." *Rutgers Law Review*, 32 (1979), 608-660.

Argues that Aristotle's views on money seem to underlie Dante's enigmatic treatment of usury in the *Inferno* (specifically Cantos XI and XVII). Because society is based on the principle of exchange (*Nichomachean Ethics*), usury represents a fundamental threat to the community: "it destroys the medium of exchange, but worse, it corrupts the relationship of exchange, by using the relationship for private profit rather than as a means to a more perfect association with others." In order to put the discussion in a historical context, Koffler attempts "to connect Dante's allusion to Caorsa in Canto XI with the international commercial, financial, and political power of the Cahorsines in later thirteenth century Christendom and with that of their Florentine successors who were likewise called Cahorsines." The article ends with a comparative analysis of capital in Aristotle, Dante, and Marx.

766   Liserre, Eugenio. *Storia e diritto in Dante (nel VII centenario della nascità)*. Milan: Marzorati, 1964.

Rhetorical, impressionistic study of history and law in Dante's thought, which is assumed to be based "sulla metafisica dell'Essere." The poet's interest in law—which cannot be separated from philosophy—is doubtless attributable to his youthful study in Bologna. Part I of the work, "La 'Volontà' metastorica di Dante," emphasizes that nothing impedes investigation of the *Commedia* as a treatise on moral philosophy; indeed, at the basis of Dante's poetic genius was his religious soul, his participation as a rational creature in the Eternal Law as defined by St. Thomas. Part II, "Dante e il diritto," reveals that throughout the *Commedia, De Monarchia*, and other works, Dante wished to unfold moral reason through art and to proceed "to the sources of Law and Justice."

767   Lomonaco, Vincenzo. *Dante giureconsulto*. Atti della Reale Accademia di Scienze Morali e Politiche di Napoli, 7. Naples: R[eale] Università, 1872.

A broad study in two parts of Dante's conception of the law. Part I examines the definition of law contained in *De Monarchia* II, 5, and its application in the *Commedia* and elsewhere. Notes that Dante, in drawing on the concepts of *concordantia* and *proportio* from Antiquity and medieval Scholasticism, constantly depicted the restoration of order as absolutely necessary. For this reason he placed Caesar and Justinian, the great promoters of civil law, in Paradise (canto VI). Similarly his system of punishments in Hell and expiations in Purgatory everywhere reflects "a rigorous geometry." Part Two of the study provides a rambling Hegelian overview of the relationships between the individual and the state, and associates

Dante's political ideas with items as diverse as Rousseau's Social
Contract and the French Revolution.

768   Lumia, Giuseppe. "La legge, il diritto, la giustizia." *Aspetti del
pensiero politico di Dante.* Università di Palermo: Pubblicazioni a
cura della Facoltà di Giurisprudenza, 16. Milan: Giuffrè, 1965, pp.
27-41.

Dante's concern for justice is manifested in his demonstration of
the need for empire, whereas his concern for right (*diritto*) affirms
that imperial power derives from the *iure* of the Roman people.
Dante's use of legal terminology is studied in the context of *lex
divina, naturalis*, and *humana.*

769   _____. "Legge, diritto e giustizia nel pensiero di
Dante." *Atti del Convegno di Studi su Dante e la Magna Curia.*
Palermo: Centro di Studi Filologici e Linguistici Siciliani, 1967, pp.
563-568.

Dante adheres closely to the thinking of Augustine and Aquinas
in his own system of divine, natural, and human law. The article
follows the argument earlier developed in Lumia's book [768].

770   Maccarone, M. "Teologia e diritto canonico nella *Monarchia,* III,
3." *Rivista di storia della Chiesa in Italia,* 5 (1951), 7-42.

771   Mariani, Andrea. "Diritto (dritto)." *Enciclopedia dantesca.* Rome:
Istituto della Enciclopedia Italiana, 1970, 2:471-472.

Studies the numerous examples of the terms *dritto* and *diritto*
and their various syntactic and semantic functions in Dante's works.
Mariani notes that the form *dritto* generally appears in poetry (*Rime,
Commedia*), and the form *diritto* in prose (*Convivio*).

772   Maurer, Karl. "Die Selbstmörder in Dantes Divina Commedia."
ZRP, 75 (1959), 306-321.

Argues that the placement of suicides in the *Inferno* can be
rationalized in terms of Augustinian and Thomistic principles of
natural law.

773 Nardi, Bruno. *Dante e la cultura medievale*. Bari: Laterza, 1942; 2nd ed., 1949.

> Shows (pp. 218-223) that Dante depended on the *Glossa ordinaria* of Accursius in the *Commedia*.

774 —————————. "Dante e il 'buon Barbarossa'." *L'Alighieri*, 7 (1966), 3-27.

> Dante agrees with the thesis held by Barbarossa against Pope Hadrian IV—that imperial power emanates directly from God. Along with the Bolognese glossators, the poet saw the pseudo-donation of Constantine as devoid of all legal and political value, bearing "mal frutto" (*Parad.* XX, 56) and therefore revocable.

775 Passerin d'Entrèves, A. *Dante as a Political Thinker*. Oxford: Clarendon, 1952.

> An introduction to Dante's political thought, treated under three headings: the City, the Empire, the Church. In addition to numerous observations throughout on the role of law in the poet's system, there is an appendix which takes up the issue of *ratio* as a technical legal term.

776 Pézard, André. *Dante sous la pluie de feu (Enfer, chant XV)*. Études de philosophie médiévale, 40. Paris: Vrin, 1950.

> In the chapter "Légistes d'enfer et saints légistes," Pézard provides a foundation study on Dante and the law from the perspective of Rome and the empire. He collects references to the jurists mentioned in the *corpus Dantescum:* Justinian, Benincasa, and Hostiensis (to name the principals), in order to reflect the more general aspects of Dante's legal philosophy. The canonist Gratian is to Francesco d'Accorso (the "unnatural lawyer" in *Inferno* XV) as Donatus is to Priscian.

777 Quinones, Ricardo J. *Dante Alighieri*. Boston: Twayne, 1979.

> Chapter 6, "*Commedia: Purgatorio*, I. *The Temporal Realm*," notes that "suffused as it is by the lyricism of memory, Purgatory is a place where one sets one's ethical nature in order by obedience to the Law. When Dante insists that both for the race as for the individual the spirit can only be reached through the Law, he is

simply recapitulating the Christian view of history: the Law preceded
the advent of the spirit. Consequently the guardian of the access to
Purgatory is Cato, whose most sacred memory Dante has already
invoked in *Convivio* IV....'Who are you,' he demands, as he
confronts Virgil and Dante, 'to come to Purgatory directly from
Hell? Are the laws of the abyss broken?'''

778   Reade, William H. V. *The Moral System of Dante's Inferno.*
       Oxford: Clarendon, 1909; rpt. Port Washington, N.Y.: Kennikat
       Press, 1969.

       Traces the various examples of penal terminology cited in the
       Inferno to Aristotle and Aquinas (e.g., *peccatum, culpa,* and
       malitia). Of particular interest is Chapter 16, "*Malitia* and Justice."

779   Renucci, Paul. *Dante, disciple et juge du monde gréco-latin.* Paris:
       Les Belles Lettres, 1954.

       This detailed examination of Dante's indebtedness to classical
       antiquity notes his admiration for the Byzantine emperor Justinian,
       whose strengthening of the law in Italy is exalted in the *Paradiso:*
       "C'est un souverain très chrétien, respectueux des droits de
       l'Eglise...." Provides a brief bibliography on "Les Notions
       juridiques acquisés par Dante."

780   Rolfs, Daniel. "Dante, Petrarch, Boccaccio and the Problem of
       Suicide." *RR*, 67 (1976), 200-225.

       While primarily a moral issue in Dante (*Inferno*, XIII), suicide is
       seen as a literary theme in Petrarch and Boccaccio (letters of the
       Famigliari; the epic poem *Africa*; the *Decameron*). Dante and
       Petrarch, despite their celebration of pagan suicide, always condemn
       the Christian self-murderer, as does canon law (sources noted).
       Boccaccio, however, alternately praises and censures the act by *both*
       groups, reveals the most extreme manifestations of this characteristic
       ambiguity, and gives full expression to its inherent irrationality.

781   Rosadi, Giovanni. *Il Canto XI dell'Inferno.* Florence: Sansoni,
       [1906].

       Denies that Dante had legal training, noting that he "non fu,
       neppure per dilettantismo, un giuresconsulto," but affirms that his

concept of injury corresponds to that of Roman sources (i.e., the *Digestum Vetus*, I.xlvii.10), which is at the base of his penal system.

782 Ruffini, F. "Dante e il protervo decretalista innominato." *Memorie della Reale Accademia delle Scienzi di Torino: Classe di scienze morali, storiche et filologiche*, Ser. II, 66 (1922), 1-69.

Provides commentary on the question of Dante's juridical background, noting that he understood "even the more subtle concepts of the law, and at times sublimated and illuminated them with the light of his genius."

783 Sapegno, Natalino. *Il canto XXIX dell'Inferno.* Florence: Le Monnier, 1952; excerpts rpt. in *Dante nella critica: Antologia di passi su Dante e il suo tempo.* Ed. Tommaso Di Salvo. Florence: La Nuova Italia, 1965, pp. 358-359.

Sapegno examines in its historical context the institution of the private vendetta, the basis for action in *Inferno* XXIX. At the time of Dante, this act of revenge was recognized by the law, and was viewed as an obligation of honor—being practiced with particular ardor by the Florentines. It comes as no surprise, then, that Dante, with his great sense of justice and desire for peace, renounces the custom in the episode of the Geri family. But while he condemns, he comprehends: examining the nature of human passion in a greater context, he is not totally without sympathy for those who become its victims.

784 Schmidt, Richard. "Dante und die strafrechtliche Praxis seines Zeitalters." *DDJ*, N. F. 9 (1936), 52-108.

A study of Dante's conception of criminal justice and its relation to the work of Albertus Gandinus.

785 Shapiro, Marianne. "An Old French Source for Ugolino?" *DSARDS*, 92 (1974), 129-147.

Dante's indebtedness to the epic tradition of Virgil and Statius is so well known and studied as to obscure the more quotidian proximity of the Old French epic. A detailed comparison of *Amis et Amiles* and *Inferno* XXXIII elucidates the thematic and structural ambience of the sacrifice of Ugolino's sons in vss. 61-63. Similarities between the judicial combats and other episodes suggest that the relationship between the account of Ugolino and the French text may well be a close one.

786   Singleton, Charles S. "Justice in Eden." *Sixty-Eighth to Seventy-Second Annual Reports of the Dante Society with Accompanying Papers*. Cambridge, Mass., 1954, pp. 3-33 [*DSARDS*, 68 (1950), 3-33.]

Beatrice's awesome arrival at the summit of Purgatory (*Purgatorio*, XXIX-XXX) discloses her to be the coming of the Word of God in history, bringing the perfection of justice. Later as she comes to stand in judgment on her lover, it is apparent that the analogy Beatrice-Christ is being extended out of the *Vita Nuova* into the last cantos of the *Purgatorio*—a second coming. Moreover, the figure of Matelda in Eden (canto XXVIII) is the living image of a justice—an *original* justice—which had once existed in our first parents. This lost justice far outweighs that which can now be had *naturally*.

787   Solari, Gioele. "Il pensiero politico di Dante." *Rivista Storica Italiana*, N. S. 1 (1923), 373-455.

A review of scholarship on Dante's political thought, including the studies by Solmi [788], Dyroff [742], Ruffini [782], and Ercole [744].

788   Solmi, Arrigo. *Il pensiero politico di Dante: Studi storici*. Florence: "La Voce," 1922.

Chapter 7, "Dante e il diritto," deals with the renaissance of the science of law during the Middle Ages and with Dante's juridical training. At Bologna he would have studied rhetoric, which encompassed the topic of the *genus iudiciale*; and would have been familiar with the *ars dictaminis*. Also examines Dante's definition of the law in *De Monarchia* II.5.1, his knowledge of Roman legal texts, and his influence on later juridical writers. Notes that in representing law as an equilibrium in the individual vis-a-vis society, Dante goes beyond definitions offered in the Justinian and Bolognese texts and perfects the Aristotelian concept of law as expounded by St. Thomas.

789 Triolo, Alfred A. "*Inferno* XXXII: Fra Alberigo in Context." *L'Alighieri*, 11 (1970), 39-70.

Provides an analysis of Dante's last human encounter in the *Inferno*, the Fra Alberigo episode, in the context of the "perversion of *veritas*" and the increased *impietas* of Tolomea. The episode follows upon a synthesis of the structural dynamics of the lower Hell—*iustitia legalis* combined with *iustitia particularis* and paralleled by *prudentia politica* and *sanctitas*.

790 Vadalà-Papale, G. "Le leggi nella dottrina di Dante Alighieri e di Marsilio da Padova." *Studii giuridici dedicati ed offerti a Francesco Schupfer*. Turin: Fratelli Bocca, 1898, 2:41 ff.

791 Vallone, Aldo. "Il peccato e la pena." *Studi su Dante medievale*. Biblioteca dell'Archivum Romanicum. Ser. I: Storia-Lettera-tura-Paleografia, 80. Florence: Olschki, 1965, 111-123.

Emphasizes the constructive capacity of the rigor of law in the *Commedia*, though it is hardly possible to distinguish what Dante owes to Roman law and what to barbarian law. The *Inferno, Purgatorio*, and *Paradiso* are perhaps best examined, respectively, in terms of reason, love, and intelligence. Far from separating itself from the law or moral/religious norms, Dante's personal poetic vision is unified, logical, and coherent.

792 Vento Palmeri, Sebastiano. *Dante e il diritto pubblico italiano*. Milan: Sandron, 1923.

793 Williams, James. "Dante as a Jurist." *The Law Magazine and Review*, 12 (1896-1897), 84-111; rpt. *Dante as a Jurist*. Oxford: Blackwell, and London: Marshal, 1906.

Offers a collection of legal terms and arguments in the *Commedia*. Concludes that the poet was a jurist and recognizes that a "complete bibliography of the books and articles on the legal aspect of Dante's works still remains to be compiled."

794 Zingarelli, Nicola. *La vita, i tempi e le opere di Dante*. (With A. Belloni, G. Bertoni, et al.) 2 vols. Milan: Vallardi, 1914; 3rd ed., 1931; rpt. in abridged version in *La vita di Dante: Con un'analisi della Divina Commedia*. 2nd ed. Milan: Vallardi, 1914.

Outlining the long juridical heritage that emanated from
Bologna, Florence, and other parts of Italy, Zingarelli indicates that
the "codice giustinianeo" and the glosses of Accursius would have
been part of young Dante's academic curriculum. Provides an
overview of the poet's concept of justice as manifested in the
Convivio, Commedia, and *De Monarchia*, and offers some
conjectures on his attitude toward certain legislation of the day (e.g.,
the *Ordinamenti della giustizia* of 1293). Volume 2, chapter 37,
provides interesting commentary on the celestial bodies of judgment
in the *Paradiso*, especially cantos XVIII-XIX.

Petrarch

795   Bergin, Thomas G. *Petrarch*. New York: Twayne, 1970.

Chapter 2 describes the young Petrarch's studies in law at
Montpellier and his reasons finally for rejecting a legal career. In his
Letter to Posterity, he states that "a profession that degraded those
who practiced it" should be abandoned. Although the theory and
study of law appealed to him, "the practice of law seemed to him to
carry with it the need for dishonesty if it were to be successful...."

796   Billanovich, Giuseppe. *Petrarca letterato: Lo scrittoio del Petrarca*.
Storia e letteratura, 16. Rome: "Storia e letteratura," 1947.

Contains a general overview of Petrarch's legal studies at
Montpellier.

797   Fedele, Pius. "Francesco Petrarca e Giovanni d'Andrea."
Ephemerides Iuris Canonici, 30 (1974), 201-225.

Provides biographical information on the epistolary relationship
between Petrarch and the Bolognese decretalist Johannes Andreae.
As a point of departure, Fedele mentions the criticism leveled by
Dante against the prestige accorded to the decretalists ("Per questo
l'Evangelio e i dottor magni/ son derelitti..." [*Parad.* IX, 133-134])
as well as the criticism by Petrarch ("Iustitiam tanto...dehonestant"
[*Epistolae de rebus familiaribus*, lib. XX, epistola iv]). Also quotes
from Petrarch's letters that describe his transition "degli studi
giuridici [i.e., those at Montepellier, 1319; and Bologna, 1323]...a
quelli letterari."

798 Maffei, Domenico. *Gli inizi dell'umanesimo giuridico*. Milan: Giuffrè, 1956.

Chapter 1 discusses the invectives directed by humanists against jurists. Petrarch himself apparently studied law under the guidance of Oldradus de Ponte and Johannes Andreae, and was also in correspondence with Lucas de Penna.

799 Tatham, Edward H. R. *Francesco Petrarca, the First Modern Man of Letters: His Life and Correspondence*. Vol. 1. London: Sheldon; New York and Toronto: Macmillan, 1925.

Contains information on Petrarch's early juridical career.

Sercambi, Giovanni

800 Sinicropi, Giovanni Andrea. "Le opere di Giovanni Sercambi." Diss. University of Toronto 1963.

A general study of the personality and works of Sercambi. Among other things, Sinicropi notes that Sercambi was twice elected "gonfaloniere di giustizia," or head of the state; and that "the experience gained during the years in which he took part in the government of the city inspired Sercambi to write the *Nota ai Guinigi*, most probably in 1392 or shortly after, at the time when the Guinigi had achieved supremacy in the political life of Lucca."

HISPANIC

General and Miscellaneous

801 Alcalá-Zamora y Castillo, Niceto. *Estampas procesales de la literatura española.* Buenos Aires: Ediciones Jurídicas Europa-América, 1961.

Sketchy examination of the relationship between medieval Spanish law and literature is made on pp. 1-74, citing examples from the *Cid, Libro de buen amor, Celestina,* and other works.

802 _____. "Nuevas estampas procesales de la literatura española." *Revista de derecho procesal iberoamericana,* 1 (1969), 303-367.

Examines legal encounters in the works of Berceo; the *Poema de Fernán González; the Rimado de Palacio* by Pero López de Ayala; the *Corvacho* of Alfonso Martínez de Toledo; the *Coplas* of Jorge Manrique; and alludes to other medieval literary lights as well in Part 2, sections A-E.

803 Armistead, Samuel G. In correspondence with C. Colin Smith. [Cited in 877, p. 176, n. 22.]

Armistead, citing parallel legalistic features of other epic poems (e.g., the *caloña* "blood-payment" in the *Siete Infantes de Lara,* the trick of the "hawk-and-horse" in the *Poema de Fernán González,* and the legalism of the *riepto* "challenge" of Zamora), views with caution Smith's argument that the *Cid* is the work of a lawyer: "That the 'author' of the *Cid* knows his law does not *en un principio* clash with the poem's traditional character." Presuming that Armistead would view these examples as isolated episodes in the texts mentioned, Smith reiterates his own view "that [*Cid*] is *consistently* legalistic, in themes, episodes and phraseology, and that this gives the poem much of its distinctive character."

804 _____. "Epic and Ballad: A Traditionalist Perspective." Paper presented at the annual meeting of the Société Rencesvals, American-Canadian Branch, New York, 29 December 1981. Cited in report on the session by H. Salvador Martínez, "Problems in the Medieval Spanish Epic," *Corónica*, 10 (1982), 250-254, at p. 251.

In the discussion following this paper, Professor Armistead argued in favor of an uninterrupted oral tradition extending from the epic poem to the ballad, emphasizing that the author of *Cid* was not necessarily trained in the law: "Icelandic sagas are even more legalistic than *PMC*.Were the authors lawyers? No. Everyone knew law; it was part of tradition."

805 Deyermond, A. D. *Epic Poetry and the Clergy: Studies on the "Mocedades de Rodrigo."* London: Támesis, 1968.

Describes the decline of Castilian epic poetry exemplified by the evolution of the figure of the Cid, Rodrigo Díaz de Bivar, from the *Cid* to the *Mocedades de Rodrigo*. Citing *MR*'s close association with the *Poema de Fernán González* (ca. 1250), Deyermond notes its emphasis on notarial documents and seals: there are eighteen references in 1200 lines, as opposed to eight in *Cid*, and sixteen in the non-epic narrative *Poema de Alfonso XI* (10,000 lines long). Moreover, King Fernando is singled out for praise in *MR* for having proclaimed *fueros* and *previllejos*. This suggests "sufficient familiarity with law..., a notarial or administrative background for the poet," but does not exclude popular aspects in the recasting or diffusion of the poem by minstrels (*juglares*). With respect to their descriptions of documents, the *MR, Cid*, and some *cuaderna vía* poems are seen to behave in much the same way.

806 _____. *A Literary History of Spain: The Middle Ages*. London: Ernest Benn, and New York: Barnes & Noble, 1971. Spanish trans. Luis Alonso López. *Historia de la literatura española: la Edad Media*. Barcelona: Ariel, 1973.

A true miracle of compression, Deyermond's indispensable guide to the literature of the Spanish Middle Ages provides critical insights into the juridical aspects of major works and the forensic training of their authors. Following Russell [869, 870] and Pattison [867], Deyermond notes that *Cid* "was composed...by a single author, a learned poet who may have well been a cleric and who had certainly had a legal and notarial training." On Berceo (after Dutton [830]), he says that this poet's service "was primarily legal and administrative...; there is good reason to believe that he was notary to the abbot [of San Millán de la Cogolla]." Regarding *La Celestina*, Deyermond believes that Fernando de Rojas, a law student from Puebla de Montalbán, did not write Act I at the same time as the rest of the work, "and probably did not write it at all," but did draw on legal sources for the remainder of the text. The *Cárcel de Amor* (1492?) by Diego de San Pedro is also viewed in terms of its juridical aspects: lovers Leriano and Princess Laureola are accused of unchastity by a jealous rival, "and the King condemns his daughter to death (*ley de Escocia*), despite Leriano's vindication of her in a judicial duel."

807   Dutton, Brian. "The Popularization of Legal Formulae in Medieval Spanish Literature." *Studies in Honor of John Esten Keller*. Ed. Joseph R. Jones. Newark, Del.: Juan de la Cuesta, 1980, pp. 13-28.

Dutton's important investigation is a "brief and limited excursion into legal formulae, principally as present in the works of Berceo [*Milagros de Nuestra Señora, Vida de Santo Domingo de Silos, Vida de San Millán de la Cogolla*, and other texts]." Indicates the mechanisms by which legal formulae were made intelligible to the general public of the day "without having to attend Law School," showing also the effects of "oral vernacularization" (after Lomax [815]) of Latin juridical terminology in commonplace documents. Notes that "legal documents were much more a part of daily life and aural experience in the Middle Ages than today. Publication implied not gazettes and classified sections in newspapers, but public proclamation and recital," such that "Romance versions of Latin legal formulae (and from about 1200, the Romance formulae used in vernacular documents) passed into commonly understood phrases, and often commonly used expressions." Extensive examples of terminology (Latin and Spanish) are provided.

808   Faulhaber, Charles. *Latin Rhetorical Theory in Thirteenth- and Fourteenth-Century Castile*. California University Publications, 103. Berkeley and Los Angeles: The University of California Press, 1972.

Observes that a knowledge of the *ars dictandi* and the *cursus*, as synthesized in Spanish rhetorical tradition during the period 1250-1300 (and now manifested in literary works and royal documents), was considered especially helpful in establishing the authenticity of royal privileges and letters.

809   García Gallo, Alfonso. "El carácter germánico de la épica y del derecho en la edad media española." *AHDE*, 25 (1955), 583-679.

Denies the thesis of Hinojosa [813] on the Germanic origins of the themes common in epic poetry ("blood vengeance," "collective responsibility for political demise," etc.), preferring instead to emphasize the importance of *juridical folklore* in Castilian epic literature.

810   García y García, Antonio. "Obras de derecho común medieval en castellano." *AHDE*, 41 (1971), 665-683.

A description of works of common law in Spain from the twelfth to the sixteenth centuries, which divides them into sources and general works; criminal law; and canonical and pastoral works, such as manuals for confessors. Important pastoral figures include Martín Pérez, canonist theologian of the fourteenth century; Pedro Gómez Barroso, author of a *Confesionario*; and Alfonso de Madrigal, "el Tostado" (1400?-1455), who became Bishop of Ávila, and who produced, among other works, the *Tractado cómo al ome es nescesario amar*, "which deals first with the inevitability of sexual love, and then with its effects: mental disturbance, illness, and even death."

811   Gautier Dalché, Jean. "Vengeance privée, composition, inimité, trahison comme facteurs d'exclusion dans les sociétés urbaines de l'Espagne Castillane." *Exclus et systèmes d'exclusion dans la littérature et la civilisation médiévales*. Collection "Senefiance," 5. Aix-en-Provence: Cuer Ma, and Paris: Champion, 1978, pp. 179-191.

Although the domain of literature is beyond its scope, this study contains a valuable glossary of legal terms (presented etymologically) apropos to the medieval Castilian epic (e.g., *calumnia-caloña* "blood-payment").

812   Hinojosa, Eduardo de. *Influencia que tuvieron en el derecho público de su patria y singularmente en el derecho penal los filósofos y teólogos españoles anteriores a nuestro siglo [XIX]*. Madrid: Real Academia de Ciencias Morales y Políticas, 1890.

Chapter 3 studies canonical influences in medieval Catalan
literature, particularly in Eiximenis' *El Crestià o Libro del Regiment*
("Guide for Princes").

813 _____. *El elemento germánico en el derecho
español.* Madrid: Centro de Estudios Históricos, 1915; rpt. in his
Obras completas. Madrid: [Ministerio de Justicia y C.S.I.C.], 1955,
2:407-470. [The Castilian text was prepared by Galo Sánchez,
Hinojosa's disciple, from the monograph "Das germanische
Element im spanischen Rechte," *ZRG*, Germ. Abt., 31 (1910),
282-359.]

Noting that our imperfect knowledge of medieval common and
local law is due largely to the dearth of edited diplomas, charters,
and such legal instruments, Hinojosa proposes the study of literary
monuments like the Castilian popular epic in order to "clarify and
complement [our knowledge of the] sources of the law"—an
investigative task that he had begun in his earlier study on the *Cid*
[859]. Commenting on the Germanic influence in Spanish law as
manifested in the epic, Hinojosa observes the excessiveness of
"blood-vengeance" in the *Siete Infantes de Lara*, in which vengeance
for an affront, while technically limited to the delinquent, also falls
on other family members.

814 Kirby, Steven D. "Legal Doctrine and Procedure as Approaches to
Medieval Hispanic Literature." *Corónica*, 8 (1980), 164-171.

This important study calls attention to juridical aspects of the
Cid; Berceo and his works; the *Lupus et vulpis, judice simio* episode
of the *Libro de buen amor* and its indebtedness to the Alfonsine *Siete
partidas*; and Fernando de Rojas' *La Celestina*. Calls for an
examination (or re-examination) of these and other works for
"traces of legal or procedural influence by persons capable of
recognizing such elements"; the production of "monographic
studies which attempt to explain the influence of law upon these
literary works"; and the publication of "dependable syntheses of the
composite findings" of these investigations. Notes that debate poems
(e.g., the *Disputa del alma y el cuerpo, Razón de amor, Elena y
María* and the *Danza de la muerte*) should also be studied for legal
elements.

815   Lomax, Derek W. "The Lateran Reforms and Spanish Literature."
       Iberoromania, 1 (1969), 299-313.

       One of the effects of the Fourth Lateran Council (1215) was to
       make available hagiographic, liturgical and paraliturgical texts in the
       vernacular. Lomax observes that the "oral vernacularization" of
       Latin legal phrases which followed had an impact both on the
       language of public documents and on the literature of the day.

816   Martínez, J. J. Victorio. "Nota sobre la épica medieval española: el
       motivo de la rebeldía." *Revue Belge de Philologie et d'Histoire*, 50
       (1972), 777-792.

       Tries to demonstrate the importance of the rebellious vassal
       theme in medieval Spain by reference to the relationship between
       hero and king in the epic. In the case of the Cid's banishment,
       Martínez notes that the mysterious exile which occurs at the
       beginning of the *Cid* can be attributed to the oath required of King
       Alfonso VI (the *jura de Santa Gadea*, in which he is forced to swear
       not to have taken part in the murder of his brother Sancho) inasmuch
       as the later *romance* dealing with the theme states that "Las juras
       eran tan fuertes/ que el rey no las ha otorgado." Although the law
       routinely required a response in such cases, the Cid's proud, harsh
       tone of voice in dealing with the monarch elicited the foreboding
       warning "si hoy me tomas la jura,/ después besarás mi mano."

817   Ossorio Morales, Juan. *Derecho y literatura*. Granada: Univ. de
       Granada, 1949.

       General study of law and literature from the medieval period to
       contemporary times.

818   Smith, C. Colin. "Latin Histories and Vernacular Epic in
       Twelfth-Century Spain: Similarities of Spirit and Style." *BHS*, 48
       (1971), 1-19.

       Examines the importance of the Latin histories of Spain
       produced during the period 1100-1150—the *Historia Roderici*, the
       Silense, the *Chronica Adefonsi Imperatoris* and others—for the
       vernacular epic. In individual words, phrasing, and syntax
       numerous parallels can be drawn, especially in the area of
       "physical" phrases [cf. 872] and comprehensive binomial pairings
       "*Moros e cristianos, grandes e chicos, hombres e mujeres...*which

shatter the abstract notion of *todos* 'everybody.'" Indeed, the presence of learned elements in the *Cid* hints "at contacts of its author with Latin histories and the language of the law...."

Alfonso X (el Sabio)

819 Bloom, Leonard. "The Emergence of an Intellectual and Social Ideal as Expressed in Selected Writings of Alfonso X and Don Juan Manuel." Diss. University of Pittsburgh 1967.

Identifies the "intellectual and social ideal as expressed in selected works of Alfonso X and don Juan Manuel"—the *Siete partidas* and *Cantigas de Santa Maria* of the former; and *El libro del caballero et del escudero, El libro de los castigos,* and *El libro de los estados* of the latter. Notes that Alfonso specified in the *Partidas* "the ideal traits which a monarch should possess, since governing by divine right, he had to make and execute sound and appropriate laws. Don Juan Manuel, on the other hand, not only emphasized the need of just laws and ideal kings to execute them, but also the need of princes to represent the judicial perfection of their lords."

820 Craddock, Jerry R. *A Bibliography of the Legislative Works of Alfonso X el Sabio, King of Castile and Leon 1252-1284.* Research Checklists and Bibliographies. Alan Deyermond, ed. London: Grant and Cutler [forthcoming].

821 Herriott, J. Homer. "A Thirteenth-Century Manuscript of the *Primera Partida.*" *Speculum*, 13 (1938), 278-294.

Mentions the "profound influence that the *fueros*, privileges, ordinances, *'fazannas, albedrios y costumbres,'* and codes promulgated or granted by the rulers and lords of mediaeval Spain have exercised...on its literature" (e.g., the influence of the *Siete partidas* on the *Caballero Cifar*).

822 Ingamells, Lynn E. "Neologisms in Book II of *El espéculo* of Alfonso el Sabio." *Medieval Hispanic Studies Presented to Rita Hamilton.* Ed. A. D. Deyermond. London: Támesis, 1976, pp. 87-97.

A linguistic study that compares first occurrences in the Alfonsine *Espéculo* with the text of the *Caballero Cifar, Gran conquista de Ultramar,* and other works cited in the *Tentative Dictionary of Medieval Spanish* (Chapel Hill, 1946), finding that the sixteen neologisms that can be documented in Book II of the legal treatise constitute a small number, an observation which "reinforces the evidence that [it] was the un-edited first draft for *Las siete partidas.*"

823   MacDonald, Robert Alan. "Kingship in Medieval Spain: Alfonso X of Castile." Diss. University of Wisconsin-Madison 1958.

The first part of this study attempts to obtain "a reasonably accurate statement of the king's political philosophy," noting that "it seems necessary to consult a greater number of the Alfonsine works, legal and non-legal, in order to confirm the authenticity of broad concepts implicitly underlying the principles and specific provisions of the *Partidas.* These works—other code texts, didactic writing and the histories—also give complementary expression to the Alfonsine ideas."

824   _____. "Legal Justice and Its Dispensation in the *Cantigas de Santa Maria.*" *Proceedings of the First International Symposium on the "Cantigas de Santa Maria"* [forthcoming].

Treats the Alfonsine concept and administration of legal justice in the *CSM:* its nature, its sources, and the means for its dispensation. Provides some examples and treatment of justice-dealing in this poetry.

825   MacKay, Angus, and Geraldine McKendrick. "Confession in the *Cántigas de Santa María.*" *Reading Medieval Studies,* 5 (1979) 71-88.

The *CSM* dates from the period after the Fourth Lateran Council of 1215 but before the reform movement began to "flourish," and so provides an interesting insight into the prevailing attitudes to confession. In particular *Cantiga* 98 reflects the dictates of Canon 21 (*Omnis Utriusque Sexus*), which established the obligation of yearly confession and communion; and of the *Siete partidas,* I.iv.34. The poem describes how the doors of the church of Santa Maria de Valverde remained shut on an unconfessed woman.

Alfonso XI

826 Seniff, Dennis Paul. "All the King's Men and All the King's Lands: The Nobility and Geography of the *Libro de la caza* and the *Libro de la montería.*" *La Chispa 81.* Selected Proceedings of the Second Louisiana Conference on Hispanic Languages and Literatures. Ed. Gilbert Paolini. New Orleans: Tulane University, 1981, pp. 297-308.

Examination of legal influences (the inclusion of juridical statutes) in the *Book of Hunting* by Alfonso XI (1312-1350). In treating the *Ordinance of the Rights that Hunters Ought to Have* (I, xlvi), a totally objective set of legal statutes governing the hunt, Alfonso illustrates his points by fanciful reference to such literary creations as Roland, the Cid, Merlin, and others.

827 _____, ed. *Libro de la monteria.* Spanish Series, 8. Madison: The Hispanic Seminary of Medieval Studies, 1983.

The introduction to this edition of Alfonso XI's hunting treatise contains a detailed study of the influence of legal treatises on its structure and didactic goals.

Alfonso de Toledo

828 Gericke, Philip Otto. "The *Invencionario* of Alfonso de Toledo: Edition, with Introductory Study and Notes." Diss. University of California at Berkeley 1965.

The *Invencionario* (ca. 1467) was composed in order "to list discoveries pertinent to man's material and spiritual well-being....Narrative continuity provided by the underlying purpose of the work is augmented by an effort to establish the chronology of the events described, either through a division of time into successive ages from Adam to eternity (Bk. I) or through the use of the theological dispensations of Law of Nature, Law of Scripture and Law of Grace (Bk. II)."

Baena (See *Cancionero de Baena*)

Berceo

829   Bermejo Cabrero, José Luis. "El mundo jurídico de Berceo."
       Revista de la Universidad de Madrid, 18 (1969), 33-52.

       Amply demonstrates Berceo's knowledge of legal language and
       procedures in fifteen of the *Milagros de Nuestra Señora*. Angels,
       demons, saints, and sinners are all subject to juridical formalities;
       and at each turn the same terms are heard: "pleitos y sentencias,
       rieptos y alzadas." The law at the basis of the *Milagros* has not been
       invented; it is, more or less, the law of Berceo's day. Similarly, the
       terminology that he uses—even those terms with multiple meanings
       (e.g., *querella, pleito,* etc.)—was used at the time in forensic
       language. Berceo's "afición jurídica" cannot be denied.

830   Dutton, Brian. "The Profession of Gonzalo de Berceo and the Paris
       Manuscript of the *Libro de Alexandre.*" *BHS*, 37 (1960), 137-145.

       Dutton shows that the description of Berceo as the "abat Johan
       Sanchez notario por nonbrado" of the Monastery of San Millán de
       la Cogolla, cited in MS. *P*, 2639d, is likely to be an accurate one,
       making him almost certainly a legal professional. "If Berceo were
       indeed a *notario*, then one would naturally expect him to be familiar
       with judicial parlance." Among the terms that he uses are
       "(d)estemar" (*Sto. Domingo* 146d), "robrar" (*Milagros*, 842c)
       "reçentar el pleito," and others.

831   Pensado, José Luis. "Los *Signa Judicii* in Berceo." *Archivum*
       (Oviedo), 10 (1960), 229-270.

       Studies Berceo's *De los signos que aparesçeran ante del Juiçio* in
       light of treatments of the theme by St. Jerome (*Signa Iudicii*), Peter
       Comestor and Peter Damian. The article includes linguistic analysis
       of legal terminology in Berceo's text, e.g., "Pero en su *derecha* será
       él muy quedado" (stz. 2).

Caballero Cifar

832 Hernández, Francisco J. "Ferrán Martínez, 'Escrivano del Rey', Canónigo de Toledo, y autor del *Libro del Cavallero Zifar*." *RABM*, 81 (1978), 289-325.

Accepts the view that "Ferrán Martínez," a priest of Toledo mentioned in the prologue to the *Zifar* (ca. 1300), is the author of the work. Several passages show the imprint of a legal mind (e.g., Chap. 170, which makes an appeal to the practice of justice: "Deuedes ser justicieros...asy commo dize en el capitulo de la justicia"). The use of diplomatic documents, seals, *procuratorios*, and "letters of obligation"—as well as *cartas de creencia, de homenaje, de ruego, de guia,* and *de convocatoria de Cortes*—confirm the notarial vocation of Ferrán Martínez.

833 Wagner, Charles Philip. "The Sources of *El Cavallero Cifar*." *Revue Hispanique*, 10 (1903), 5-104.

Notes that the author of "the earliest Spanish novel that has come down to us, *El Cavallero Cifar*" (ca. 1300), used as a source Alfonso el Sabio's *Siete partidas*.

Cancionero de Baena

834 Cummins, John G. "Methods and Conventions in the 15th-Century Poetic Debate." *HR*, 31 (1963), 307-323.

Based on Cummins' M.A. thesis (Univ. of Manchester, 1961), "The *Pregunta* and *Respuesta*: A Study of the Debate-Form in 15th-Century Spanish Poetry," this work examines the question-answer poetic technique in which the replying poet adheres to the rhymes and verse-forms of his opponent. Characteristic of these debates was the legalistic *sentencia* handed down by a "judge" to determine the winner (see *C. de Baena*, 259): after a summing up of the arguments in the terminology of the courtroom, the verdict would be given, the winner often being entitled to "damages" from wealthy opponents (see "Villasandino vs. Carrillo" [*Baena*, 111]). The allegorical "Court of Love" was often the setting for these debates.

835   Marino, Nancy F., ed. *Dezir que fizo Juan Alfonso de Baena.*
       "Albatrós" Ediciones, 3. Valencia: Hispanófila, 1978.

       Notes the allusion in Baena's *dezir*, v. 4c, to Bartolus, the
       "famous Italian jurisconsult of the fourteenth century, whose legal
       works dominated in the university of that time."

Cantigas de Santa Maria (See Alfonso X)

Cartagena, Alonso de

836   Boarino, Gerald Louis. "Alonso de Cartagena's *Doctrinal de los
       caballeros:* Text, Tradition and Sources." Diss. University of
       California at Berkeley 1964.

       "The primary purpose of the treatise was to collect excerpts
       from legal works which treated some phase of chivalry and to
       arrange these laws in some organic whole....Cartagena...laments the
       excessive emphasis which knights placed on jousts and tournaments,
       oftentimes neglecting what the author viewed as their primary duties:
       the defense of the Church and the monarchy." Numerous chronicles
       and doctrinal treatises, including the literary-historical compilations
       Primera crónica general and the *Crónica de Lucas de Túy*, served
       Alonso as source material.

Celestina (Fernando de Rojas)

837   Bermejo Cabrero, José Luis. "Aspectos jurídicos de *La Celestina*."
       *"La Celestina" y su contorno social: Actas del I Congreso
       Internacional sobre "La Celestina."* Ed. Manuel Criado de Val.
       Barcelona: Hispam, 1977, pp. 401-408.

       Bermejo classifies *La Celestina* with other works that reveal
       juridical knowledge (i.e., those of Berceo and of the Archpriests of
       Talavera and Hita). In noting Celestina's caution in disguising her
       profession as *alcahueta*, he observes that it is Melibea herself who
       describes the punishment—burning at the stake—that the procuress
       should receive: "Quemada seas, alcahueta falsa, hechicera, enemiga
       de la honestidad y causadora de secretos yerros." With respect to the

binding *promesa* between Sempronio and Pármeno, Bermejo notes that Celestina, demanding justice while being murdered at the hands of the servants, "tiene un morir triunfal, con la justicia de su parte." In short, the juridical aspects of the work, and of Calisto in particular, have been adapted to literary ends without display of superfluous erudition.

838 Deyermond, A. D. *The Petrarchan Sources of "La Celestina."* Oxford Modern Languages and Literatures Monographs. Oxford: Oxford University Press, 1961.

Chapter 6, "The Stylistic Consequences of the Borrowings," notes that "Calisto's legalistic borrowing in his soliloquy after the seduction of Melibea ('antes muestran que es menor yerro...,' ii. 125; 242) would be out of place in most contexts, but is fully in keeping with the section in which it appears, and it helps to build up the impression of a confused and divided mind, of a man profoundly disturbed by the passion which is to destroy him." Also contains a brief mention of Rojas' legal career.

839 Dunn, Peter N. *Fernando de Rojas.* Boston: Twayne, 1975.

Provides information about Rojas' legal training at Salamanca. In discussing the title "Bachelor" (*bachiller*) found in the acrostic at the beginning of the *Argumento* to the *Celestina*, Dunn notes that Rojas held this degree by 1500, and that the work itself was composed after 1496. Concludes that it is reasonable to suppose that Rojas began studies at Salamanca "by 1493 or 1494."

840 Gilman, Stephen. "Fernando de Rojas as Author." *RF*, 76 (1964), 255-290.

Notes in passing the "conventional legal career'" of Fernando de Rojas.

841 _____. *The Spain of Fernando de Rojas: The Intellectual and Social Landscape of "La Celestina."* Princeton: Princeton University Press, 1972.

Extensive study of the *converso* ambience—and tension—that was part of the personal and professional development of Fernando de Rojas, prepared largely on the basis of legal documents. Chap. 2 ("The Case of Álvaro de Montalbán") comments on the legal

proceedings against Rojas' father-in-law on a trumped-up charge.
Chap. 6 ("Salamanca") offers a broad panorama on what Rojas'
legal studies would have been like. Yet the study provides
surprisingly little commentary on juridical matters in *La Celestina*
itself—a notable exception being the discussion of the term *justicia* in
the go-between's scriptural citation "los que padecían persecución
por la justicia" (p. 93). Appendix III contains "The *Probanza de
hidalguía* ["Deposition of Nobility"] of Licentiate Fernando de
Rojas"; Appendix IV, "The Bachelor's *Libros de leyes*" [a list of
forty-four legal texts belonging to Rojas].

842   Menéndez y Pelayo, Marcelino. *Orígines de la novela*. 4 vols. 2nd ed.
      Madrid: Bailly-Baillière, 1905-1915.

      Notes in volume 3, perhaps with excessive caution, that "las
      alusiones a las costumbres jurídicas" in *La Celestina* are rare (p. 241,
      n. 1).

843   Russell, Peter E. "*La Celestina* y los estudios jurídicos de Fernando
      de Rojas." *Temas de "La Celestina" y otros estudios. Del "Cid" al
      "Quijote."* Ed. Peter E. Russell. Colección "Letras e Ideas."
      Barcelona: Ariel, 1978, pp. 323-340.

      Stressing the importance of Rojas' professional background to
      his literary production, Russell examines the salient juridical aspects
      of the *Tragicomedia*. The bawd Celestina herself has spent most of
      her life beyond the law, and others commit infractions of civil or
      canon law throughout the work. The characteristic attitude of the old
      woman toward justice is one of disdain. Legal themes are present,
      however, in the fourth and seventh *auctos*, commentary in the latter
      being provided on Pármeno's mother, "ajusticiada como
      bruja"—the punishment for which was generally burning at the
      stake. The *alcahueta* receives summary justice in the end amidst her
      own ironic discourse ("¡Justicia, justicia, señores vezinos!"); while
      Calisto's judicial rhetoric is evident throughout (cf. his monologue in
      aucto fourteen).

844   Stinson, Robert. "Precepts for Punishment of Crimes in the
      Twelfth-Century *Fuero de Cuenca*." *Proceedings of the 32nd
      Mountain Interstate Foreign Language Conference*. Ed. G. C.
      Martín. Winston-Salem: Wake Forest University Press
      [forthcoming].

Provides an overview of the nature of municipal *fueros* or compendia of juridical statutes, promulgated throughout Spain during the eleventh through the thirteenth centuries. Describes the importance of the *judicium Dei* to the realization of justice in the *Fuero de Cuenca,* e.g., the bearing of a hot iron by the woman accused of adultery, and notes the manifestation of such tests in certain literary works. In the *Celestina,* for example, the "hot iron test" would have been applied to the old go-between as suggested by Melibea's indictment "quemada seas."

845   Valis, Noël M. "'El triunfo de Celestina': The Go-Between and the Penal Code of 1870." *Celestinesca,* 5 (1981), 35-39.

Valis surveys the legal status in Spain of the procuress, or *celestina,* immortalized in Rojas' 1499 work, from the medieval period through the nineteenth century. By the latter 1800's celestinesque figures "had acquired a modicum of legal acceptability, although it was not always reflected within the society itself."

Cid (Poema de mio Cid)

846   Burt, John R. "Honor and the Cid's Beard." *Corónica,* 9 (1981), 132-137.

The Cid's beard is seen to have a dual role: it reflects both the hero's inner strength or virtue and his exterior honor, which is worthy of kings. It grows longer and more "frightening" throughout the first and second *cantares,* and in the third reaches its most prepossessing state during the Cid's appearance at the Cortes de Toledo, at which point the aggravation to his daughters and the earlier affront to the beard by García Ordóñez are vindicated. It thus symbolizes both the Cid's personal honor and the justice that he has received and can mete out himself.

847   Chasca, Edmund de. *Estructura y forma en "El Poema de Mio Cid." (Hacia una explicación de la imitación poética de la historia de la epopeya castellana).* State University of Iowa Studies in Spanish Language and Literature, 9. Iowa City: State University of Iowa Press, and México, D. F.: Patria, 1955. Pp. 116-121 rpt. in *El arte*

juglaresco en el "Cantar de mio Cid." Biblioteca románica hispánica. Madrid: Gredos, 1967, pp. 140-144.

Brief discussion of the Cid's appearance before the Cortes de Toledo. Emphasizes the dramatic aspect of the speeches given by his partisans—the rapid inculpations and rebuffs between plaintiffs (the Cid and his retinue) and the defendants (the Infantes de Carrión and partisans)—all of which is seen to have been accomplished by the art of the minstrel (*juglar*). The Cid stands as a "giant among dwarves" in his brilliant—although limited—discourse by virtue of its gradation, juridical astuteness, legal strategy, cogency, and majestic fury. These proceedings are a solemn, dramatic formality to re-emphasize the merit of the Cid.

848   _____. "Composición escrita y oral en el *Poema del Cid.*" *Filología* (Buenos Aires), 12 (1966-1967), 77-94.

Rejects Russell's arguments [869] for the poet's juridical vocation on the grounds that they exclude "a consideration of what style can signify as an indication of authorship, either by a possible cleric-poet, a minstrel, or both." Chasca argues instead for oral composition or, less likely, for composition by a "minstrel-cleric" (*clérigo ajuglarado*).

849   _____. *The Poem of the Cid.* New York: Twayne, 1976.

Chapter 1, "The Cid of History," notes that on his father's side the Cid "was descended from Laín Calvo, one of the judges who according to tradition was elected by the Castilians to govern their country when, at the beginning of the tenth century, they rebelled against the king of León." Chasca follows traditional Pidalian views on the oral (minstrel) origins of *Cid*, despite his recognition of the importance of the poem's detailed legal commentary.

850   Corominas y Montaña, Pedro. "Las ideas jurídicas en el *Poema del Cid.*" *Revista general de legislación y jurisprudencia,* 97 (1900), 61-74; 222-247; and 389-411.

Rejects in an uncritical fashion the work of Hinojosa on the legal aspects of *Cid*.

851   Deyermond, A. D. "La decadencia de la epopeya española: *Las Mocedades de Rodrigo." Anuario de estudios medievales*, 1 (1964), 607-617.

Uses the history of the theme of the Cid from the *Cid* to the *MR* as an example of the decline of the Spanish epic. Of particular interest are the allusions to Castilian judges Nuño Rassura and Layn Calvo in the prose introduction to the *MR*. Examining the primitive version of the *MR* contained in the prose *Crónica de los reyes de Castilla* (which lacks the trial scene), Deyermond notes that, in contrast to the *Chanson de Roland* where Ganelon is tortured and executed, the malefactors of *MR* are exiled and later pardoned. Erudite influence in the original version of *MR* is highly likely, given its emphasis on the importance of *fueros* and *privilegios*; in addition, it appears to be a work of propaganda for the Diocese of Palencia, afterwards revised by *juglares* to achieve maximum diffusion, and as such was conserved in the extant codex (Bibl. Nat. [Paris] Esp. no 12).

852   Dunn, Peter N. "*Poema de Mio Cid*, vv. 23-48: Epic Rhetoric, Legal Formula, and the Question of Dating." *Romania*, 96 (1975), 255-264.

Points out that since the legal phrases found in *Cid* would remain familiar to hearers long after dropping out of usage, they are useless for dating purposes.

853   Entwistle, William J. "My Cid—Legist." *BHS*, 6 (1929), 9-15.

Strongly rejects the black reputation of the "historic Cid" put into circulation by R. Dozy (source undocumented) and affirms the "remarkable legal sense of Ruy Díaz el Campeador," who, "however right or wrong his deeds may have been...is admitted by all to have taken pains to be formally right." King Alfonso's advance on Valencia after the Cid's conquest was a "flat breach of legal agreement" for which the Cid's "ruthless, but legally correct" action of initiating private war against another noble was justifiable. Significantly the Cid's final triumph is not on a field of battle but in a court of chivalric justice.

854   Fletcher, Richard. "Diplomatic and the Cid Revisited: The Seals and
       Mandates of Alfonso VII." *Journal of Medieval History*, 2 (1976),
       305-337.

       A renewed examination of matters diplomatic in the *Cid* after
Russell [869]. "The royal chancery of the kingdom of León-Castile
appears to have adopted the use of the seal towards the middle of the
twelfth century" during the reign of Alfonso VII (1126-1157). Such
seals may have been used on administrative mandates like the *carta
fuerte mientre sellada* that was sent to the citizens of Burgos by
Alfonso VI and denied the Cid all hospitality (*Cid*, vss. 21-28). The
implication is that dates proposed for the composition of the poem
during the early thirteenth century, e.g., that of Colin Smith (1207
[cf. item 874, p. xxxiv]), should possibly be moved to an earlier
period.

855   Galbis, Ignacio R. "Don Ramón Menéndez Pidal y el perfil jurídico
       del Cid." *REH*, 6 (1972), 191-210.

       Rephrasing of Menéndez Pidal's views [864] on the legal aspects
of the *Cid*. Galbis provides a sketch of the legal ambience based on
ancient Roman law prevailing in the peninsular Christian kingdoms
at the time of the work's composition (but "en el siglo xv"?). In
order to establish Rodrigo Díaz as a true expert in the law, Galbis
cites the testimony of the *Historia Roderici* and types of duels in
which the historical Cid is known to have participated.

856   García González, Juan. "El matrimonio de las hijas del Cid."
       AHDE, 31 (1961), 531-568.

       Discusses the accuracy with which the *Cid* represents
contemporary marriage law, revising some of Hinojosa's earlier
views [859]. Topics include the betrothal of the Cid's daughters
Elvira and Sol to the *Infantes* of Carrión; economic aspects of the
arrangement; and dissolution of the match after the young wives
have been beaten and abandoned by their husbands. The article also
notes why the girls' *arras* ("donation of the husband in remuneration
for the dowry") was not claimed by the Cid during the Toledo court
proceedings, but it fails to examine the re-betrothal procedure to the
princes of Navarre and Aragon.

857   Garci-Gómez, Miguel. "Don Rachel e Vidas, amigos caros. Replanteamiento." *RFE*, 56 (1973), 209-228.

Ingenious argument which rejects the reading of the Raquel e Vidas episode as either anti-Semitic or comic, because the *Cid* nowhere states that the pair *are* Jews; because no interest is charged on the 600 marks that the Cid "borrows" from them (therefore there is no usury); because of the episode's place in the *Cid*; and because, as the law decrees, they have not yet opened the *arcas*, which are full of sand (vss. 1433-1438), left as collateral by the Cid after the first of three years. Garci-Gómez attempts to rationalize etymologically the Cid's default, "Desfechos nos ha el Çid" (v. 1433), citing a passage from the *Siete partidas* forbidding usury.

858   _____. "La *Afrenta de Corpes:* su estructura a la luz de la retórica." *KRQ*, 24 (1977), 125-139.

Call to dissuade scholars of *exocrítica*, i.e., of external evidence, from examining *Cid* as a rare juridical, folkloric, or geographic document. Recommends instead the spirit of *endocrítica*, with the *Rhetorica ad Herennium* as a guide. Thus, the apparent tragedy of the Cid's daughters, for example, is counterbalanced out of rhetorical necessity by a "happy ending" (*iucundus exitus rerum*) which accords with justice from the kingdom, the king, and God.

859   Hinojosa, Eduardo de. "El derecho en el *Poema del Cid.*" *Homenaje a Menéndez y Pelayo*. Madrid: Suárez, 1899, 1: 541-581; rpt. in Hinojosa's *Estudios sobre la historia del derecho español*. Madrid: Imprenta del Asilo de Huérfanos del Sagrado Corazón de Jesús, 1903, pp. 73-112; and in his *Obras completas*. Madrid: [Ministerio de Justicia y C.S.I.C.], 1948, 1:181-215.

A classic study of legal influence in the *Cid*, which is seen to be almost a legal text itself because of its accurate and constant representation of many juridical matters. Section I, "Las clases sociales," treats the hierarchy of nobility in the work. Section II, "El Rey y las Cortes," notes that the Toledo Court scene represents "the transition between primitive Germanic law, under which the judgment was based on combat between the two parties...and later law, in which the intervention of [the judge or tribunal] is more direct and effective." Part III, "La familia," examines aspects of the betrothal and dowry of the Cid's daughters. Given the legal state that it reflects, the *Cid* must have been redacted in the second half of the twelfth century.

860   Lacarra de Werckmeister, María Eugenia. "Ideology and Social Conflict in the *Poema de Mío Cid*" (Spanish Text). Diss. University of California at Los Angeles 1976.

"The first of the three chapters compares the legal institutions as they appear in [the *Cid*] with those which actually existed according to historical research, and which can be assessed from legal codes, royal documents, and local grants of rights. The key concepts are *ira regia*, loot, marriage, *Cortes*, and *riepto*. The chapter leads to the conclusion that the *PMC*'s conception of law reflects the legal institutions of the late twelfth and early thirteenth centuries; [too,] the influence of Roman law, which became prevalent at that time, can be clearly traced. The *PMC* also reflects some of the more recent municipal *fueros* peculiar to Castile, differing from earlier and later territorial law codes....The third chapter [concludes] that the *PMC* was written in or about 1207 by a legally-trained author born in Molina de Aragón and probably attached to the chancery of the Lara family."

861   Marín/Granada, Nicolás. "Señor y vasallo. Una cuestión disputada en el *Cantar del Cid*." *RF*, 86 (1974), 451-461.

Impressionistic examination of *Cid*, v. 20, "¡Dios qué buen vasallo/ si oviesse buen señor!" emphasizing that only the Cid could have been aware of the empty basis for Alfonso VI's *ira real* on exiling him; that the rupture of the feudal link between the two was, therefore, invalid; and that the later act of humility of the Cid in bending to kiss his feet—but made instead to kiss his hands (vss. 2028-2029)—was an "acto jurídico decisivo" to gain him, eventually, the royal pardon. Follows Menéndez Pidal's view [864] that the Cid appears in the Cortes de Toledo, in accordance with the historical figure of the *Historia Roderici*, as a "sabidor en derecho."

862   Menéndez Pidal, Ramón, ed. *Poema de Mio Cid*. ("Clásicos Castellanos," [24].) Madrid: La Lectura, 1913; 12th ed., Madrid: Espasa-Calpe, 1968.

The introductory section notes that the episode of the Cid and Raquel e Vidas is not a manifestation of medieval anti-Semitism, and that the poet does not fall into the "vulgaridad jurídica" that inspired papal bulls and royal privileges regarding the disposition of debts contracted with Jews, inasmuch as it is stated (v. 1436) that the Cid will repay his loan.

863 _____. "Una duda sobre el duelo en el *Poema del Cid.*" *Acta Salmanticensia*, 16 (1962), 15-19.

Rejects the opinion of P. Merêa [865], who maintains that the duel following the Cortes de Toledo scene in the *Cid* is merely one of vindication rather than a formal rendering of sentence and punishment.

864 _____. *La España del Cid.* 2 vols. Madrid: Plutarco, 1929; 7th ed., Madrid: Espasa-Calpe, 1969.

Emphasizes legal aspects in the background of both the Cid of history, Ruy Díaz de Vivar (d. 1099), and of the poetic legendary figure of the *Cid.* Establishes that the Cid is "sabidor en derecho" inasmuch as in the *Historia Roderici* (ca. 1100-1150) he reveals "scrupulous subtlety of juridical thought," accomplished through the use of legal formulae in extricating himself from an accusation of failure to aid Alfonso VI; through his actions as judge (*pesquisidor*) at the duel of Langreo; through his extraction of the oath from Alfonso in the church of Santa Gadea, which absolves the monarch of regicide (*lesa majestad*); and through his arbitration of the cattle dispute between the Abbot of Cardeña and several noblemen of Orbaneja Valley.

865 Merêa, Paulo. "Relendo o *Poema do Cid (Algumas notas acerca do duelo na história do direito).*" *Miscelânea de Estudos a Joaquim de Carvalho*, No. 4 (1960), pp. 394-398.

Influenced by the opinion of Cabral de Moncada (*O duelo na vida do dreito*, 1925), Merêa argues against defining the duel after the Cortes de Toledo scene as a judicial process, since it carried neither sentence nor punishment (both of which were necessary to satisfy the true challenge process).

866 Michael, Ian, ed. *Poema de Mio Cid.* Madrid: Clásicos Castalia, 1976.

In studying the background of the poet of the *Cid*, Michael imagines that he was a cleric; that he was educated by the

Benedictines; and that he perhaps was notary of the abbot, becoming familiar "con documentos y disputas legales." The work was written probably between 1201 and 1207.

867   Pattison, D. G. "The Date of the *Cantar de Mio Cid:* A Linguistic Approach." *MLR*, 62 (1967), 443-450.

Emphasizes that the author of the *Cid* may have been in the legal profession, for he uses legal language and reveals a knowledge of juridical procedure. In particular the poet's use of the suffixes *-ura* and *-ada* is studied in the light of legal documents of the twelfth and thirteenth centuries—e.g., *apreçiadura* ("payment in kind"), which has the same meaning in the *Cid* as in the *Fuero de Guadalajara* (1219).

868   Richthofen, Erich von. "La Justice dans l'épilogue du *Poème du Cid* et de la *Chanson de Roland*." *CCM*, 3 (1960), 76-79.

Maintains that the poet of the *Cid* based the Cortes de Toledo episode on the trial of Ganelon in the *Chanson de Roland*. The *cortes* scene reflects the customary way of dealing with breach of faith in Frankish law: trial by combat in the presence of the king and the nobility. Also discussed is the function of the Cid's swords, *Colada* and *Tizón*, as symbols of justice (human and divine).

869   Russell, Peter E. "Some Problems of Diplomatic in the *Cantar de Mio Cid* and Their Implications." *MLR*, 47 (1952), 340-349. Spanish trans. "Algunos problemas de diplomática en el *Poema de Mio Cid* y su significación." *Temas de "La Celestina" y otros estudios. Del "Cid" al "Quijote."* Ed. Peter E. Russell. Colección "Letras e Ideas." Barcelona: Ariel, 1978, pp. 13-33.

Groundwork study for the importance of chancery procedures in the dating of the *Cid*. At v. 24, the citizens of Burgos receive a letter from Alfonso VI, described as "fuertemientre seellada," in which they are instructed to refrain from providing the hero with any hospitality, lest they be severely punished; the poet's audience would probably have visualized a large pendant seal at the bottom of a short *mandato*, or royal decree. Russell, examining diplomatic practices and the use of seals at the time, argues that the poet's description of such a legal instrument is very difficult to reconcile with a composition date as early as 1140 (proposed by Menéndez Pidal and others), and that the period ca. 1180 is probably the earliest date consistent with the diplomatic evidence. [Russell's date has since been challenged by Fletcher; see item 854.]

870 _____. "San Pedro de Cardeña and the Heroic History of the Cid." *Medium Aevum*, 27 (1958), 57-79.

Claims proof that the Cid sometimes acted on behalf of the monastery of San Pedro de Cardeña in legal disputes in the time of the abbot Sisebuto, and may even have been a *miles*, or protector of Cardeña.

871 Smith, C. Colin. "Did the Cid Repay the Jews?" *Romania*, 86 (1965), 520-538.

Holds that the Cid was an unusual hero who was an excellent lawyer, but that he did not repay the Jews and never intended to. The episode was meant to poke fun at them, and to show the Cid as being free from *petit bourgeois* morality.

872 _____ and J. Morris. "On 'Physical' Phrases in Old Spanish Epic and Other Texts." *Proceedings of the Leeds Philosophical and Literary Society, Literary and Historical Section*, 12 (1967), 129-190.

Extensively documented study of physical phrases (i.e., those dealing with the hand, eye, mouth, etc.) in Old Spanish literary texts—particularly the *Cid*—French epics, Latin texts, and legal works. Finds that some of these have a legal origin: for example, *ver de los ojos, llorar de los ojos, aver a ojo*, and others may have derived from *decir de la boca*. Thus, the "author of the *PMC* must have had some sort of training in the law or close contacts with the world of law."

873 _____. "The Personages of the *Poema de Mio Cid* and the Date of the Poem." *MLR*, 66 (1971), 580-598.

The key figures of the *Cid* often have a different character from their historical counterparts (viz. the poet's negative depiction of the Count of Barcelona, García Ordóñez). Smith suggests that the author was probably "a lawyer by profession," who had access to legal documents in Burgos and/or Cardeña, and dates the poem as early thirteenth century rather than 1140 (assigned by Menéndez Pidal).

874   _____, ed. *Poema de Mio Cid.* Oxford: Clarendon, 1972.

In the Introduction, Smith argues that the poem was probably composed in 1207 for a Burgos audience by an author with legal training. In his view, "the author cannot have been other than a lawyer, or at least a person who had been trained in the law and had considerable technical knowledge of it. Scholars have recognized that the *PMC* gives a detailed and accurate account of many legal and social matters...."

875   _____. "Per Abbat and the *Poema de Mio Cid.*" *Medium Aevum*, 42 (1973), 1-17.

Argues for the composition of the *Cid* in 1207, proposing as author (*refundidor*) a well-documented Pedro Abad, layman and lawyer, connected with the monastery of Santa Eugenia during the relevant period.

876   _____. "Literary Sources of Two Episodes in the *Poema de Mio Cid.*" *BHS*, 52 (1975), 109-122.

Finds classical, literary sources (particularly Sallust) for the episodes of the captures of Castejón and Alcocer in the first *cantar* of the *Cid*, noting that such influences "surely remove the last possibility of its composition by a *juglar* or by a series of *juglares*, and make us look towards an author who was not only lettered but relatively learned too." A prime candidate is Per Abad, "author of the poem in 1207 and...some kind of literary lawyer. [The poet] would have had the training in Latin and in rhetoric, and the access (in whatever form) to Sallust and Frontinus...."

877   _____. "On the Distinctiveness of the *Poema de Mio Cid.*" *"Mio Cid" Studies.* Ed. A. D. Deyermond. London: Támesis, 1977, pp. 161-194.

Evaluates the literary qualities and learned features of the *Cid* and the evidence of a legal mind behind the poem. Reiterates that, in comparison with other Spanish epics, it is in matters of detail and phraseology that a case can best be made for the work's legalistic nature—e.g., its mention of written documents, the descriptions of feudal relationships, the naming of places (particularly as influenced by legal documents), the Cortes de Toledo, and general phraseology (e.g., word-pairings and binary phrases such as *malo e traidor* [v. 3383]).

878   _____. "El derecho, tema del *Poema de mio Cid* y profesión de su autor." *Estudios cidianos*. Ed. C. Colin Smith. Madrid: Cupsa, 1977, pp. 63-85.

Smith has reworked and expanded an earlier essay [877] in providing more information to corroborate his theory that the author was Per Abad, a lawyer who composed the poem in 1207.

879   _____. "Realidad y retórica: El binomio en el estilo épico." In *Estudios cidianos*. Ed. C. Colin Smith. Madrid: Cupsa, 1977, pp. 161-217.

Surveying the epic (especially the *Cid*), Berceo's works, the *Libro de Alexandre*, various *Crónicas* and numerous other texts in Romance (including Old French) and in Latin, Smith shows how many of the most common binomial phrases are in fact common formulae found in legal documents written in these languages—e.g., *sanus et salvus, sano y salvo, sain et sauf, safe and sound*. Other phrases include *mugeres e varones, legos e coronados, casadas e por casar*.

880   Socarrás, Cayetano J. "The Cid and the Bishop of Valencia (An Historical Interpretation)." *Iberoromania*, 3 (1971), 101-111.

Discusses vss. 1278-1301 on the constitution of the bishopric of Valencia and the designation of its occupant. The "distortion consists of two elements: first, the bishopric...was not established by the Cid; second, the procedure of the designation of the bishop as mentioned by the poet departs from the actual historical procedure of the period." Avers (p. 104, n. 9) that the "minstrel [!] shows without doubt a remarkable knowledge of the laws and juridical institutions of the times."

881   Sola-Solé, Josep M. "De nuevo sobre las arcas del Cid." *KRQ*, 23 (1976), 3-15.

Claims that the Raquel e Vidas episode actually happened; that the poet was not anti-Semitic, merely anti-bourgeois; and, given the evidence of contemporary legal contracts where the Jewish wife signs with the husband and before him, that Raquel is the wife of Vidas, and not another Jewish moneylender.

882   ter Horst, Robert. "The Meaning of Hypothesis in the *Poema de Mio Cid.*" *RHM*, 37 (1972-1973), 217-228.

The Cid enters into two contracts involving bad faith. In the first of these, the *arcas de arena*, the Cid shows bad faith towards the Jewish moneylenders Rachel and Vidas; in the second, the marriage of his daughters, he is shown bad faith by the *infantes* Fernando and Diego de Carrión. Concludes, after the arguments of Colin Smith [874], that a legalistic frame of reference is important for understanding the work: "the idea of a legally trained author of the *Poema* enriches rather than impoverishes our understanding of [its] singular depth...." Based on a hypothesis that depends on "a series of valid and invalid contracts" for its unity, the poem possesses "a strength of ideal structure."

883   Walker, Roger M. "The Role of the King and the Poet's Intentions in the *Poema de Mio Cid.*" *Medieval Hispanic Studies Presented to Rita Hamilton.* Ed. A. D. Deyermond. London: Támesis, 1976, pp. 257-266.

Notes Alfonso VI's prodigious respect for the Cid in ordering the Court of Toledo, in which the monarch himself intervenes to make a significant change in juridical procedure to benefit his vassal. "In contrast with Alfonso's activity, the Cid takes very little part in the action" during the trial. "It is his men who issue the challenges to the Carrión party and it is the King who arranges the venue for the duels, guarantees safe conduct for the Cid's champions, and supervises the actual combat. The Cid himself does not even witness the duels, but returns to Valencia...."

884   Walsh, John K. "Epic Flaw and Final Combat in the *Poema de Mio Cid.*" *Corónica*, 5 (1977), 100-109.

Careful examination of the judicial combat following the Cortes de Toledo scene in light of similar contests described in other Romance epic poems (e.g., *Couronnement de Louis, Siete Infantes de Lara*). Ascertains the reversal of behavior—"the structural flaw" in the finale of the *Cid*—on the part of the heretofore cowardly Infantes de Carrión, who are now "accommodated in the full pattern of a standard epic sequence. In the end, they enter the combat with the bravery and vigor that would have sent the earlier Infantes rushing in panic, or scurrying behind the nearest beam."

885 Zahareas, Anthony N. "The Cid's Legal Action at the Court of Toledo." *RR*, 55 (1964), 161-172.

The Cortes de Toledo scene crowns the poet's treatment of "the problem of justice which pervades the *Poema*." Herein, the Cid achieves a greatness based not on his earlier heroism in battle, but on the legal procedure which he employs in obtaining satisfaction from the Infantes de Carrión. "The development of legal control is mirrored by the psychological development of the Cid: the skillful transition from the wounded father to the clever lawyer brings again to mind the importance of law to man....[T]he trial scene is a document of Spanish history not because it contains facts but because it captures the spirit of the age."

Danza de la muerte

886 Whyte, Florence. *The Dance of Death in Spain and Catalonia*. Baltimore: Waverly, 1931.

Traces the genesis of literary manifestations of the dancing mania in the Iberian peninsula to French models (e.g., the *Danse Macabre*, known in Catalonia before 1480 by means of a translation). Whyte notes that in the *Dança general de la muerte* a lawyer "is summoned to a region where edicts are of no avail. He is accused of not playing the game, for he has accepted bribes from both sides! The canon emphatically refuses to participate in the dance, but Death, taking him by the hand, ironically divests him of his fine linen vestment...." Also treated is the Catalan *Romiatge del Venturos Pelegrí ab Les Cobles de la Mort*, a version of the Legend of the Three Living and the Three Dead: the Pilgrim is led by Death "before the Celestial court where God the Father presides as Judge," the scene followed by a dispute between Devil and Angel over his soul. Discussion of the satire of the legal profession found in the later (1557) *Las Cortes de la Muerte* is provided as well (Chap. 4).

Díaz de Toledo, Pero

887 Riss, Barbara A. "Pero Díaz de Toledo's *Proverbios de Seneca:* An Annotated Edition of MS S.II.10 of the Escorial Library." Diss. University of California at Berkeley 1979.

Pero Díaz de Toledo was a jurist who translated Seneca's *Proverbs* for King Juan II.

Elena y María

888 Menéndez Pidal, Ramón, ed. *"Elena y María (Disputa del clérigo y el caballero).* Poesía leonesa inédita del siglo XIII." *Revista de filología española,* 1 (1914), 52-96; rpt. Madrid: C.S.I.C., 1965.

Places the poem among those of the twelfth and thirteenth centuries which discuss whether the love of a knight is preferable to that of a cleric, in particular *Phillis et Flora* and *Le Jugement d'amour.* In the French works, a court judgment is made to resolve the issue. Interestingly, the Spanish (Leonese) text is the first to have its litigious members plead their own cases. The description of the birds in *EyM,* vss. 301-315, seems to derive from a text similar to the reworking of the *Jugement* found in Bibl. Nat. [Paris] Fr. 795, the cleric of which is declared expressly to be a lawyer.

Hernando de Talavera

889 Nyholm, Hannah Marie. "An Edition of Fray Hernando de Talavera's *Tractado prouechoso que demuestra commo en el uestir y calçar comunmente se cometen muchos peccados y aun tanbien en el comer y beuer."* Diss. University of Wisconsin-Madison 1955.

Analysis of Hernando de Talavera's treatise (1477) "on the sins that man commits in connection with two of his basic needs for self-preservation—food and clothing...." The work is partly a defense of positive human law.

Juan Manuel

890   Caldera, Ermanno. "Retorica, narrativa e didattica nel *Conde Lucanor*." *Miscellanea di Studi Ispanici*, 14 (1966-1967), 5-120.

Broad study of the intellectual heritage and milieu of Don Juan Manuel. Though marginal to a juridical interpretation of his works, the study is indispensable for rhetorical analysis of the *obra juanmanuelina* and for an understanding of the identical training in the *trivium* that Don Juan and his legal counterparts received.

891   Tate, R. B., and I. R. Macpherson, eds. *Libro de los estados*. Oxford: Clarendon, 1974.

The excellent Introduction provides a clear statement about the influence of Dominican thought in the works of Juan Manuel. Notes that the legalistic *Libro de los estados*, or "Book of Estates," "opens with a debate between Turín and Julio on the law of nature and natural justice in which is included, as in Calderón's *Vida es sueño*, the argument about the superiority of natural law among animals [e.g., "los cavallos...non...se llegan los maslos a las fenbras, sinon en tienpo que an de e[n]gendrar, segund su naturaleza"], and the correct response to it." Observes, however, that it "is probable, no more, that such vague identities as exist between the *Libro de los estados* and Aquinas's *Summa* may derive from the broad current of evangelical works which flowed down through southern France into Aragon...."

Jura de Santa Gadea

892   Horrent, Jules. "La jura de Santa Gadea. Historia y poesía." *Studia Philologica: Homenaje ofrecido a Dámaso Alonso*. Madrid: Gredos, 1961. 2:241-265; rpt. in *Historia y poesía en torno al "Cantar del Cid."* Barcelona: Ariel, 1973.

Studies the historical and literary aspects of the oath that the Cid forced King Alfonso VI to swear—namely, that he was innocent of complicity in the murder of his brother Sancho II. The *Jura* may have been composed for the purpose of linking the *Cantar de Sancho II* and the *Cid*.

Libro de buen amor (See Ruiz, Juan)

Libro de la montería (See Alfonso XI)

López de Ayala, Pero

893   Sears, Helen L. "The *Rimado de Palaçio* and the 'De Regimine
      Principum' Tradition of the Middle Ages." *HR*, 20 (1952), 1-27.

      The importance of the visual impression of a sealed document
      "is regarded by López de Ayala [in the *RP*, MS. *N*, 606] as a matter
      of great importance, and he includes, among the nine things by
      which the king's majesty is known, [this instrument]: '...your
      messenger's letter,/ On very beautiful form, the true word,/ In
      well-formed script, and with beautiful wax/ Closed, well sealed, with
      the day, month and year'" [trans. D.P.S.].

Llull, Ramón

894   Bauzá y Bauzá, Rafael. "Doctrinas jurídicas internacionales de
      Ramón Llull." *Estudios Lulianos*, 2 (1958), 157-174; 3 (1959),
      181-184; 5 (1961), 171-175 and 295-304; 13 (1969), 37-49; and 14
      (1970), 37-45.

      This extensive study, published over the span of twelve years,
      provides a synthetic view of Llullian concepts of international society
      (studied in the *Llibre de Blanquerna*), diplomatic law (viewed in the
      "Cardenal de la Paz" of the *Blanquerna* novel), unity of language,
      war and peace (couched in terms of canon law), and other concerns
      as manifested in his political, philosophical and literary works.
      Provides a list of Llull's writings (14 [1970], 44-45).

Martínez de Toledo, Alfonso

895 Bermejo Cabrero, José Luis. "La formación jurídica del Arcipreste de Talavera." *RFE*, 57 (1974-1975 [1976]), 111-125.

Systematic examination of the legalistic nature of *El Corbacho* (1438) and the strong juridical understanding of its author, Alfonso Martínez de Toledo, Archpriest of Talavera. The frequently misogynistic accounts of the "wiles of women" as they murder, mutilate, and entrap their male victims are often corroborated by the Archpriest's own eye-witness accounts. Notarial allusions, legal definitions, and the mention of well-known figures in canon law substantiate Bermejo's thesis that the Archpriest makes a constant display of his juridical knowledge throughout the work. Also provides legal documentation for the Archpriest's *Vidas de S. Ildefonso y S. Isidoro*.

896 Del Piero, Raúl A. "El 'Arcipreste de Talavera' y Juan de Ausim." *BH*, 62 (1960), 125-135.

Maintains that Alfonso Martínez de Toledo, being *bachiller en decretos*, must have known the work of Nicolaus de Auximo, a specialist in canon law, whom he cites (in all probability) as the legal authority designated "Juan de Ausim, authority on *buen* and *mal amor*" at the beginning of the prologue to the *Corbacho*.

Poema de mio Cid (See *Cid*)

Rojas, Fernando de (see *Celestina*)

Ruiz, Juan (*Libro de buen amor*)

897 Bermejo Cabrero, José Luis. "El saber jurídico del Arcipreste." *El Arcipreste de Hita: El libro, el autor, la tierra, la época. Actas del I Congreso Internacional sobre el Arcipreste de Hita*. Ed. M. Criado de Val. Barcelona: S.E.R.E.S.A., 1973, pp. 409-415.

Juan Ruiz's reworking of the Aesopic fable *Lupus et vulpis, judice simio* in the *Libro de buen amor* reveals a serious (not parodic) display of legal erudition. Specifically, he adapts poetically the legal *sentencias* of the epoch according to metrical exigencies. The Archpriest's knowledge of Roman and canon law makes the work unusual in medieval Spanish literature: only in the fifteenth-century *Cancionero de Baena*, for example, can anything be found regarding the legal theory of exceptions, present in the *Libro de buen amor*. Numerous less erudite juridical aspects appear in the work's *exempla* and legends.

898   Chapman, Janet A. "Juan Ruiz's 'Learned Sermon.'" *"Libro de buen amor" Studies*. Ed. G. B. Gybbon-Monypenny. London: Támesis, 1970, pp. 29-51.

       Libro de buen amor's first three vernacular *auctoritates* are attributed to Gratian's *Decretum*, and "are followed by the phrase 'eso dize el decreto' (5, x, xv, xvii)." Other authoritative statements are attributed also to the *Decretum*, to common law, and to St. Gregory.

899   Deyermond. A. D. "Some Aspects of Parody in the *Libro de buen amor*." *"Libro de buen amor" Studies*. Ed. G. B. Gybbon-Monypenny. London: Támesis, 1970, pp. 53-78.

       Noting that parodies in the *Libro de buen amor* are either ecclesiastical or secular in nature, Deyermond describes the treatment accorded legal procedure and notarial style in the trial of the wolf vs. the vixen (stzs. 326 and 348-366).

900   Eizaga y Gondra, Martín. *Un proceso en el Libro de buen amor*. [Bilbao]: Junta de Cultura, Diputación de Vizcaya, [1942].

       Studies juridical procedure in the *Libro de buen amor* in light of legal texts of the period: the *Siete partidas, Fuero real,* and *Leyes del estilo*. Pays close attention to the *pleito* between the wolf and the vixen (stzs. 321-371) heard by the ape-judge, Don Ximio.

901   Eugenio y Díaz, Francisco. "El lenguaje jurídico del *Libro de buen amor*." *El Arcipreste de Hita. El libro, el autor, la tierra, la época. Actas del I Congreso Internacional sobre el Arcipreste de Hita*. Ed. M. Criado de Val. Barcelona: S.E.R.E.S.A., 1973, pp. 422-433.

       Solid discussion of legal terminology employed in the *Libro de buen amor*, which emphasizes that beneath the lively, colloquial language of the work lies a "verdadero saber de letrado, de docto, de erudito...." The study is organized around three concepts: *derecho* and related terms (*ley, fuero, costumbre, uso, derecho*); *tuerto* and related terms (*tuerto, yerro, pecado, maleficio, malfetría*); and *pleito* and related terms (*pleyto, juicio, fallo* [*letrado, abogado, querella, alguacil, demanda*]). The author concludes with a call for further socio-linguistic investigation of the law: the task of discovering what values and beliefs of juridical significance are contained within a specific language.

902 Hamilton, Rita. "The Digression on Confession in the *Libro de buen amor.*" *"Libro de buen amor" Studies.* Ed. G. B. Gybbon-Monypenny. London: Támesis, 1970, pp. 149-157.

The controversy over penance and absolution—and ecclesiastical jurisdiction over these matters—was considerable throughout the Middle Ages. In *Libro de buen amor*, following the battle of Doña Cuaresma and Don Carnal, Juan Ruiz discusses the form and matter of the Sacrament of Penance, giving a definition (stzs. 1128-1143) similar to that found in Gratian's *Decretum* and providing an explanation (stzs. 1144-1161) of the administrative jurisdiction over this sacrament, a matter so important that St. Thomas Aquinas, in defining the sacrament in the *Summa theologica*, included the warning that priests must have jurisdiction over the penitent involved. Clearly, Juan Ruiz had the best interests of his colleagues at heart—mere "clérigos synples"—in exhorting them not to fall into error ("de mi parrochiano non seades confesor" [1154b]).

903 Kassier, Theodore L. "On the Archpriest's Legal Knowledge and Situation." Paper presented at the South-Central Modern Language Association, 27-29 October 1977 [Abstract from *Corónica*, 6 (Fall 1977), 12].

"Throughout the *Libro de buen amor* numerous passages bespeak the Archpriest's familiarity with, and concern for, legal questions. Although critics have studied some of these passages, such as the lawsuit between the wolf and the vixen, and the so-called 'digression' on confession..., new study of passages such as the astrological prediction of the prince's death (stzs. 128-139), whose legal aspects have been completely overlooked, makes clear that legal matters constitute a more central theme and preoccupation than has previously been realized." The study also examines legal aspects of

Doña Endrina's widowhood and Don Melón's expertise in the law. In addition it "casts some light on the troublesome question of the Archpriest's imprisonment."

904   Kelly, Henry Ansgar. *Canon Law and the Archpriest of Hita.* Medieval and Renaissance Texts and Studies. Binghamton: SUNY Center for Medieval and Early Renaissance Studies, 1983.

Kelly documents the citation by Juan Ruiz of Johannes Andreae's *Novella,* produced in Bologna in 1338, and emphasizes that the Archpriest himself had extensive knowledge of the subject. Also interprets the "year of the Era" mentioned in MS. *S* (stz. 1634) as alluding to Christian rather than Caesarian chronology (a thirty-eight year difference), thereby assigning a date to the *Libro de buen amor* of 1381—and not ruling out a date as late as 1389.

905   Kirby, Steven Darrell. "The Artistic Utilization of Law and Rhetoric in the Don Ximio Episode of Juan Ruiz's *Libro de buen amor.*" Diss. University of Kentucky 1976.

Key study of how "legal and rhetorical doctrines contribute to the total meaning and artistry" of the *Libro de buen amor.* Examines closely the Don Ximio episode, stzs. 321-371, and posits as its source the Alfonsine *Siete partidas,* noting that "No other single code, or probable combination of codes, can explain the legal doctrines expounded." On the basis of the "unwavering concern with the law" throughout the book, Kirby suggests that Juan Ruiz "was trained as a lawyer." Provides in an appendix transcripts of the notarial documents which prove the authenticity of the "legal proceedings and terminology used by Juan Ruiz" in the episode of the wolf, vixen, and ape judge.

906   _____. "Juan Ruiz, Don Ximio and the Law." *Studies in Language and Literature: The Proceedings of the Twenty-Third Mountain Interstate Foreign Language Conference.* Ed. Charles L. Nelson. Richmond, Ky.: Dept. of Foreign Languages, Eastern Kentucky University, 1976, pp. 295-300.

Concludes that "Juan Ruiz's sole legal source for his Don Ximio fable [stzs. 321-371] is the *Siete Partidas* of Alfonso el Sabio. The Archpriest reveals this fact in two ways. First, he adapts, almost verbatim, prescriptive and formulaic passages from the code. Second, he explicitly mentions the year when it was completed."

907 _____. "Juan Ruiz and Don Ximio: The Archpriest's Art of Declamation." Abstract in *Corónica*, 4 (1975), 3; published in revised form in *BHS*, 55 (1978), 283-287.

Asserts that Juan Ruiz based the legal elements in the Don Ximio story (*Libro de buen amor*, stzs. 321-71) on the *Siete partidas*. Moreover, Kirby views the tale as "a clear display of legal and rhetorical erudition, closely akin to the elder Seneca's *Controversiae*. Both the structure and content of the Archpriest's fable closely parallel Seneca's forensic *Declamations*....[Juan Ruiz] most likely learned declamatory techniques when he studied law, probably at Toledo....If indeed the fable is a declamatory exercise, then this conclusion suggests significant implications with regard to Juan Ruiz's use of rhetorical techniques, his probable sources and his audience."

908 Lecoy, Félix. *Recherches sur le "Libro de buen amor" de Juan Ruiz, Archiprêtre de Hita*. Paris: Droz, 1938; rpt. with prologue and comprehensive bibliography by A. D. Deyermond, Farnborough: Gregg International, 1974.

Studies (pp. 129-130) the parodic nature of the *pleito* of the wolf and vixen [stzs. 321-371], which Juan Ruiz uses to attack "les avocats chicaneurs" and to praise "les juges honnêtes et conciliateurs." Lecoy notes the Archpriest's use of the *Decretals* as a source.

909 Murillo Rubiera, Fernando. "Jueces, escribanos y letrados en el *Libro de buen amor*." *El Arcipreste de Hita. El libro, el autor, la tierra, la época. Actas del I Congreso Internacional sobre el Arcipreste de Hita*. Ed. M. Criado de Val. Barcelona: S.E.R.E.S.A., 1973, pp. 416-421.

Brief outline of the judicial selection process during the High Middle Ages which notes that from the tenth-century judges could be chosen by the king, by his representatives, or by judicial assemblies. Stzs. 142-147 provide an exposition of the monarch's role as judge and legislator. Rubiera notes that from 1348 on, remunerated justices were called *corregidores*. In stzs. 321-371, local proceedings are parodied in the court of Don Ximio, "Alcalde de Bugía." The *abogados* (*letrados*) and *notarios* are depicted humorously from the popular perspective as being specialized solely in argumentation, having been transformed into a greyhound and a mastiff. Mentions that similar diatribes are found in López de Ayala's *Rimado de Palacio* against the *letrados* who spoil for legal action so as to attract their clients' money.

910   Polaino Ortega, Lorenzo. "El derecho procesal en el *Libro de buen amor.*" *Revista de Derecho Procesal* (Madrid), 3 (1947), 581-621.

Treats the relationship between the *Siete partidas* and the *Libro de buen amor*, particularly the court scene of the wolf, vixen, and Don Ximio (stzs. 321-371).

911   Walsh, John K. "The Names of the Bawd in the *Libro de buen amor.*" *Florilegium Hispanicum: Medieval and Golden Age Studies Presented to Dorothy Clotelle Clarke*. Ed. John S. Geary, Charles B. Faulhaber, and Dwayne E. Carpenter. Madison: The Hispanic Seminary of Medieval Studies, 1983, pp. 151-164.

Notes that a possible "frame for parody in the list of nicknames [of the *Libro de buen amor*] is that of a specific legal formulation. To Juan Ruiz and his congregation of devotees, legal parodies were as operative and familiar as religious parodies." Walsh details the importance of local *fueros* prohibiting insults and abusive names ("especially those with sexual connotations") and cites the *fueros* of Usagre, Alcaraz, Alarcón ("Todo aquél que a otro dixiere 'malato' o 'cornudo' o 'fodido'..., peche .II. moravedís..."), and other areas.

912   Zahareas, Anthony N. "Structure and Ideology in the *Libro de buen amor.*" *Corónica*, 7 (1979), 92-104.

Points up the conflict between the ideology of celibacy and the persistence of concubinage in the *Libro de buen amor*. Alfonsine legal sources are crucial to an understanding of sections like the "Clerics of Talavera" episode at the end of MS. *S*.

Sánchez de Arévalo, Rodrigo

913   Law, John Richard. "El *Espejo de la vida humana* de Rodrigo Sánchez de Arévalo (1404-1470): Estudio y edición crítica." Diss. University of Texas at Austin 1980.

Rodrigo Sánchez de Arévalo was cleric, bishop, and doctor of the "two laws." In the *Espejo*, he "expresses his concept of the political and social structure of Christian society."

914   Tate, Robert B. "Rodrigo Sánchez de Arévalo (1404-1470) and His *Compendiosa Historia Hispanica*." *NMS*, 4 (1960), 58-80.

Arévalo's *Compendiosa* draws on texts like the *Historia Gothica*, on fanciful popular traditions (e.g., the snake-belt given by King Pedro the Cruel to his first wife), and on his earlier views on the laws of monarchical succession laid down in Book II of *De Monarchia*. As a historiographer trained in canon law, Arévalo writes with "the experiences of the jurist, the moral philosopher, ambassador and papal politician."

Vidal mayor (Navarrese)

915   García-Granero Fernández, Juan. "*Vidal mayor*: Versión romanceada navarra de la *Maior Compilatio* de Vidal de Canellas." *AHDE*, 50 (1980), 243-264.

A study of the authorship, linguistic aspects, and artistic qualities of the legal text *Vidal Mayor*, a Navarrese translation (thirteenth century) of the Latin *Compilatio Maior* and *In Excelsis Dei Thesauris* written by Vidal de Canellas. The 156 miniatures of the version contained in MS. Perrins 112 [now Aachen Sammlung Ludwig MS. XIV, 4] constitute "un cuerpo unitario integrado" of text and art depicting the juridical aspects described in each chapter. Argues that the "Michael Lupi de Çandiu" of the *explicit* was not just a simple copyist, but rather a trilingual (or quadrilingual) notary who probably had legal training, possibly being a *licenciado* in Roman law. The language of the work (e.g., the term *paramiento*) indicates that the writer-translator used Navarrese rather than Aragonese, as was previously thought. The combination law-art in such a text is an extreme rarity in the Iberian peninsula.

INDEXES

AUTHOR INDEX

Brall, Helmut 482
Branca, Vittore 711, 712
Brandileone, F. 729
Braun, Werner 108
Bray, Gerald 116
Breslin, Carol Ann 196
Bressie, Ramona 322
Bresslau, H. 613
Brévonnes, Roland 671
Brockett, Mervyn Neil 706
Brockman, Bennett A. 239
Brook, Leslie C. 614
Brown, Ursula 515
Bründl, Peter 450
Bryant, Lucie M. 651
Bumke, Joachim 335
Burdach, Konrad 336, 432
Burger, André 615, 707
Burrell, Margaret A. 616
Burrow, John A. 319
Burt, John R. 846
Burton, Dorothy Jean 294

Cabaniss, Allen 70
Caluwé, Jacques de 650
Caldera, Ermanno 890
Calin, William 605
Campo del Pozo, Fernando 78
Cancelli, Filippo 730
Carmignani, Giovanni 731
Carruthers, Ian Robert 255
Carruthers, Mary 197
Carson, M. Angela 280
Chandler, Arthur Bayard 240
Chaney, William A. 143, 172
Chapman, Janet A. 898
Chasca, Edmund de 847-849
Chiappelli, Luigi 717, 732, 733
Chiaudano, Mario 734
Chroust, Anton-Hermann 43
Ciklamini, Marlene 516
Clanchy, M. T. 4
Clifton-Everest, J. M. 498
Cohen, Gustave 636, 652
Coleman, Janet 295
Combridge, Rosemary 391, 396
Cometta, Marina 451
Conley, John 241
Cons, Louis 672
Cook, Albert S. 73, 198

Corominas y Montaña, Pedro 850
Cospito, Antonio 735, 736
Coster, Charles Henry 85
Coulin, Alexander 576
Coville, Alfred 682
Cowgill, Bruce Kent 199, 200
Craddock, Jerry R. 820
Cramer, Thomas 401
Crowe, Michael Bertram 124, 125
Culbert, Taylor 144
Cummings, Michael Joseph 326
Cummins, John G. 834
Cunningham, Stanley B. 71
Curtius, Ernst Robert 44

Dahl, Willy 517
Daly, L. J. 134
Daucé, Fernand 577, 673
Davis, Robert Evan, Jr. 307
De Antonellis, Ciriaco 737
de Chasca, Edmund see Chasca, Edmund de
De Florio, Anthony 738
Delachenal, Roland 578
Delany, Sheila 308
Delhaye, Philippe 739
Del Piero, Raúl A. 896
De Mattei, Rodolfo 740
Dembowski, Peter 606
Derrett, John Duncan M. 5, 6
De Smet, Imogene L. 242
Desobry, Jean 661
Dessau, Adalbert 579
Deyermond, A. D. 805, 806, 838, 851, 899
Dickinson, John 96
Dohse, Jutta 337
Dombois, Hans 76
Donadoni, Eugenio 741
Donahue, Charles 173
Donaldson, E. Talbot 296
DuBruck, Edelgard 692
Duncan, Annelise Marie 518
Dunleavy, Gareth W. 201
Dunn, Peter N. 839, 852
Dutton, Brian 807, 830
Dyroff, Adolf 742

Eden, Kathy Hannah 7
Ehrismann, Gustav 338, 425
Einarsson, Bjarni 519
Eizaga y Gondra, Martín 900

SUBJECT INDEX